Cinema at the

Edited by
Dina Iordanova, David Martin-Jones, *and* Belén Vidal

wayne state university press
detroit

14 13 12 11 10   5 4 3 2 1

Library of Congress Cataloging-in-Publication Data

Cinema at the periphery / edited by Dina Iordanova, David Martin-Jones, and Belén Vidal.
p. cm. — (Contemporary approaches to film and television series)
Includes bibliographical references and index.
ISBN 978-0-8143-3388-4 (pbk. : alk. paper)
1. Motion pictures and transnationalism. 2. Motion pictures and globalization. 3. Culture in
motion pictures. I. Iordanova, Dina. II. Martin-Jones, David. III. Vidal, Belén, 1974–
PN1995.9.T6855C56 2010
791.43'611
2009023918

Typeset by Maya Rhodes
Composed in Adobe Garamond and Myriad Pro

Contents

Part 2. Peripheral Visions: (Re-)conceiving Identities and Histories

Acknowledgments

It all started on a beautiful sunny day in June 2006, when an international group of film studies academics gathered together in St. Andrews for what was to become an enduring discussion on matters of peripheral cinema. Later on, when we decided to pursue this intellectual project even further and publish a book, more scholars came on board.

We would like to thank all those friends and colleagues who confirmed that cinema at the periphery is an important topic to study, by coming to the conference and contributing to the volume, for their great scholarship and for their patience! We are grateful to the University of St. Andrews in Scotland for the generous funding that allowed us to hold the event.

In the course of our work, we received vitally important funding from the British Academy, the Arts & Humanities Research Council (AHRC), and the Leverhulme Trust; besides the financial assistance the backing of these organizations came as an important moral reward. We would also like to thank the anonymous reviewers of the volume; Richard Dyer; Barry Keith Grant; Robert Burgoyne; and the wonderful Annie Martin for her unwavering support. Our thanks to Dawn Hall and Kristin Harpster Lawrence and to Yun-hua Chen for her excellent work on the bibliographies and index contained in this volume.

Introduction

A Peripheral View of World Cinema

The revision and questioning of established canons has been the driving force behind some of the most innovative theory and practice in film history. Released to coincide with the celebrations of cinema's centenary, Peter Jackson and Costa Botes's mockumentary *Forgotten Silver* (New Zealand, 1995) illustrates this point with a disarming flair. The film opens with Jackson standing in front of an abandoned, overgrown shack in provincial New Zealand. A neighbor of his parents has reportedly called him to check out some decaying film cans left there by one Colin McKenzie, an enterprising kiwi filmmaker originating from the rural area who died in 1937 at the age of forty-nine. What emerges from Jackson's inspection of the cans is a discovery that turns the entire history of cinema as we know it upside down. As per Jackson's account, we gradually begin to realize that key technological discoveries driving the evolution of the cinematic medium have been, in fact, the fruit of the independent endeavors of this pioneering New Zealander.

McKenzie's work, clips of which are featured in the film, was apparently filmed on a film stock that, having since been affected by various degrees of nitrate decomposition, looks technically convincing. Backed by such persuasive evidence and by supporting highbrow commentary from the likes of film historian Leonard Maltin, mogul Harvey Weinstein, and New Zealand's own Sam Neill, Jackson proceeds to credit McKenzie with the independent and accidental discovery of the film camera at the age of twelve, in 1900. McKenzie's discovery, consequently, allows him to capture on film the early aviation attempts of other ingenious New Zealanders, who, apparently, managed to fly a few months before the Wright Brothers! Other idiosyncratic discoveries and inventions attributed to McKenzie include film stock

1

(produced from raw eggs); the technique for recording sound (in 1908); color film stock made using local berries (in 1911); tools of cinematographic narration such as montage and the close-up; key film genres such as the slapstick comedy and the epic costume drama, as well as pioneering production breakthroughs such as international financing deals (with the Soviets), the use of extras and of stand-in shooting locations (across the Pacific).

Forgotten Silver constructs a witty alternative take on the history of the cinematic medium, where all key events are attributed to one single person who belongs to a singular and peripherally positioned nation.[1] It is a clever proposition that challenges entrenched canons of film historiography. However, what if a Colin McKenzie had actually existed? What would have happened if it turned out that all these innovations were indeed introduced in the context of sidelined cinematic traditions? Would not such an alternative historiography then turn upside down all tacit conventions of who are the leaders and who the followers in world culture? Would this not also impact upon what are currently considered the *center* and *periphery* of world cinema? Would it compel us to acknowledge that there are multiple possible avenues to an artistic status quo, and that the outer peripheries could be as ingenious as the universally acknowledged centers on which the spotlight usually lands?

Ironically, less than a decade later, Peter Jackson, the man behind the hoax, transcended the confines of his island's national cinema to reposition himself centrally when he became the best-known New Zealander in Hollywood with his blockbuster trilogy *The Lord of the Rings* (New Zealand/USA, 2001–3). Unlike the films of his imaginary predecessor Colin McKenzie, Jackson's films would play simultaneously on hundreds of screens around numerous territories.

At the same time, however, there are still filmmakers around the world whose work exists in a singular mode. The hoax of *Forgotten Silver* is all the more plausible because the circumstances in which McKenzie's forgotten work might have been created are not hugely different from the conditions of infrastructural dearth in which many filmmakers from the periphery work today. Even in our present age of advanced communications, important alternative efforts can easily remain obscure, due to an absence of international exposure and distribution.

The fiction that structures *Forgotten Silver* has its historical counterpoint in the subject matter of the documentary *Al-Film al-Mafkoud/The Lost Film* (Joana Hadjithomas and Khalil Joreige, Lebanon/France, 2003), discussed by Laura U. Marks in this volume. *The Lost Film* documents the loss of a print of the filmmakers' first film and their efforts to retrieve it. Rather than the story of a miraculous finding, *The Lost Film* constitutes a sui generis "chronicle of a disappearance" of a piece of filmmaking whose existence, by an ironic turn of fate, is reduced to the excerpts removed by censorship.

A film-about-a-lost-film like this one uncovers unrelated but parallel histories of invisibility, struggle and resourcefulness taking place in a multitude of forms, conditions, and places. Such irregular histories constitute the subject matter of the contributions to this volume. The collection addresses cinematic traditions that, like the lost film in question or the shack full of Colin McKenzie's reels, could remain in obscurity until the moment they are unearthed and brought to light to challenge entrenched hierarchical takes in film appreciation.

The recent wave of uncovering the multiple, previously hidden facets of diverse forms of cinematic creation has been called many things in film studies. *Accented, interstitial, intercultural, underground,* or *minor cinemas* are just some of the terms used by various authors to advocate the mounting urge to conceptualize cultural production that takes into consideration the global interchange of players, be they big or small, prevailing or frail.

At the onset of this movement, there was *Unthinking Eurocentrism* (1994). The groundbreaking work by Ella Shohat and Robert Stam questioned the implicit positioning of Euro-centrism as a limiting straitjacket passing for a commonsensical norm used to assess every kind of creativity by implicitly measuring up to its own standard. Shohat and Stam appealed for the mobilization of "multicultural media studies," a field that "has been gaining momentum but has been barely named." Their supple interdisciplinary approach allowed for the exploration of multiple interacting cultural peripheries, subsuming the much-maligned "*institutional* multiculturalism" in favor of transnationalism and postcolonialism.[2] Their edited collection *Multiculturalism, Postcoloniality, and Transnational Media* (2003) thus outspokenly aimed to overcoming the "neat binarism" that "ironically repositions whiteness and Westernness as normative interlocutors." This work puts forward the relations among various peripherally positioned film traditions that were not necessarily correlated to a tacit Western norm, but asked to be assessed on their own terms.[3]

Our present volume builds upon this work. Like Shohat and Stam, we want to see the entrenched binarism that pits "a rotating chain of marginalized communities against an unstated white norm"[4] challenged and redrawn in favor of scholarship that unveils and acknowledges a vibrant multitude of creative voices and forms of expression that originate and dwell beyond and outside the commonly celebrated cultural hubs.

Shohat and Stam saw Western-based educators as the main agents of this project and called to them for a more enlightened polycentric vision, one that would include recognition of diverse cultural strands alongside the study of the Western mainstream.[5] Further to this, the present volume proposes a scholarly space where the multiple peripheral strands may *speak* for themselves without having to face the onerous burden of constantly explaining themselves in the context of a Eurocentric construct that inevitably puts them in the position of "defensive apology" and "shamefaced disavowal."[6] The project that this volume is trying to put in motion is, therefore, to place the research in cultures entirely rooted within the periphery, thus sparing the need of the investigation to constantly engage with the center, and effectively bracketing the center out.

This collection branches out from the formative roots established by diverse strands of postcolonial discourse. Edward Said's pronouncements on Orientalism and on the exoticism imbuing cross-cultural representations, Homi Bhabha's take on narrating the nation, or Dipesh Chakrabarti's project of "provincializing Europe" in the discourse on history and memory have been augmented by present-day interpretations that extrapolate the postcolonial condition onto a much wider range of phenomena. In effect, postcolonialism has evolved into a comprehensive category that is not restricted to instances of straightforward domination on the basis of race or colonial dependencies. Today we are able to talk of previously unrecognized dimensions of the dynamically changing periphery, such as postcolonial *whiteness,* and see liminality not only beyond but also within former colonial strongholds.

Evolving globalization theory drew the attention to the "flatness" of the world, to the increasingly dynamic mutual penetration of previously isolated spheres, and to the vigor of interacting peripheries. This links to the clear realization that the shifting configurations of power are perennially recasting the peripheries into new patterns. The need to reassess these transcultural relationships was first recognized within a number of cognate disciplines, especially media and cultural studies, anthropology, cultural geography, and other social sciences.[7] In disciplines adjacent to film studies, studies such as Armand Mattelart's political economy treatise *International Image Markets* (1984) or globalization investigations like John Sinclair and Stuart Cunningham's *Floating Life* (2001) questioned entrenched hierarchies, mapped out new power grids and spatial interfaces, and outlined new circuits of cultural creation, circulation, and consumption. Toby Miller's group project on *Global Hollywood 2* (2005) revealed the extent to which even this preeminently positioned focal point of cultural power had grown reliant on a fiscal lifeline of proceeds flowing in from the trivial peripheries. Transforming the view on the dialectics of global cinema was accompanied by a concerted move of the attention from the national onto the postnational and the transnational echoed, for instance, in such works as Sheldon Hsiao-peng Lu, *Transnational Chinese Cinemas* (1997); Laura U. Marks, *The Skin of the Film* (2000); Hamid Naficy, *An Accented Cinema* (2001); and Elizabeth Ezra and Terry Rowden, *Transnational Cinema* (2006). Like those predecessors, this volume wants to expand the reflection on alternative cinemas initiated by others with a multinational focus, including: Scott MacKenzie and Mette Hjort, *Cinema and Nation* (2000); Stephanie Dennison and Song Hwee Lim, *Remapping World Cinema* (2006); Paul Willemen and Valentina Vitali, *Theorising National Cinemas* (2006); and Mette Hjort and Duncan Petrie, *The Cinema of Small Nations* (2007).

The variety of contributions to such collections is a welcome consequence of collective research that addresses concepts of global significance. *Cinema at the Periphery* seeks to contribute to these multifarious debates by foregrounding a body of cinematic practices, traditions, and texts often overlooked in dominant histories—from Australian Aboriginal cinema to Palestinian documentary; from the unrelenting efforts of indigenous filmmaking to the minority-language endeavors of Scottish-Gaelic or Québécois cinema. The driving concept is the exploration and theorization of cinemas and practices located in positions marginal to the economic, institutional, and ideological centers of image making. Our emphasis is on the vibrant *periphery* as it manifests itself in a variety of contexts worldwide, be it within a national, regional, or global framework, and our focus on contemporary filmmaking. Moreover, the collection aims to formulate the potential ways in which the periphery can function as a critical paradigm that allows for a commonality of meanings to emerge from what are, effectively, radically diverse historical processes. Thus contributions are not only drawn from different disciplines (film studies, cultural studies, anthropology, and such), but also they, and their interests, are derived from all around the world. The films examined deploy an array of local references and tell very different stories from those of the world's established film industries. This is not to say that we are simply positing an age-old binary: independent or art cinema (or rather, all those various international films that circulate via film festivals and independent cinema networks) against the global might of Hollywood. Likewise, this collection does not simply seek to reinstate established notions of oppositional, postcolonial, or third world cinemas. Such approaches would exclude crucial areas of inquiry: for example, the mammoth film producing industry of India whose films do not easily fit into either category; indigenous film cultures and industries (such as Aboriginal Blak cinema) that necessitate a frame of reference other than the modern nation-state; or the contribution of marginalized artists and modes of production to the formation of new hubs of (economic, cultural) influence, such as the impact of the Chinese Sixth Generation filmmakers on the international film festival circuit.

Amid the diversity of filmmaking that takes place at the periphery such rigid oppositions lose their epistemological value. This volume offers instead an attempt to shift established paradigms of world cinema, to turn film history on its head *by making the periphery the center of our study,* and to allow the investigation to take off, wherever possible, from a point that is radically marginal. By changing the perspective we are able to ensure that concerns and voices traditionally sidelined will have the chance to, at least temporarily, take center stage. The various films discussed may or may not appear at film festivals or obtain commercial distribution. While some of these films could be considered art cinema, some most assuredly could not. The chapters that follow take the first steps of a process of mapping out the different layers and territories occupied by these as yet often isolated instances of filmmaking that experience themselves as peripheral. Brought into contact in this way, the films examined begin to resonate with shared concerns. Before we begin, however, there is first the matter of this slippery term, *periphery.*

Where Is the Periphery?

A: "Where is Ulan Bator?"—B: "Capital of Outer Mongolia."
A: "Where is Outer Mongolia?"—B: "Up north, past Inner Mongolia."
A: "And farther north?"—B: "USSR."
A: "And farther north?"—B: "The sea, I guess."
A: "And farther north?"—B: "What the fuck are you on about?"
A: "Farther north is here, Fenyang. 18 Wujia Lane . . . Zhang Jui's house . . .
So, we are all north of the sea."
Dialogue between friends while smoking in Zhang Jui's house.

—*Zhantai/Platform* (Jia Zhangke, China, 2000)

The cinematic periphery is a constantly shifting constituent in a dynamically evolving relationship. It is elusive and intangible, as the center to which it relates keeps redefining itself. In the context of globalization and the realities of the post–cold war world, the relationship between center and periphery is no longer necessarily a straightforward, hierarchical one, where a center seeks to subsume its margins. It is often not even a case of margins struggling toward a center by virtue of some actively functioning centripetal force. As Ezra and Rowden note, "capitalism, as the catalytic agent in the expansion of popular culture has undermined the viability of cultural or national insularity."[8] Accordingly, many new films from the periphery subvert traditional hierarchies of location, as they come from, and/or are set in, places traditionally deemed remote, dependent, subaltern, minor, small, or insular. Their key themes and narratives are defined by a growing awareness of instability and change, by homelessness or incessant journeying and border crossing, counteracting the certainty of fixed coordinates. Accordingly, the theoretical concerns of the collection foreground questions of place, space, passage, and migration in a concerted move toward making new localities and vantage points imaginable.

This volume seeks to create a dynamic tapestry of snapshots that substantiates the peripheral condition in terms of locations, practices, methods, and themes. This allows room for a multifaceted approach to the concept beyond the limits set by an exclusive focus on the minor or the postcolonial; what makes a colossal country like China peripheral in the context of globalization is very different from the relationships that make indigenous filmmakers peripheral; Brazil's marginality differs from the liminality of Denmark or Palestine. Clearly, some chapters do focus on geographically remote case studies. Contributions by Duncan Petrie and Mette Hjort discuss small national cinemas located at the global margins (New Zealand and Scotland respectively). Although prosperous economies, these small nations are marginalized in terms of film production. Other chapters explore filmmaking emerging from peripheral cultures (be they social of filmic) that are internal to nations and therefore depend on an industrial infrastructure the access to which is predicated on their marginal position within the whole. These peripheral cultures may or may not feel that the nation or state speaks with the same voice as they do, and, accordingly, their cinematic output often represents a different view from yet another peripheral position. Examples include Kay Dickinson on Palestinian "stateless" cinema, Faye Ginsburg on Australian Aboriginal films, Bill Marshall on cinema from Quebec, and David Martin-Jones on Scottish-Gaelic cinema. At times the discussion of "indigenous" production that can be classed as "peripheral" is the sole focus of the piece, but at others peripheral films are considered in relation to other cinemas that make films in and/or about the same locations (for instance, Patricia Pisters on films about Tangier). This diversity of definitions of the periphery gives us flexibility in opening up unexplored territory as a way of questioning how many types of periphery are out there rather than prematurely narrowing the potential of the discussion. The major strength of this approach is that it enables diverse ways of thinking (and rethinking) notions of center and periphery in the configurations of world cinema. The concept of periphery is not fixed and static but dynamically adjusts to a range of shifting patterns of dominance in spheres such as industry, ideology, and taste.

The multiple meanings of this cinematic periphery suggest that there are many connections to be drawn among different approaches to cinema that prove to be mutually enriching and among different types of marginally positioned cinematic productions. This type of synergizing, which aims to highlight mutual interrelatedness, is easier to facilitate through open-ended categories than through more restrictive geographical or economic classification. This rationale determines the two key areas into which the book is divided—industries and markets on the one hand, and identities and histories on the other. This organization facilitates the exploration of various spatial, cultural, and filmic configurations that become peripheries in the context of those dynamically changing relations of hierarchy and power that more narrowly defined geographical or economic definitions would not permit us to conceptualize. It also reflects the very particular conditions of filmmaking at the periphery, the inextricable interrelationship that exists between peripheral production modes and circulation channels, and the emerging narratives of histories and identities they enable. These areas function as the interlocking pieces of the yin and yang circle or as the intertwined surface of a Möbius strip. It is the specific industrial and distributional formations of the periphery that condition certain visions, just as peripheral films require a certain type of infrastructure to enable them to enunciate themselves. The two sections are not intended to demonstrate a causal relationship, as it were, with marginal industries and markets being considered the sole determinants of subliminal narratives of memory and identity. Rather, this is a symbiotic feedback loop, the two sections of the book each emphasizing a different side of the mutually enabling equation.

Inevitably, as is seen in several of the contributions, discussion of individual peripheral contexts that define specific narratives of history and identity will involve some examination of the industrial and market conditions that affect these projects. The reverse is also true of pieces that focus on industrial and distributional issues first and foremost. Thus, the two different ways of approaching cinema at the periphery that determine the volume's structure are intended to demonstrate the necessity of exploring both aspects of peripheral cinema as reciprocally formative and entwined.

Whereas the point of departure for the concept of periphery lies, most commonly, in realities of location, the different case studies included in this volume explore the connotations of the peripheral as a mode of practice, as a textual strategy, as a production infrastructure, and as a narrative encoded on the margins of the dominant modes of production, distribution, and consumption. In this respect, our aim is to contextualize and cancel the presumed binary dichotomy of "center" and "periphery" by offering a collection of "relational studies that do not always pass through the putative center."[9] The selected case studies "attempt to spell out the workings of globalization in particular contexts."[10] As they map out the periphery as a relational and shifting concept, they uncover the multiplicity of interactions that take place around and beyond the centers of power.

Structure of the Collection

In part 1, "Peripheral Positions: (Re-)drawing Industries and Markets," we find different modes of production from Australia, New Zealand, and China rubbing shoulders with examples of Danish coproduced and Québécois filmmaking that are, quite literally, a world apart both in size and on the map, even though in various ways similar in their economic peripherality and the strategies they adopt to overcome it. Part 2 sees discussion of such geographically disparate locations as Tangier, Scotland's Gaeldom, Palestine, or Brazil. These liminal locations share many similarities in the way filmmakers narrate space and place to examine peripheral identities, in particular in their explorations of history through the landscape. Here the periphery is often approached almost as a condition, a mental state that can throw into question linear histories promoted by established national powers. In this respect, the contributions to this part stress the continuous shifting of perspectives that results from the excavation of histories of suppression and domination.

The first part is concerned with the industrial set-ups of diverse cinemas and the multifarious ways in which various peripheries interact with one another, be it in the process of production or in the area of distribution. Globalization, international coproduction, and funding opportunities raise questions about the nature of contemporary cinema and the role it plays in both major and minor cultural frameworks. How do subnational film industries—such as those of Scotland or Quebec, or those of nomadic or aboriginal cultures—function in the context of multinational nation-states? Is cross-financing mutually empowering to production and distribution mechanisms across peripheral nations, or does this very process tend to move cultural production inevitably back toward a homogenizing center? Is there evidence that we are witnessing a, to use Fareed Zakaria's popular phrase, "rise of the rest" in the area of film production and circulation?

Most of the contributors cannot help observing the limitations of international distribution, caused not only by the fact that small domestic audiences do not provide sufficiently sizable markets but, first and foremost, also by the limited access to established international distribution channels. Throughout a variety of industry models—from situations with a well-developed production base to situations with an almost absent production infrastructure—the control over distribution remains only partial at best. Would the growing recognition of alternative distribution routes change the picture? Dina Iordanova's contribution raises questions regarding the way in which we study the channels of international penetration available to peripherally positioned cinemas. Taking off from the premise that most research into film's global distribution patterns is carried out in Western-based hubs and effectively traces only the flow of mainstream entertainment, her investigation aims to highlight and bring into account the growing importance of less acknowledged diffusion channels (such as the festival and the diasporic circuits, as well as the new digital downloads) that have traditionally been dismissed as lacking substantial penetration and thus remain underexplored. In order to highlight the cumulative impact of such additional routes available to customarily ignored cinematic outputs, her study positions the investigative point of view outside of the traditional model of "the West and the rest" and delves into the peripheral domain of the "Long Tail" of distribution.

In her investigation of Danish cinema's response to globalizing processes in *Small Nation, Global Cinema* (2005), Mette Hjort makes an important point that can be applied to the field in general: the major trends and broad characteristics of globalization in relation to cinema have been outlined successfully so far; what is needed now is a closer scrutiny on concrete cases. Therefore, the real understanding of globalization necessitates, "a broadly diversified empirical engagement with the central issues." Rather than making wide-ranging statements on globalization, Hjort notes, at this point it would be more useful to acknowledge that globalization's tendencies "are not uniform across contexts and thus become apparent only in somewhat more particularist accounts that are properly attuned to the empirical realities of specific local situations."[11]

Hjort's close-up study on the *Advance Party* gives life to the above methodological observation. It focuses on a concrete instance of cinematic collaboration between two nations at the periphery of European cinematic culture, one with an independent state (Denmark), the other enjoying a relative autonomy as a result of a devolutionary process (Scotland). Taking a bird's-eye view within these two national contexts, the scrutiny is on the transnational interaction between agents located in key cities (Copenhagen and Glasgow) and film producing companies (Zentropa Film Productions and Sigma Films). The detailed empirical analysis of the resulting affinitive and "milieu-building" transnationalism reveals that while cultural policy is an important part of the picture, the emphasis falls not so much on state actors but on a different type of more concrete-level agency. The case study reveals that on the periphery there are promising transnational initiatives that film companies operating within the parameters of national, subnational, or supranational frameworks can undertake in order to develop a filmmaking milieu in cities that are of strategic importance for the countries where they are situated.

Duncan Petrie, whose earlier work on Scottish cinema has also been preoccupied with issues of periphery, here explores the case of New Zealand, another peripherally positioned nation that has recently enjoyed an unprecedented level of international visibility. His chapter focuses on the subtle branding of New Zealand's cinematic culture. Starting off with the premise that peripheral cinemas face a constant struggle to secure a visible share of their own domestic markets, Petrie systematically reveals the various constraints, opportunities, and dilemmas that they are confronted with. State support for the film industry makes a difference only when it comes hand-in-hand with the cultivation of outside markets. Where New Zealand films are intended to compete in the global arena, they can capitalize on the specific subtleties that play out within the cultural nationalism of a settler society as manifested in the domestic Pakeha-Maori stratification, as well as on the "international division of cultural labor,"[12] ultimately creating an alternative kind of cinema that has its own local resonance and global audience. Petrie's investigation highlights the complexities of a situation where emerging alternative opportunities and integrated cultural and economic initiatives are being mobilized for the benefit of local filmmaking endeavors. The emphasis on the national brand reflects on the conscious efforts to negotiate the intricate interaction between local and global considerations, as it plays out within a small and peripheral nation's attempt to appropriate creative ways of embracing new opportunities for reaching out to international image markets. It also raises real concerns about how effectively the moving image can engage with the underlying multifaceted cultural issues that continue to define and trouble New Zealand as a rapidly changing nation.

Keeping the Pacific in focus, Faye Ginsburg goes a degree below the national in a case study that looks into the developing infrastructure of aboriginal filmmaking in Australia over the past two decades, looking beyond the text in search of offscreen dimensions of cultural and political labor of Aboriginal activists. She traces the ways in which resourceful indigenous cinematic activism has managed to take advantage of the state's cultural policy framework and to mobilize the discursive evolution in conceptualizing diversity and the expanding (if contested) understanding of Australia as a culturally heterogeneous nation. This filmmaking offers alternative narratives that undermine the established yet fictional accounts of harmonious and universally accepted national development; by doing this it contributes to a superior process of self-representation and mastery of policy and industry contexts. Ginsburg also offers a case study—the career of indigenous filmmaker Rachel Perkins—and thus asserts the trend of close-up investigations into cinema at the periphery. Both contributions stress the importance of government support and of branding in the context of complex identity negotiations.

In contrast, Sheldon H. Lu explores the paradoxical status of independent "underground" filmmaking in the People's Republic of China vis-à-vis the state apparatus: subject to censorship in the national market, but supported and given exposure by alternative transnational circuits of film culture, such as the network of bigger and smaller film festivals. Lu calls for a reassessment of old dichotomies. Periphery and center, marginal and mainstream, opposition and co-optation are not clearly delimited areas anymore. Whereas formerly resistant directors move into the mainstream and reinvent themselves as successful producers of new Orientalizing spectacles for Western consumption, Sixth Generation filmmakers position themselves strategically in the national and international markets balancing formal adventurousness with the limitations imposed by economic necessity. For Lu, the work of underground directors encapsulates a distinct peripheral cinema emerging into mainstream circuits in China, which still exhibits an uncompromising aesthetic and unflinching social focus in spite of the pressures of economic censorship.

Finally, Bill Marshall discusses the specifically *internal* peripheral status of filmmaking in Quebec, a tradition that is known for its ambiguous relationship with its own national power structures and the dominant forms of identity they promote. For Marshall, Quebec cinema's peripheral status, both nationally and internationally, is a result of a complex nexus of unique historical and geographical circumstances. He traces the development of this subnational tradition in relation to the global film industry, and—beginning the transition to part 2—the many ways the minor Québécois cinema negotiates its identity in relation to Anglophone North America, metropolitan France, and the rest of the French-speaking world. Marshall explores the interconnections between industrial and distribution opportunities available to Québécois filmmakers and the narratives they enable, where state aid at both federal and provincial levels facilitates a peripheral vision that is able to crossover into Francophone markets. In a way that complements Faye Ginsburg's investigation, Marshall's analysis shows the difficulties faced by Québécois filmmaking within the domestic market, where (in spite of stiff competition from Hollywood), it continues to thrive against the odds. In closing, the question of Quebec cinema's exportability is examined, in particular the strategic role of coproductions as a mechanism that allows the targeting of wider markets.

Part 2, "Peripheral Visions: (Re-)conceiving Identities and Histories" investigates the distinctive narratives and iconographies that visualize silenced voices, hidden and forbidden histories, and emerging identities. In the films set in Palestine, Scotland's Gaeldom, Tangier, and Brazil, *place* takes on an equal role to that of the *protagonist*. Location now functions not only as a plot device but also provides a symbolic framework within the film's diegesis. Liminal, tangential, or even extreme borderlands function as the setting for narratives that signify isolation and marginality, presuppose a context of frontier and displacement, or remythologize peripheral histories. An exploration of the strategies of aesthetic resistance via language, intertextual appropriation, and visualization of the hidden processes of identity overlaps and develops this trajectory of analysis in particular in the last three chapters on Brazilian, Spanish, and Arab case studies. Together, these six pieces examine the extent to which marginal and peripheral filmmaking constructs new identities in the ever-changing geopolitical configurations of globalization.

In the first entry in this section, Kay Dickinson discusses the Palestinian road movie, an example of national filmmaking that survives in the interstices of intricate and fragile transnational production and distribution infrastructures. She concentrates on a selection of films from the period of the Second Intifada, from the international art cinema hit *Yadon ilaheyya/ Divine Intervention* (Elia Suleiman, France/Morocco/Germany/Palestine, 2002) to smaller documentaries such as *Going for a Ride?* (Nahed Awwad, Palestine, 2003). Through repeated ironic reference to the supposed freedoms of "the road" as conceptualized by the global genre of that name, these movies thwart any such easy insinuations about liberty through concrete reference to the many road blocks suffered under the Occupation (itself a larger metaphor for the prohibition of returning refugee Palestinians). Dickinson explores how, in recent Palestinian cinema, "the road" generates meaning as a symbolic and a geopolitical entity in the Israel-Palestine conflict. She offers the impeded, ever-changing, and often dangerous space of "the road" not only as a recurrent narrative conceit but also as a clue to understanding how the increasingly complex center/periphery divide shapes filmic analysis.

The second piece in the section is by David Martin-Jones, and examines several recent Gaelic-language films, focusing in particular on *An Iobairt/ The Sacrifice* (Gerda Stevenson, UK, 1996) and *Seachd: The Inaccessible Pinnacle* (Simon Miller, UK, 2007). Produced on the periphery of Scotland, the production and distribution context of Gaelic films is yet another example of fragile yet remarkably vital infrastructure that enables creativity that would otherwise remain unvoiced. As this contribution shows, the engagement of certain of these films with the Gaelic oral storytelling tradition enables an innovative examination of peripheral identities on a par with that found in certain African cinemas. The chapter begins with a brief introduction to the history of cinematic representations of Scotland's remote islands before sketching in the context of the Gaelic Renaissance taking place in the Gàidhealtachd (Gaeldom) and the place of Gaelic cinema in this process. A consideration of Gaelic films' treatment of historical time and landscape (in particular their use of bleak, isolated locations that propel their narratives) demonstrates how these films deploy epic, mythical tales to reconsider stereotypical conceptions of life on Scotland's remote edges. Rather than lost in the past, or bypassed by the teleological progression of modernity, these films consider how, through the oral storytelling tradition, the periphery's past remains active in the present (in line with a Bergsonian or Deleuzian view of time), as a way of explaining the presence of various layers of history in contemporary Scottish-Gaelic cinema and ensuring the continued engagement with the specific past of this particular periphery in the greater context of the Gaelic Renaissance.

Remaining with the notion of a layered view of the past, Patricia Pisters investigates cinematic representations of Tangier, a city that cinema has revisited at various points in time, and in the context of various transnational production contexts. Initially Pisters makes use of the Bergsonian view of time to discuss a number of different films depicting key moments in the history of this most peripheral of cities, as though they were, precisely, virtual layers of the past. In the context of the examination of peripheral cinemas, this versatile model of time (as further developed by Deleuze) is used here as a metaphor for the archiving of different "histories" of Tangier through cinema. With this contextual sketch of the city's cinematic archive in place she then embarks upon a postcolonial critique, informed by Homi Bhabha's work on the way in which nostalgia is deployed in *Casablanca* (Michael Curtiz, USA, 1942), which is used as a springboard for discussion of the return of postcolonial agency that has recently arisen in films set in Tangier. Revisionist perspectives on the history of Tangier are examined in films like Rachid Benhadj's *El Khoubz el Hafi/For Bread Alone* (France/Italy/Morocco, 2005) and André Téchiné's *Loin/Far* (France, 2001), showing how, in both instances, these films of the periphery reinvest the past with new meaning through an examination of its active presence in the present, thereby challenging the archive of previous depictions of the city created by other Western filmmaking centers.

The vertical axis of temporal exploration offers a suggestive contrast with the shifting horizons in Lúcia Nagib's analysis of the retelling of Brazil's myths and Portugal's imperial history from the viewpoint of the excluded. Moving into matters of cultural discourse, Nagib examines the ways in which the crisis of the national project in the early 1990s led Brazilian art cinema, for the first time, to look at itself as periphery and reapproach the old colonial center, Portugal. Through an in-depth analysis of Walter Salles and Daniela Thomas's *Terra estrangeira/Foreign Land* (Brazil/Portugal, 1995), a film shot in São Paulo, Lisbon, and Cape Verde, her chapter examines the reversals in historical perspective that may reveal hidden histories of peripheral identities through the encounter of Lusophone peoples who find common ground in their marginality. As much as the former colonies, Portugal is defined by its location at the edge of Europe and by myths such as Sebastianism, which date back to a tumultuous history of imperial subjugation of Portugal by its closest neighbor, Spain. The dialogues in *Foreign Land* combine Brazilian, Portuguese, and Creole linguistic peculiarities into a common dialect of exclusion. Language puns trigger visual rhymes, which refer back to the Cinema Novo repertoire and restage the imaginary of the discovery turned into unfulfilled utopia. The film's Christian iconography, reminiscent of the colonial past, defines a circuit of exchange, which is also that of the globalized cinema, a realm in which this film, made of citations and homage to other cinemas, tries to retrieve a sense of belonging.

The search for a sense of belonging within histories of exclusion is also the guiding thread in Belén Vidal's chapter on the aesthetics and politics of contemporary Spanish retro-comedy. The chapter focuses on *Torremolinos 73* (Pablo Berger, Spain/Denmark, 2003), a film whose plot revolves around an unlikely axis of interacting peripheries. Vidal teases out the reverse side of what Hjort calls "affinitive transnationalism" in a film that pokes fun at the difficulties entailed by transnational collaboration in Europe in the face of uneven socioeconomic development. Vidal examines how, through arch irony and careful period reconstruction, *Torremolinos 73* retrieves a tradition of despised popular comedies reflecting (and masking) realities of cultural isolation. She looks in particular at cinephilia as a thematic strategy that brings to the fore unexpected iconic and narrative intersections among pornography, art cinema, and indigenous popular films—intersections that challenge linear accounts of Spanish national cinema. This reimagining of the national as peripheral within Europe allows for a negotiation of processes of historical exclusion (signified by the protracted Francoist dictatorship) through an empowering, if double-edged fantasy of filiation to European art-cinema traditions. The chapter argues that the mechanisms of retro-comedy in *Torremolinos 73* foreground a strategic use of cinephilia in order to reframe a marginalized national tradition in dialogue with an imagined landscape of European film culture.

Laura U. Marks closes the collection with an illuminating theoretical examination of nonindustrial, artisanal, and auteurist modes of Arab cinema against the background of imperialist and neo-Orientalist preemptive interpretations that inform the politics of funding, distribution, and exhibition. She examines forms of cinema that, dependent on a combination of local and foreign funding, circulate complexly among Arab participants with vying interests and between Arab and Western audiences, all of whom tend to regard Arab films through the eyes of the others. In this context, *enfolded* modes of experience manifest through instances of politically and economically marginalized filmmaking that, more often than not, evokes virtual spaces and virtual events. Arab filmmakers are highly aware that the perceptible world is constructed by political interests, and that it is almost impossible for an Arab filmmaker to speak of the Arab world without simultaneously deconstructing or negating it. Marks deploys a triadic model based on Charles Sanders Peirce's epistemology and a Deleuzian and Guattari-inspired cinema of immanence in order to examine an enfolded model of knowledge divided into three epistemological levels: Experience, Information, and Image. From the Syrian documentary *Toufan fi Balad al-Baath/A Flood in Baath Country* (Omar Amiralay, 2004) to the Egyptian epic *Bab al-Shams/The Door to the Sun* (Yousry Nasrallah, 2004), Arab cinema thus takes on the delicate task of unfolding or explicating—from these insufficient images and across a thick layer of imperialist predisposition—hitherto virtual events, data, and sensations.

The Periphery—A New Center?

The framework we propose is meant to be a flexible one, encouraging a diversity of approaches and dialogues between and across the two parts into which the book is divided. Throughout the two sections, a number of reading itineraries are possible, and indeed, desirable. The most obvious are established through cultural proximity and affinity. The Pacific Rim (examined by the chapters by Petrie and Ginsburg), as well as the cinemas from the Arab world (focus of the pieces by Dickinson and Marks) or Scotland (as a model case of European periphery, as variously examined by Hjort and Martin-Jones) figure prominently in our preoccupation with the periphery as geopolitical reality(-ies). There are dialogues that concern the North (Quebec, Denmark, Scotland) and dialogues that concern the South (Morocco, Brazil, Spain), as well as explorations that bring large yet peripherally positioned traditions, like China and Brazil, in correlation to each other. Likewise, dialogues emerge around conceptual clusters such as the ongoing currency of a Deleuzian methodology for the exploration of peripheral histories (embedded in the arguments by Pisters, Martin-Jones, Marshall, Nagib, and Marks); the ambivalent relationship of subnational and oppositional cultures within the wider frame of the nation-state (touched upon by Hjort, Ginsberg, Martin-Jones, Marshall, and Lu); the metaphorical and actual narratives of displacement and traveling (in Dickinson and Nagib); the legacy of the colonial past (in Nagib and Pisters); the impact of war and political oppression (in the pieces by Dickinson, Lu, and Marks); the dependency on the distribution infrastructure (Iordanova, Marks, Ginsburg, Petrie); or the connections between local and transnational histories that arise through intertextual reframing (Pisters, Nagib, Vidal). These microitineraries, with their focus on the particular, the analysis at close range, or the single case study, are framed in the wider picture offered by Iordanova in her analysis of the cumulative effect of networks and clusters established at the periphery.

From Hjort's taxonomy of transnationalisms, to Marks's model of the enfolded image that unearths suppressed histories and modes of experience in the Arab world, the collection aims to substantiate a cinema at the periphery that, by drawing a complex map of global case studies, goes from the particular to the general, in the form of myriad strategies for methodological reflection. The notion of periphery advocated by the collection thus takes the shape of a productive relational framework informed by contextual and textual factors alike.

Notes

1. See Duncan Petrie, "New Zealand," in *The Cinema of Small Nations,* ed. Hjort and Petrie, 160–61.

2. Shohat and Stam, Introduction to *Unthinking Eurocentrism: Multiculturalism and the Media,* 6.

3. In their introduction, Shohat and Stam interrogate, for example, the underexplored connections between Indian and Egyptian cinema, or between Chinese and Japanese cinema, in order to ascertain how race and caste may be formulated in other national contexts. Shohat and Stam, eds., *Multiculturalism, Postcoloniality, and Transnational Media,* 4.

4. Ibid.

5. "Such studies would go a long way toward deprovincializing a discussion that has too often focused only on United Statesian issues and Hollywood representations. Multiculturalizing and transnationalizing the media studies curriculum opens up fascinating possibilities. Rather than focus exclusively on the Hollywood musical comedy, for example, why not devise courses that feature Brazilian chanchadas, Mexican cabaret films, Egyptian belly-dance films, and Bombay musicals?" Introduction to Shohat and Stam, eds., *Multiculturalism, Postcoloniality, and Transnational Media,* 4.

6. As brilliantly articulated by Rosie Thomas in her classical text on Indian cinema's reception in the West. See Thomas, "Indian Cinema: Pleasure and Popularity," in *The Bollywood Reader,* 22.

7. See, among many others, Appadurai, *Modernity at Large: Cultural Dimensions of Globalization;* Ong, *Flexible Citizenship: The Cultural Logics of Transnationality;* Hedetoft and Hjort, eds., *The Postnational Self: Belonging and Identity;* or Shohat and Stam, eds., *Multiculturalism, Postcoloniality, and Transnational Media.*

8. Ezra and Rowden, "General Introduction: What Is Transnational Cinema?" in *Transnational Cinema, The Film Reader,* 3.

9. Shohat and Stam, Introduction to *Multiculturalism, Postcoloniality, and Transnational Media,* ed. *Shohut and Stam,* 4.

10. Hjort, *Small Nation, Global Cinema: The New Danish Cinema,* 24.

11. Ibid.

12. Miller et al., *Global Hollywood 2,* 200.

Bibliography

Appadurai, Arjun. *Modernity at Large: Cultural Dimensions of Globalization.* Minneapolis: University of Minnesota Press, 1996.

Bhabha, Homi K. "Dissemination: Time, Narrative, and the Margins of the Modern Nation." In *Nation and Narration,* edited by Homi K. Bhabha. London: Routledge, 1990, 291–322.

Chakrabarti, Dipesh. *Provincializing Europe.* Princeton, NJ: Princeton University Press, 2000.

Cunningham, Stuart, and John Sinclair, eds. *Floating Lives: The Media and Asian Diasporas.* Denver, CO: Rowman and Littlefield, 2001.

Dennison, Stephanie, and Song Hwee Lim, eds. *Remapping World Cinema: Identity, Culture, and Politics in Film.* London: Wallflower, 2006.

Ezra, Elizabeth, and Terry Rowden, eds. *Transnational Cinema: The Film Reader.* London: Routledge, 2006.

Hedetoft, Ulf, and Mette Hjort, eds. *The Postnational Self: Belonging and Identity.* Minneapolis: University of Minnesota Press, 2002

Hjort, Mette. *Small Nation, Global Cinema: The New Danish Cinema.* Minneapolis: University of Minnesota Press, 2005.

Hjort, Mette, and Scott McKenzie, eds. *Cinema and Nation.* London: Routledge, 2000.

Hjort, Mette, and Duncan Petrie, eds. *The Cinema of Small Nations.* Edinburgh: Edinburgh University Press, 2007.

Lu, Sheldon Hsiao-peng, ed. *Transnational Chinese Cinemas: Identity, Nationhood, Gender.* Honolulu: University of Hawai'i Press, 1997.

Marks, Laura U. *The Skin of the Film: Intercultural Cinema, Embodiment, and the Senses.* Durham, NC: Duke University Press, 2000.

Mattelart, Armand, Xavier Delcourt, and Michele Mattelart. *International Image Markets: In Search of an Alternative Perspective.* London: Comedia, 1984.

Miller, Toby, Nitin Govil, John McMuria, Ting Wang, and Richard Maxwell. *Global Hollywood 2.* London: British Film Institute, 2005.

Naficy, Hamid. *An Accented Cinema: Exilic and Diasporic Filmmaking.* Princeton, NJ: Princeton University Press, 2001.

Ong, Aihwa. *Flexible Citizenship: The Cultural Logics of Transnationality.* Durham, NC: Duke University Press, 1999.

Shohat, Ella, and Robert Stam. *Unthinking Eurocentrism: Multiculturalism and the Media.* London: Routledge, 1994.

Shohat, Ella, and Robert Stam, eds. *Multiculturalism, Postcoloniality, and Transnational Media.* New Brunswick, NJ: Rutgers University Press, 2003.

Thomas, Rosie. "Indian Cinema: Pleasure and Popularity" (1985). In *The Bollywood Reader,* edited by Jigna Desai and Rajinder Dudrah, 18–28. London: Open University Press, 2008.

Said, Edward W. *Orientalism.* 1978. London: Penguin, 2003.

Willemen, Paul, and Valentina Vitali, eds. *Theorising National Cinema.* London: British Film Institute, 2006.

Part 1

PERIPHERAL POSITIONS

(Re-)drawing Industries and Markets

Rise of the Fringe
Global Cinema's Long Tail

In 2007 and 2008 I visited a variety of countries. Quite naturally for a film buff like me, I wanted to know what was at the cinemas wherever I went. The film theaters in my native city of Sofia, Bulgaria's capital, seemed to be playing mostly Hollywood films. But this seemed to be the case only in this far-flung corner of southeast Europe. In other places, Hollywood's stranglehold seemed to be loosening. During my stay in Paris people were standing in line for tickets to see the smash hit *Welcome to the Sticks*. In Tokyo, all the headlines were for Japanese blockbusters such as *Hero* or *Always*, whereas in Thessaloniki, *El Greco* was by far the most popular film. All the film theaters in Hong Kong prominently displayed posters for Ang Lee's *Lust, Caution* while the cinema in Copenhagen played the new Ken Loach, *It's a Free World*. Berlin's twenty-odd specialized cinemas could not have carried a more diverse fare, from the Chinese Berlinale-winner *Tuya's Marriage* to the GDR-nostalgic documentary about American dissident singer Dean Read, *The Red Elvis*.[1]

It is not the fleeting impressions of these travels on which I will be building my argument here, however. Having spent twenty years studying international film, I am more than convinced that we operate with a flawed understanding of the dynamics of world cinema, and that the field of film studies would greatly benefit from the introduction of a more acute peripheral vision. We have been led to believe that, as far as film is concerned, the world is divided into Hollywood, powerful and thriving, and the rest, weak and fading. If, however, we were to become more perceptive to the snowballing evidence coming from multiple but scattered data streams and strands of scholarship, we would finally see and acknowledge the effects of other routes of film distribution, we would change our view on the balance of powers and enhance our understanding of how these traditionally ignored flows are changing the global dynamics of cinema in circulation. In order to see this, one would need to consolidate the multiple peripheral circulation strands into one and juxtapose them as a solidly conjoined stream to Hollywood's chart-buster culture.[2]

It is about time to acknowledge the new realities. A quarter of the world's most commercially successful films come from sources other than Hollywood; many are more profitable and bring higher per-screen averages than the studio blockbusters. Not only are many more peripheral films being produced, many more of them are also seen and appreciated, due to the vitality of growing alternative channels of dissemination.

Since the end of the Cold War, global migration and diasporic cultural consumption has intensified, and new technologies have reshaped the media worlds of people around the globe.[3] Countries that used to be traditional sources of emigration have turned into countries of immigration; worlds that were unlikely to touch or collide, now intersect and overlap. Yet our concepts of the pattern of comprehensive cultural exchanges are inconsistent and patchy, and the studies that propose a comprehensive picture of the "alternative modernities" (Larkin) at the periphery are still a handful in comparison with the scholarship on mainstream modernity.[4]

We need a better understanding of the essence and the effects of transnational cultural circulation originating from the periphery. These are processes that one can see best if one transcends the strictly defined framework of the national, which treats national traditions as a mosaic of discrete cultural phenomena. One increasingly recognizes that the localities of production are spatially disjointed and audiences increasingly scattered around the globe. This is where studies of peripheral cinema come into the picture, with a call to approach the cycle of film production, dissemination, and reception as one dynamic process that transcends national borders, reflecting the mobility of human existence in the global age.[5]

The growing number of studies that highlight aspects of the complexities of global cinematic circulation allow for a fuller grasp of the situation. Besides the traditionally weak channels of ordinary commercial (theatrical and ancillary) distribution, we need to take into account several further channels that function together but are still studied as discrete phenomena and considered independently from one another. There is the overlooked but nonetheless influential system of the international film festival circuit. Then, the thriving system of diasporic distribution of films from various alternative production centers that integrates theatrical distribution, DVD sales in shops and online, as well as low-power TV and satellite television outlets. And, last but probably most important, there is the increased significance of the new Internet-enabled channels.

Some of these have been covered in the media and studied by academics in a steadily growing body of scholarship, while others have only recently become the object of attention. In most cases the focus has been on a single distribution channel that, for the purpose of convenience, is taken out of its complex context. Typically, one strand would study the diasporic distribution at the expanse of one specific national or linguistic group without correlating it to the multiplicity of channels that other diasporic groups operate simultaneously; another strand would study European or A-category festivals but not their complex hierarchical interactions with all the other smaller and geographically dispersed players in the circuit. Thus, due to methodological constraints, we have only limited comprehension of the dialectical interactions of these multiple circuits in a global context. In order to comprehend the real global dynamics, we would need to focus on merging the scattered strands of knowledge into a consolidated *long tail*.

My goal in this chapter is simple and straightforward: to point out the ascendant global presence and impact of cinema from the periphery that, by virtue of entrenched perceptions of ageless hegemony, is often regarded as secondary and, even where acknowledged, still classified as lacking impact. In doing this, I hope to begin correlating discussions of cultural hybridity and postmodern practices of appropriation to the emerging empirical evidence that increases our awareness of the global dynamics of cinema. The methodologies for studying these processes are still imperfect, and the data we can use in our assessment are incomplete and insufficient. Increasingly, however, things are changing, as new figures become available, and new scholars interested in peripheral cinemas enter the field and produce scholarship that rapidly improves the level of our understanding. The suppressed treasure trove of cinematic content of peripheral cinema, sidelined into the margins by the enduring blockbuster culture, is about to break through and reveal all its glorious richness and diversity, in large measure due to shifts in the manner of distributing film content.

Global Dynamics

Scholarship as well as popular wisdom has it that Hollywood product enjoys unrivaled dominance over world markets and stifles all other cinematic outputs. Little is known of the distribution dynamics of other film traditions or of other audiences, however, and many of the transnational channels used for distributing non-Hollywood cinema are still to be properly examined. In addition, the instances where alternative strands have been explored and written on are usually presented as discrete individual case studies with little further correlation to a global and evolving context. Yet more and more studies on these understudied channels of distribution are coming about, and a range of publications present findings that, if taken together, enable us to discover a far more diverse picture of the dynamics of peripheral cinema. It is about time to raise the issue of the impact of non-Hollywood cinema as cumulative totality.

Film studies has produced a respectable and thorough body of work outlining the functioning of Hollywood, both as an industrial set-up,[6] and globally.[7] Viewed in a worldwide context, this scholarship tells an important part of the story: that Hollywood is ubiquitous, that it is the only truly global film distribution operation that capitalizes successfully on its position within the international marketplace, and that at least half of its revenues come from abroad (which makes preserving its strong international marketing position particularly important). Year after year the world's top-grossing pictures come from major Hollywood studios; their international saturation releases are often scheduled a year in advance, and, after being intensely hyped up, they triumph on multiple screens across various countries. International films can get a similar kind of exposure only if picked up by Hollywood distributors. It is a remarkable and truly comprehensive marketing machine.

More importantly, Hollywood is the only film marketing enterprise that directly monitors all aspects of its operation, by keeping a close watch on a variety of statistics produced from meticulous reporting on all domestic and international box-office and auxiliary revenues. It has been engaged in such scrutiny for decades now; scholars who examine Hollywood's global expansion and analyze its global presence and impact owe the reliability of their studies to this inexorable monitoring, most of which is on hand from an assortment of publicly available reports, financial information, budget data, box-office statistics, weekend tables of theatrical revenues, international release charts, auxiliary markets revenue records, and so on.

No similar data have been available to researchers who are observing other aspects of the global dynamics of film circulation. While some countries produce statistics, putting together a picture that compares the available data is a mammoth task.[8] Thus, compiling a comprehensive picture of the global movements of films is altogether impossible due to the absence of reliable inclusive data. While we know part of the story on global cinema, the one relating to Hollywood, we do not know enough about the other part of the equation related to non-Hollywood. It is a void we can fill up with speculative narratives, simply because we do not have sufficient information. If we ever really want to see the whole picture, we will have to put up with inconsistent methodologies. On the one hand we will have the reliable, sturdily measured and extensively covered Hollywood, and on the other hand we will have the anecdotal, episodic, and scattered evidence that is gathered from diverse outlets throughout the rest of the world.

Still, the little that is known gradually grows bigger. Slowly and painstakingly, this knowledge is helping to construct a picture that differs from the one of Hollywood's unshakable global hegemony. In countries like France, Italy, Spain, the United Kingdom, Russia, Poland, and in particular in smaller markets (where national films have difficulties recouping their budgets due to the smaller size of audiences) like Denmark or Greece, domestic productions have begun to attract a significant proportion of the audience, at the expense of Hollywood's share of the market. Whereas just a few years ago the box-office revenue from domestic films for many of these areas stood at around 15 percent or less, it has now doubled across most of Europe, and trebled in some of the key territories.[9] In addition, it is likely that we may see further improvement of the circulation of European films across borders to other European countries, as in 2007 new measures for supporting the circulation of European products were taken in the context of the new phase of the MEDIA program, with over 65 percent of the program's budget now being allocated for improving distribution to levels that would match rising production. In other parts of the world, India's domestic market still remains inaccessible to Hollywood with more than 90 percent of revenues going to domestically produced films, whereas the revenues based on the increased international presence of Indian cinema have significantly risen; South Korea released over ten films in 2007 with revenues of more than U.S. $25 million domestically; and more than 60 percent of Japan's box-office revenues (yielding the world's third biggest total) come from domestic productions.[10]

Many of the international films that make it to the top forty weekend gross box-office statistics of *Screen International* bring spectacular revenues: in 2007, France's *La Môme/La vie en rose* (Olivier Dahan, 2007) earned U.S. $75 million, Germany's *Lives of Others*—U.S. $65 million, South Korea's *Dragon Wars: D-War* (Hyung-rae Shim, 2007)—U.S. $58 million, India's *Om Shanti Om* (Farah Khan, 2007)—U.S. $35 million. Since these films have been made on budgets that represent a fraction of the average Hollywood budget, they clearly are also more lucrative because a significantly larger proportion of the returns represent profit. The success of such non-Hollywood blockbusters is signaling a bold move toward an increased heterogeneity that has been a feature of some of the established national film industries that, like France or India, remain marginalized in the wider global context and are eager to devise ambitious hits that nonetheless engage with specific cultural legacies and concerns. An example of such effort is Dany Boon's runaway success *Welcome to the Sticks,* a film made for €11 million (euros) (U.S. $15 million), which, released in March 2008, returned more than U.S. $230 million by the end of the year, a return that is worth the investment fifteen times over. The biggest globally coordinated marketing launch for an Indian film also occurred in 2008: UTV's release of *Jodhaa Akbar* in February 2008 secured simultaneous opening for the film across twenty-six territories and on over 1,500 screens, a launch that is fully compatible with high-profile Hollywood releases. Whereas Hollywood continues to mimetize, absorb, and reconfigure peripheral traits and talent in order to reinforce its own dominance, the peripheral industries focus on producing more of these types of blockbusters that are culturally recognizable at home, yet manage to play like a global chart buster.

One of the factors that prevent us from seeing such momentous variations outside global Hollywood is that these are treated as peripheral and often not covered, even in the specialized media. The remake of the musical *Hairspray* (Adam Shankman, USA/UK, 2007) received extensive international coverage and market analysis in the trade press, and ended its five and a half months run in 2007 with theatrical revenues of about U.S. $71 million from distribution in thirty-five territories; over the same period, Japanese *Hero* made U.S. $76 million from only five territories, yet the film's only English-language review by a professional assessor (in the trade magazine *Variety*) remarked that "this highly accessible crowd-pleaser unfortunately looks likely to bypass Western marts."[11]

Since 2004, *Screen International* has endeavored to monitor and present figures that outline the state of the international box office in more comprehensive and compatible terms. It is a challenging task, especially since it is only recently that data have become available for China, India, Russia, and other East European countries.[12] Even though the number of monitored areas is steadily increasing, there is no information from all countries, and not all information is reliable due to the propensity of some distributors to underreport revenues.[13]

Following these reports makes for intriguing reading because several trends emerge clearly. Like, for example, that currently about 25 percent to 30 percent of the forty top grossing global films come from countries other than the United States or the United Kingdom. People who closely monitor the global situation described 2007 as a record-breaking year for the international box office.[14] It is not that such trends were not there before; but it is only now that they are finally coming into the picture. Even if it covers only a short period of time, the table below gives an interesting glimpse into this changing dynamic and reveals that this increased availability of international data change what we see in our monitoring of the global dynamics of non-Hollywood cinema. Data provided in the context of the table allow us to conclude that about 7.5 percent of the recent revenues from the domestic North American market have gone to international producers, and that Hollywood seems to control less than 70 percent of the international market. Both figures undermine the widely spread beliefs (commonly repeated in the classroom) that only 1 percent of the North American market is open to foreign-made content and that Hollywood's level of penetration is at 90 percent in most countries. If international producers find ways to expand their traditionally limited global operations, and if they manage to preserve the healthy market share in their own countries, these statistics are likely to change even further. Such expansion is a scenario that should not be ruled out, especially in view of swift developments that take place in various parts of Asia or Africa.

Writing about the rapidly changing reality of film and media production and entertainment consumption patterns in China, Michael Curtin, remarks:

Hollywood today is . . . very much like Detroit 40 years ago, a factory town that produces big, bloated vehicles with plenty of chrome. As production budgets

Global market comparison (January 1–April 30, 2007)

Theatrical Revenues	Box Office	Percentage of BO
Total	$7.2 bn	100
U.S. majors	$4.8 bn	66.7
Int'l Prod.	$2.4 bn	33.3

Domestic North American market	Box Office	Percentage of BO
Total	$2.8 bn	100
U.S. majors	$2.5 bn	90
Int'l producers	$0.2 bn	7.5

Source: *Screen International*, June 22, 2007, 7.

mushroom, quality declines in large part as a result of institutional inertia and lack of competition. Like Detroit, Hollywood has dominated for so long that many of its executives have difficulty envisioning the transformations now on the horizon.[15]

According to Curtin, Hollywood myopically continues to view the global future "as a world brought together by homogenous cultural products produced and circulated by American media."[16] Other, competing scenarios should be considered, however. As new media conglomerates that aim to become global players emerge in Asia, Curtin notes, this century-long hegemony could be substantially shaken, and it may well turn out that global audiences are more susceptible to new, alternative models that may come from elsewhere. It may be wise to drop the presumption that Hollywood's hegemony is forever, and operate instead with a more flexible vision of the future.[17]

The Festival Circuit

> On more familiar ground, film festivals, as they proliferate in greater numbers than ever before, are becoming the alternative distribution channel for challenging, experimental and otherwise "un-marketable" films.
>
> —Ben Slater[18]

Hollywood films do not need the festival network to get to their audiences. Many play at festivals in copies provided by (or rented from) the distributor that has been attached to the project from inception. Most of the films made in other countries, however, depend on festival participation as it secures them circulation beyond their original environment. The Berlinale Golden Bear for German-Turkish director Fatih Akin's *Gegen die Wand/Head On* in 2004 secured festival showings at more than one hundred other festivals and later on theatrical and DVD distribution deals for a wide range of countries. The award strongly enhanced the profile not only of this director but also of German-Turkish cinema as a whole. Even if the film had stayed within the festival network, it would have had a significant networking effect for its creators. Festivals have been talked up as an alternative distribution network for a while now, yet they remain seen mainly as a showcase that may open doors to real distribution. Only since recently is the increasingly interconnected festival phenomenon being recognized as an autonomous circuit with its own set of nodes, connections, and tenets.[19]

Over the past twenty years, festivals have proliferated all over the world, and they work in an interrelated hierarchical manner. It is nearly impossible to provide an exact quote on the number of festivals in operation, but it is clear that it is well over one thousand and more likely somewhere in the range of two thousand. France alone has over 350 film festivals, approximately one for each day of the year. Several large and well-established festivals function as key hubs in a global network, as it is here where the growing army of professional programmers from other festivals gather to see the new films and decide what will be seen by the audiences they hold the access to.

A select few of the festivals play a key role in the global circulation of certain types of non-mainstream cinematic products. Sundance, which takes place in January in Utah, is the most important site where new work by American independents is being showcased and invited for showings at other festivals, while Toronto in Canada in early September is where a selection of the best of all festivals in Europe and Asia from the previous year is screened to North American journalists, programmers, and distributors, who pick up the films to bring to their respective audiences at smaller festivals or cinematheques. The most exciting new films from across Asia are showcased at the festival in Pusan, Korea in October, where a selection is picked up and presented at Rotterdam at the end of January, so that European and American programmers can take their picks and proliferate the films' exposure by scheduling them for further screenings. And so on . . .

Thus, besides the official film markets that accompany some of the big festivals and that remain the domain of film industry professionals and clear-cut distributors, there is the informal but increasingly networked and efficient system of international flow through festival links, where a small film from an obscure source is picked up by a succession of festivals and shown consecutively in various countries, thus getting truly global exposure, even if this exposure does not bring along measurable financial gains. A randomly chosen example would be the work of Portuguese director Pedro Costa, known for remarkable films about protagonists on the social margins. Whereas not available in official distribution, in recent years his films have been shown across continents at festivals in Hong Kong, Buenos Aires, Belgrade, Toronto, Tokyo, Thessaloniki, Locarno, and beyond.

It is noteworthy that the Internet Movie Database (www.imdb.com) lists festival showings under the "release dates" category, which treats official distribution and festival showings on equal footing. The cases where the predominant distribution of a film is through systematic festival showings are many; one can often stumble across information about films that have achieved international festival exposure over all continents.

Sight & Sound's veteran film industry commentator Nick Roddick recently remarked that "the current distribution system of films not only fails to supply any interest in non-mainstream cinema but is also completely incapable of measuring it."[20] Based on his attendance at an extensive string of festivals, however, there was evidence "that there is a vast audience out there with a healthy appetite for the kinds of films that don't get shown in the multiplexes." This "healthy appetite," he admits, could not be easily measured nor was it "recorded with the slavish attention-to-detail the studios devote to weekend gross reports," yet it clearly testifies that the festival circuit is the closest one can get in the distribution of this alternative kind of films—a structure that provides the most systematic and consistent exposure for peripheral cinema.[21]

Today, the international film festival circuit not only supports and facilitates the distribution of non-Hollywood cinema; it has also expanded sufficiently to be regarded as the distribution network itself. Even if working without any special coordination between them, festivals have come in close collaboration with other channels that we discuss here, like various diasporic networks (many of which have embraced the festival model, for example, Los Angeles's Greek Film Festival or Chicago's Polish Film Festival, and thus function as part of the festival circuit), and, as of lately, work together with an array of online initiatives. It would take some closer scrutiny to show the span of these processes more persuasively, due to the fact that the festival system lacks clear governance or coordinating institutions. As long as the framework for the study of the international festival circuit is set up, the rest of the evidence will come easily into place.[22]

Diasporic Trails

The system of diaspora-aimed and diaspora-driven distribution of films from various production centers attracted scholarly attention about a decade ago. The groundbreaking work of Australians Stuart Cunningham and John Sinclair, and more specifically the project *Floating Lives,* traced global channels catering to the increasingly active diasporic audiences around the world.[23] Since then, there has been a great increase in the number of diasporic trails linking production to consumption across continents, as well as in the number of studies exploring the intricacies of these various channels. The most wide-ranging explorations that followed these patterns through were realized in the area of transnational television and looked into the proliferation of both local and global satellite channels as distribution sites.[24]

Film production centers may be located in one country, yet in planning and generating outputs they operate with the consciousness that the consumption of what is created "here" will most likely be taking place somewhere else, among audiences who are scattered in different locations around the world. It is an export-import business model that, in order to effectively link production and distribution, relies on dedicated outlets that target specific user groups for certain cultural imports.

The countries of the Chinese Asian diasporic spread known as Nanyang, as well as the expansions to North America and Europe (and, lately, with more recent migrations to various countries in the African continent), are regularly receiving and exchanging a significant share of Mandarin- and Cantonese-language cultural exports. These cross-border circuits have been observed and studied in the context of progressively growing scholarship that applies the transnational paradigm to the cinematic phenomena it explores.[25]

The most visible case of diasporic distribution, however, remains the ever-rising international presence of Bollywood. A number of studies explore various aspects of Bollywood's mounting leverage, with contributions from the areas of political economy of media,[26] cultural studies,[27] transnational anthropology,[28] and media sociology,[29] not to count the numerous articles in academic journals and mainstream and trade media that talk up various aspects of this diaspora-driven phenomenon.

Replicating Hollywood's operation in many respects, with its own studio and star systems and formulaic genre conventions, Bollywood has made huge advances in the area of international distribution since the mid-1990s. With new blockbusters opening simultaneously in over fifteen territories, the Bombay industry is the only non-U.S. film production and distribution entity that more or less replicates Hollywood's widespread mechanisms of international penetration. And while about half of Hollywood's revenues come from abroad, in the case of Bollywood blockbusters that cater to the twenty-odd million nonresident Indian communities scattered around the globe, the share of overseas takings is even higher.

The distribution of many of these products may be diaspora driven, but the situations where their exposure expands beyond the members of the immediate ethnic group that is targeted to cross over and reach mainstream audiences are on the increase. The interest in Bollywood films in the United Kingdom, for example, nowadays routinely transcends the Indian community, with more and more fans among other immigrant communities and young people of English or Scottish ethnicity being converted into liking the Bollywood fare, an interest that is particularly easy to cater to not least because of the wide availability of DVDs targeting a global market with zone coding 0, which permits the use of any player and eliminates zoning restrictions. New Bollywood releases routinely play at mainstream multiplexes, capitalizing on the crossover potential of the venues, often breaking past per-screen revenue records and generating media coverage claiming that they outperform "their foreign counterparts, British films and even Hollywood productions."[30] Along with the traditionally available Hollywood and European films, large DVD stores across Western Europe nowadays also carry a selection of Bollywood films. This success of Bollywood's mainstream entertainment brings better visibility to a range of other Indian-produced films, be it Hindi-language independents or those filmed in languages like Bengali, Telugu, or Malalayam, allowing smaller players to ride on the trail of networks established by bigger commercial producers.

The high visibility of Hindi-language cinema should not obscure the fact that there are also other viable diasporic circuits; there are many other instances where diasporic communities—such as Turks, Poles, Pakistanis, or Vietnamese—have embraced the imports of filmed entertainment from their countries of origin.

Videos and DVDs are often imported alongside ethnic groceries and are featured alongside the traditional foodstuffs on the shelves of convenience stores catering to the immigrant community.[31] It is notoriously difficult, therefore, to chart the full extent of diasporic film distribution, as many of its manifestations fly below the radar of reliable media consumption records or box-office statistics. One possible way to study these channels is by following the pathways of the diasporic extensions of certain film-producing nations. A systematically conducted cumulative range of empirically grounded case studies could, with time, lead to a more or less comprehensive picture of the dynamics of diasporic distribution as it is present in today's multicultural realities. One can track the functioning of clandestine channels by tracing the social impact of some diasporic cultural imports (Islamic radicalization among Western Muslim youth may well be one of these effects).[32] One can grow more sensitive to the cross-cultural dynamics of peripheral intermingling across networked ethnic communities in multicultural metropolitan areas, as observed by globalization sociologists and anthropologists.[33] Whatever pathway one takes, it would certainly take an extensive and painstaking tallying in order to arrive at a comprehensive picture of the real dimensions of these still furtive trails.

The Periphery at Web 2.0

Things on the Internet, and in particular in the domain of the so-called Web 2.0, the sphere taken up by interactive services, are shifting very fast indeed. And while the evidence that the advancements in online distribution are changing the picture of media consumption is still inconclusive, it is clear that content that was traditionally barred from the mainstream channels of distribution is finding its way here, and is becoming easily accessible online. Whether this ease of access will lead to steady changes in consumption patterns, as Chris Anderson prophesizes in *The Long Tail,* is still to be seen. Again, it is crucial to find ways to reliably measure consumption in this rapidly evolving environment.

The implications of new technologies for film distribution are enormous. In the new mode of distribution they enable, a vast number of products are now obtainable from Internet-based distributors in command of huge on-demand inventories that expand existing markets and cater to niche consumer interests. Markets become liberated from the "tyranny of geography": the new distribution set-up permits unrestrained availability of distinctive products, and the remote village residents can have access to cultural goods as easily as those in the most central metropolitan locations.

The success of DVD rental and download sites that operate online, such as Netflix or Lovefilm (and the proliferation of many more similar enterprises), has confirmed the advantages of a radically novel and disruptive business model. The importance of these services is not only in the technological innovation, though. Precisely as Anderson describes it in *The Long Tail,* they easily make niche material that is not likely to be stored in the physically limited space of traditional video stores as available as the mainstream holdings. In addition, such niche material is now available to a much wider client base than could be reached previously.

An increasing variety of studio-produced films are accessible on the Internet for downloading, but the content is not limited to these mainstream choices.[34] A huge range of alternative international offerings is now equally accessible. Long before many of the Japanese manga animations appeared on DVD in Western stores, one could view all episodes of popular series such as *Hagane no renkinjutsushi/Full Metal Alchemist* (Seiji Mizushima, Japan, 2003), *Nodame Cantabile* (Hideki Takeuchi and Kawamura Yasuhiro, Japan, 2006) or *Desu nōto/Death Note* (Shusuke Kaneko, Japan, 2006) via You-Tube (www.youtube.com) or other similar sites. Such sites serve as trailers announcing the existence of an untapped universe of alternative cinematic material. They carry musical video clips not only of popular Western artists but also of other well-known musicians like androgynous Japanese idol Kimutaku of SMAP (star of the 2007 top-grossing international blockbuster *Hero*), or trailers for blockbusters like Spanish horror *El orfanato/The Orphanage* (Juan Antonio Bayona, 2007), which, with hundreds of thousands of viewings, tremendously assist their popularity. More and more rare films are made available in their entirety on YouTube, cut into ten-minute-long segments, while file sharing via BitTorrent has enabled the formation of lively communities that converge around partaking rare material in a variety of languages.

How does this new online reality benefit peripheral cinemas? Most of all, by putting them on par with the big players, who may control the international theatrical distribution but have no efficient way of barring alternative content from seeking exposure on the Internet. In recent years various inventive online channels for the distribution of independent cinema have mushroomed, and niche products—such as independently produced features or international documentaries—have come within easy reach.[35] In an unprecedented move to gain access to wider audiences, many more filmmakers bypass the gatekeepers and jump on the bandwagon; for the first time in history they have at their disposal the means to reach out to previously inaccessible audiences that may not be particularly large but are sufficient to give them the modest revenue needed to keep them going. More and more previously unavailable international films are becoming available for online purchase, from small distributors based either in diaspora or in their respective countries.[36] More importantly, these films become available to clients based in locations that were previously out of reach for such niche material, just by virtue of remoteness.

It is no longer possible to ignore the importance of this channel of cultural distribution, as more and more audiences are turning to the Internet for cultural consumption that transcends borders. With the growing impact of cyberspace word-of-mouth publicity in the context of new virtual communities, these vernacular but vibrant channels of dissemination are only likely to proliferate. Marketing strategies change profoundly as online word-of-mouth and blog-based film criticism gradually becomes the make-or-break focus of marketing efforts. It can push up a small independent feature as easily as it can undermine a multimillion-dollar production.[37]

"Repertory cinema has relocated into cyberspace," proclaimed a recent article intended to highlight this "new cinephilia."[38] The Internet not only provides a solution for special interests by making available a wide range of classic and contemporary non-mainstream cinema and by allowing fans who are located away from metropolitan centers to gain access to films that were previously out of reach. Cinephiles are becoming ever more active in the context of forums that bring them together and allow them to meet others of similar awareness and knowledge. They participate in various discussions, or run their own specialized and increasingly respected sites. In doing this, they increasingly embrace the host of new opportunities that sometimes supply them with eminence that equals or even supersedes the authority of officially sanctioned film criticism.[39] While Austin, Texas–based Harry Knowles of *Ain't It Cool News* has been the best-known amateur cinephile directly influencing Hollywood's fortunes for a while (www.aintitcool.com), a host of new cinephile bloggers have taken over the film discussions in cyberspace, more and more bringing the cinema of the periphery into focus:

As a reaction against the Hollywood hegemony and the chauvinism of the classic art-house canon, young cinephiles who live in the cinematically less well traveled regions (South-East Asia, Eastern Europe, the Middle East) are able to reconsider the films of their home countries in a level of depth and detail that visiting programmers and critics can never muster. They champion ground-breaking young directors, as well as excavating marginalised masters of the past.[40]

Even players with outspoken commercial ambitions have discovered the commercial potential of the periphery. *Jaman,* a Silicon Valley–based enterprise that launched in January 2007, is engaged in the easy download and online access to feature films. It promptly licenses content from international cinema, which is made available to global audiences via its unique online service. Adding more than five hundred full-length films during their first year in existence and assertively putting in place content agreements with a variety of international rights holders to peripheral cinematic content, *Jaman* insistently capitalizes on international and independent film content that remains in the periphery of distribution, by taking future licensing deals for libraries featuring Hong Kong, Indian, cult, and art-house titles. They also work with film festivals, aiming to take exclusive rights for online showings of films that are screening at certain festivals (Tribeca, San Francisco IFF, Cinequest), thus converging with the festival distribution circuit and extending the festival exposure to something that may soon come to resemble a true global distribution pattern.

The business proclaims itself "the best place to discover, enjoy and share world cinema," and simultaneously invests in cultivating an international user community of film buffs who are interested in non-mainstream cinema (and who are invited to publicize their own work via the site). Started by an entrepreneur of Indian origins, Gaurav Dhillon, *Jaman* does not even try to woo Hollywood's big players to license content but rather targets niche audiences with a variety of international films, Sundance and other indies, or Bollywood classics. "Less than 1 percent of the films produced on planet earth get distribution in the United States," they say in their promotional materials. It is the untapped 99 percent of peripheral cinema, the periphery, which *Jaman*'s team sees as an alluring market opportunity, that they are committed to pursuing.

Peripheral Cinema's Budding Channels

The channels of circulation of global cinema function together but are still being studied independently from one another. Yet, there is a growing and overarching acknowledgment that they increasingly interact and interlink, in a hybrid and flexible, mercurial and mutating manner. The result is a more complicated picture, but also one that leads to clearly realizing it is necessary to underpin the last leg of our argument by dynamically correlating the peripheral strategies discussed here.

While some aspects of these channels have been well researched, others have only recently become the object of study. There is extensive scholarship on Hollywood's global reach. In recent years there have been a number of publications that focus on diasporic distribution practices, mostly exploring global Bollywood and other Asian transnational networks. Only lately have studies begun to acknowledge the importance of film festivals as an alternative global distribution circuit, as well as the global reach and specifics of Internet-enabled distribution channels.

Throughout the existing scholarship the focus may remain on a single distribution channel, mostly because of the methodological difficulties involved in reconciling the scrutiny and analysis of diversely structured operations. The next endeavor will be to pursue all these different strategies and trends that come under the periphery umbrella and examine, on the basis of cinema, their complex interactions in order to get closer to understanding the true dynamics of global cultural flows. Unlike earlier studies that have investigated the workings of a singular system, the cycles of all four distinct circuits should be correlated to show the patterns of active interaction.

Global Hollywood no longer exclusively promotes the products of large U.S. studios but actively seeks out box-office winners from alternative sources; it increasingly recognizes the importance of the festival circuit, of the Internet, and of diasporic channels of distribution, and acts accordingly in order to keep stakes in all these burgeoning areas. The networked nature of the international film festival circuit is increasingly recognized for its definitive role in the circulation of non-mainstream works; the instances where key players of the festival circuit consciously take advantage of its potential to serve as an alternative distribution channel are on the increase. Festivals often pair with various diasporic distribution outlets and online film initiatives. Diasporic distribution of films from various alternative production centers increasingly employs Hollywood-tested models, but it also uses the festival network to its advantage. It eagerly embraces the distribution advantages supplied by new technological developments in local and transnational satellite television and the Internet. Internet-enabled channels of distribution are used to carry both Hollywood and alternative or niche content. There are a growing number of instances where festivals use the Internet for dissemination, and where online communities similar to those created by festivals thrive. The comprehensive comparison of these distribution circuits will not only bring along challenges and insights but will also provide a much-needed contextual assessment of the processes that take place within the *long tail* of global film circulation at the periphery.

Notes

I am grateful to Belén Vidal and David Martin-Jones for perceptive editorial feedback on the piece, but most of all for their enduring generosity and collegiality that make for an enviably supportive working environment. I would like to thank Faye Ginsburg for her friendly responsiveness, great suggestions, and help with editing, as well as Yun-hua Chen for her efficient assistance in sorting out the bibliographies and referencing. My research has been funded, in part, by the Leverhulme Trust, the Carnegie Trust, and the Arts & Humanities Research Council in the United Kingdom, as well as by the University of St. Andrews that generously granted a period of research leave.

1. *Bienvenue chez les Ch'tis/Welcome to the Land of Sticks* (Dany Boon, France, 2008); *Hero* (Masayuki Suzuki, Japan, 2007); *Always zoku san-chōme no yūhi/Always: Sunset on Third Street 2* (Takashi Yamazaki, Japan, 2007); *El Greco* (Yannis Smaragdis, Greece/Spain, 2007); *Se, jie/Lust, Caution* (Ang Lee, USA/China/Taiwan/Hong Kong, 2007); *It's a Free World* (Ken Loach, UK/Italy/Germany/Spain/Poland, 2007); *Tuya de hun shi/Tuya's Marriage* (Quanan Wang, China, 2007); *Der rote Elvis/The Red Elvis* (Leopold Grün, Germany, 2007).

2. It would result in a drawing looking like Chris Anderson's *Long Tail,* with its graphical presentation of a chart where the tall vertical of the blockbuster-type distribution is neatly balanced out by the long horizontal "tail" of multiple diverse peripheral counter-flows. If the chart were folded, the two graphs would overlie and overlap, providing a striking visual model of an elusive balancing act.

3. Ginsburg, Abu-Lughod, and Larkin, eds., *Media Worlds: Anthropology on New Terrain.*

4. Larkin, "Indian Films and Nigerian Lovers: Media and the Creation of Parallel Modernities," 350–78; Larkin, "Itineraries of Indian Cinema. African videos, Bollywood and Global media," 170–92; Roof, "African and Latin American Cinemas: Contexts and Contacts," 241–73; Woll, "The Russian Connection: Soviet Cinema and the Cinema of Francophone Africa" 223–41; Iordanova, "Indian Cinema's Global Reach: Historiography through Testimony," 113–40.

5. Iordanova, "Transnational Film Studies," 508–9.

6. Balio, *Hollywood in the Age of Television;* Wyatt, *High Concept: Movies and Marketing in Hollywood;* Wasko, *How Hollywood Works;* Grainge, *Brand Hollywood: Selling Entertainment in a Global Media Age.*

7. Balnaves et al., *The Global Media Atlas;* Miller et al., *Global Hollywood,* 2nd ed.; MacDonald and Wasko, eds., *The Contemporary Hollywood Film Industry;* Miller, ed., *The Contemporary Hollywood Reader.*

8. The only company that specializes in producing research summarizing such international data, Dodona Research (www.dodona.co.uk/), sells its reports at prices that are out of reach for academic researchers.

9. All statements related to box-office performance and revenues made throughout this text are derived from *Screen International* and are based on continuous monitoring of their weekly reports since 2002.

10. Note that Japan's box office is the third sizable in the world, followed by France's (fourth), Germany's (fifth), Spain's (sixth), Italy's (seventh), and South Korea's (ninth).

11. Elley, review of *Hero* (Japan).

12. Klady, "The Global Perspective," 6–7.

13. Phone communication with Diana Lodderhose, *Screen International's* box-office reporter, January 3, 2008.

14. Klady, "Growing Pains," 6–8.

15. Curtin, *Playing to the World's Biggest Audience: The Globalization of Chinese Film and TV,* 4.

16. Ibid.

17. "What if the future were to take an unexpected detour on the road to Disneyland, heading instead toward a more complicated global terrain characterized by overlapping and, at times, intersecting cultural spheres served by diverse media enterprises based in media capitals around the world?" (ibid.). Curtin refers to studies of media penetration around the world looking into Japan, India, the Arab world, and Latin America that have begun presenting adequate evidence that this may indeed be happening.

18. Slater, "The New Cinephiles," 26–27.

19. Elsaesser, "Film Festival Networks: The New Topographies of Cinema in Europe," 82–108

20. Roddick, "Cinema on Demand," 14.

21. Various contributions to this volume recognize the importance of festival exposure, from Faye Ginsburg's observations of how a modest made-for-TV aboriginal film is changed by festival participation (and how networks of indigenous filmmakers forged by festivals determine further developments), to Sheldon H. Lu's com-

ments on the way in which new Chinese directors like Jia Zhangke ride the circuit and use festival success in renegotiating their position within the national cinematic status quo.

22. The analysis of the networked festival phenomenon is in the focus of a growing new area in film studies. The framework for the study of festivals is being set up in the writings of Stringer, "Global Cities and the International Film Festival Economy," 134–44; Harbord, *Film Cultures;* Elsaesser, "Film Festival Networks: The New Topographies of Cinema in Europe," 82–108; De Valck, *Film Festivals: From European Geopolitics to Global Cinephilia;* and in edited collections by Porton and Iordanova published in 2009.

23. Cunningham and Sinclair, eds., *Floating Lives: The Media and Asian Diasporas.*

24. Sinclair, *Latin American Television: A Global View;* Sinclair and Turner, eds., *Contemporary World Television;* Iwabuchi, *Recentering Globalization: Popular Culture and Japanese Transnationalism;* Iwabuchi, ed., *Feeling Asian Modernities: Transnational Consumption of Japanese TV Dramas;* Keane et al., *New Television, Globalisaton, and the East Asian Cultural Imagination;* Curtin, *Playing to the World's Biggest Audience.*

25. Mitchell, "In Whose Interest? Transnational Capital and the Production of Multiculturalism in Canada," 219–55; Ong, *Flexible Citizenship: The Cultural Logic of Transnationality;* Ang, *On Not Speaking Chinese: Living between Asia and the West;* Lu and Yueh-Yu Yeh, eds., *Chinese-Language Film: Historiography, Poetics, Politics;* Berry and Farquhar, *China on Screen: Cinema and Nation;* Gina Marchetti, *From Tian'anmen to Times Square: Transnational China and the Chinese Diaspora on Global Screens, 1989–97;* Curtin, *Playing to the World's Biggest Audience;* Keane et al., *New Television, Globalisaton, and the East Asian Cultural Imagination.*

26. Pendakur, *Indian Popular Cinema: Industry, Ideology, and Consciousness.*

27. Desai, *Beyond Bollywood: The Cultural Politics of South Asian Diasporic Film.*

28. Kaur and Sinha, eds., *Bollyworld: Popular Indian Cinema through a Transnational Lens.*

29. Dudrah, *Bollywood: Sociology Goes to the Movies.*

30. *The Times,* December 19, 2007.

31. Iordanova, "Expanding Universe: From the Ethnic Foodstore to *Blockbuster,*" 54–70.

32. It is only in rare cases that such diaspora-generated cultural imports cross over into mainstream distribution. A recent example of a product that was imported for consumption by the diaspora but ended up with a wider impact concerns the Turkish blockbuster *Kurtlar vadisi-Irak/Valley of the Wolves: Iraq* (Serdar Akar, 2006), an outspoken anti-Western action-adventure that presents the deeds of American private mercenaries in Iraq in a deeply controversial manner. The film, which featured well-known American actors and relied on special effects by Hollywood professionals, was released theatrically in Germany and the Netherlands through mainstream channels, then distributed to another ten territories in Europe, the Arab world, Asia, and Latin America, and is available internationally in a subtitled DVD version. As it shows an alternative viewpoint of the war, it became extremely popular among wider Muslim communities and beyond, thus causing a public controversy.

33. Appadurai, *Modernity at Large: Cultural Dimensions of Globalization;* Hannerz, *Transnational Connections: Culture, People, Places;* Ginsburg et al., eds., *Media Worlds: Anthropology on New Terrain;* Sassen, *The Global City: New York, London, Tokyo,* 2nd ed.

34. There are a large number of sites that make video material available for download, using either BitTorrent, the online file sharing system, or other new technologies of peer-casting (iTunes, Babelgum, Joost, Veoh, GONG, to name just a few). Many of the download sites choose to comply with restrictions of territorial nature and geo-blocking (e.g., Movielink, CinemaNow, or Amazon's Unbox are mostly available in the United States, whereas content from Lovefilm, BFI, Channel 4, SkyAnytime, and BTVision is restricted for use in the United Kingdom).

35. Some examples of pioneering online distribution models for independents could be seen at the sites of Withoutabox (www.withoutabox.com), serving the international community of independents, or Dogwoof (www.dogwoofpictures.com), a new distributor making significant inroads into the UK market. See more details at *Screen International*'s London conference on the future of distribution, July 2007. Available at www.futurefilmsummit.co.uk/homepage.asp (all accessed January 2, 2008). Amazon.com-owned Internet Movie Database (www.imdb.com) acquired Withoutabox early in 2008.

36. For example, most of the previously rare Polish or Hungarian cinema is now available from various distributors online; rare documentaries from Malaysia can be ordered at Red Films, www.redfilms.com.my/company.htm (accessed January 2, 2008).

37. As *Screen International* reported recently, mainstream distributors are growing conscious of the reputation of films in the domain of Internet conversations, paying specific attention to the buzz a film generates on social networking sites like MySpace or Facebook and monitoring postings to millions of blogs, supposedly with the intent to influence the reputation of their releases and taking advantage of services such as Blogpulse.com (which tracks nearly 40 millions blogs) and Technorati.com (which claims to monitor 57 million blogs).

38. Slater, "The New Cinephiles," 26; Rosenbaum and Martin, eds., *Movie Mutations: The Changing Face of World Cinephilia.*

39. Issues related to the decreasing clout of institutionalized film criticism and the increasing influence of online criticism and bloggers have been in the center of attention of a number of international film forums and festivals throughout 2007 and 2008. Both UK-based *Sight & Sound* and U.S.-based *Cineaste* magazines dedicated extended discussions on the matter (*Cineaste:* "Film Criticism in the Age of the Internet, A Critical Symposium," 33, no 4, 2008, 30–47; *Sight & Sound,* October 2008: "Who Needs Critics," available at www.bfi.org.uk/sightandsound/feature/49479 and "Critics on Critics," available at www.bfi.org.uk/sightandsound/feature/49480, accessed January 8, 2009). In all these discussions, however, the focus is still almost exclusively on white male critics whose native language is English and who are still predominantly familiar with Western cinematic canons and traditions. We are still to see a forum that would bring together the really diverse group of critics from the periphery who have been contributing to the increasing diversity of film criticism

on the Internet over the past few years, and of whom Slater is talking in the article quoted here.

40. Slater, "The New Cinephiles," 27.

Bibliography

Anderson, Chris. *The Long Tail: How Endless Choice Is Creating Unlimited Demand.* London: Random House, 2006.

Ang, Ien. *On Not Speaking Chinese: Living between Asia and the West.* New York: Routledge, 2001.

Appadurai, Arjun. *Modernity at Large: Cultural Dimensions of Globalization.* Minneapolis: University of Minnesota Press, 1996.

Balio, Tino. *Hollywood in the Age of Television.* Boston: Unwin Hyman, 1990.

Balnaves, Mark, et al. *The Global Media Atlas.* London: British Film Institute, 2000.

Berry, Chris, and Mary Farquhar. *China on Screen: Cinema and Nation.* New York: Columbia University Press; Hong Kong: Hong Kong University Press, 2006.

Cunningham, Stuart, and John Sinclair, eds. *Floating Lives: The Media and Asian Diasporas.* Lanham, MD: Rowman and Littlefield, 2001.

Curtin, Michael. *Playing to the World's Biggest Audience: The Globalization of Chinese Film and TV.* Berkeley: University of California Press, 2007.

Desai, Jigna. *Beyond Bollywood: The Cultural Politics of South Asian Diasporic Film.* London: Routledge, 2004.

De Valck, Marijke. *Film Festivals: From European Geopolitics to Global Cinephilia.* Amsterdam: Amsterdam University Press, 2007.

Dudrah, Rajinder. *Bollywood: Sociology Goes to the Movies.* New Delhi, Thousand Oaks, London: Sage, 2006.

Elley, Derek. Review of *Hero* (Japan), directed by Masayuki Suzuki. *Variety,* October 6, 2007. Available at www.variety.com/review/VE1117935012.html?categoryi d=31&cs=1&p=0 (accessed February 1, 2008).

Elsaesser, Thomas. "Film Festival Networks: The New Topographies of Cinema in Europe." In *European Cinema: Face to Face with Hollywood,* 82–108. Amsterdam: Amsterdam University Press, 2005.

Ginsburg, Faye, Lila Abu-Lughod, and Brian Larkin, eds. *Media Worlds: Anthropology on New Terrain.* Berkeley: University of California Press, 2002.

Grainge, Paul. *Brand Hollywood: Selling Entertainment in a Global Media Age.* London: Routledge, 2007.

Hannerz, Ulf. *Transnational Connections: Culture, People, Places.* London: Routledge, 1996.

Harbord, Janet. *Film Cultures.* London: Sage, 2002.

Iordanova, Dina. "Expanding Universe: From the Ethnic Foodstore to Blockbuster." *Framework: The Journal of Cinema and Media* 41 (Autumn 1999): 54–70.

———. "Indian Cinema's Global Reach: Historiography through Testimony." *Journal of South Asian Popular Culture* 4, no. 2 (2006): 113–40.

————. "Transnational Film Studies." In *The Cinema Book,* edited by Pam Cook, 508–9. London: British Film Institute, 2007.

Iordanova, Dina, with Ragan Rhyne, eds. *Film Festival Yearbook I: The Festival Circuit.* St. Andrews: St. Andrews Film Studies, 2009.

Iwabuchi, Koichi. *Recentering Globalization: Popular Culture and Japanese Transnationalism.* Durham, NC: Duke University Press, 2002.

Iwabuchi, Koichi, ed. *Feeling Asian Modernities: Transnational Consumption of Japanese TV Dramas.* Hong Kong: Hong Kong University Press, 2004.

Kaur, Raminder, and Ajay J. Sinha, eds. *Bollyworld: Popular Indian Cinema through a Transnational Lens.* London: Sage, 2005.

Keane, Michael, Anthony Fung, and Albert Moran. *New Television, Globalisaton, and the East Asian Cultural Imagination.* Hong Kong: Hong Kong University Press, 2007.

Klady, Leonard. "The Global Perspective." *Screen International* 22 (June 2007): 6–7.

————. "Growing Pains." *Screen International* 14 (December 2007): 6–8.

Larkin, Brian. "Indian Films and Nigerian Lovers: Media and the Creation of Parallel Modernities." In *The Anthropology of Globalization: A Reader,* edited by Jonathan Xavier Inda and Renato Rosaldo, 350–78. Oxford: Blackwell Books, 2002.

————. "Itineraries of Indian Cinema: African Videos, Bollywood, and Global Media." In *Multiculturalism, Postcolonialism, and Transnational Media,* edited by Ella Shohat and Robert Stam, 170–92. New Brunswick, NJ: Rutgers University Press, 2003.

Lu, Sheldon H., and Emilie Yueh-Yu Yeh, eds. *Chinese-Language Film: Historiography, Poetics, Politics.* Honolulu: University of Hawai'i Press, 2004.

MacDonald, Paul, and Janet Wasko, eds. *The Contemporary Hollywood Film Industry.* Oxford: Blackwell, 2007.

Marchetti, Gina. *From Tian'anmen to Times Square: Transnational China and the Chinese Diaspora on Global Screens, 1989–97.* Philadelphia: Temple University Press, 2006.

Miller, Toby, ed. *The Contemporary Hollywood Reader.* London: Routledge, 2009.

Miller, Toby, Nitin Govil, John McMurria, and Richard Maxwell. *Global Hollywood,* 2nd ed. London: British Film Institute, 2005.

Mitchell, Katharyne. "In Whose Interest? Transnational Capital and the Production of Multiculturalism in Canada." In *Global/Local: Cultural Production and the Transnational Imaginary,* edited by Rob Wilson and Wimal Dissanayake, 219–55. Durham, NC: Duke University Press, 1996.

Mowitt, John. *Re-Takes: Postcoloniality and Foreign Film Languages.* Minneapolis: University of Minnesota Press, 2005.

Ong, Aihwa. *Flexible Citizenship: The Cultural Logic of Transnationality.* Durham, NC: Duke University Press, 1999.

Pendakur, Manjunath. *Indian Popular Cinema: Industry, Ideology, and Consciousness.* Cresskill, NJ: Hampton Press, 2003.

Porton, Richard, ed. *Dekalog 03: On Film Festivals.* London: Wallflower Press,

2009.

Roddick, Nick. "Cinema on Demand." *Sight & Sound,* October 2007, 14.

Roof, Maria. "African and Latin American Cinemas: Contexts and Contacts." In *Focus on African Film,* edited by Françoise Pfaff, 241–73. Bloomington: Indiana University Press, 2004.

Rosenbaum, Jonathan, and Adrian Martin, eds. *Movie Mutations: The Changing Face of World Cinephilia.* London: British Film Institute, 2003.

Sassen, Saskia. *The Global City: New York, London, Tokyo,* 2nd ed. Princeton, NJ: Princeton University Press, 2001.

Sinclair, John. *Latin American Television: A Global View.* New York: Oxford University Press, 1999.

Sinclair, John, and Graeme Turner, eds. *Contemporary World Television.* London: British Film Institute, 2004.

Slater, Ben. "The New Cinephiles." *Screen International* 30 (November 2007): 26–27.

Stringer, Julian. "Global Cities and the International Film Festival Economy." In *Cinema and the City: Film and Urban Societies in a Global Context,* edited by Mark Shiel and Tony Fitzmaurice, 134–44. Oxford: Blackwell, 2001.

Wasko, Janet. *How Hollywood Works.* Thousand Oaks, CA: Sage, 2003.

Woll, Josephine. "The Russian Connection: Soviet Cinema and the Cinema of Francophone Africa." In *Focus on African Film,* edited by Françoise Pfaffe, 223–41. Bloomington: Indiana University Press, 2004.

Wyatt, Justin. *High Concept: Movies and Marketing in Hollywood.* Austin: University of Texas Press, 1995.

Affinitive and Milieu-Building Transnationalism

The *Advance Party* Initiative

The field of transnational cinema studies is a burgeoning one, and I would like to contribute to some of the lively ongoing debates by looking at the ways in which film professionals belonging to small, relatively privileged nations and/or states have responded to the challenges and opportunities of transnational filmmaking. My focus will be on two nations, one with an independent state (Denmark), the other with a degree of autonomy as a result of a devolutionary process (Scotland).[1] And within these two national contexts, the emphasis is on cross-border interaction between agents located in key cities: Copenhagen and Glasgow. While cultural policy is an important part of the picture, the emphasis here is not on state actors but on a quite different type of agency. The point is to draw attention to promising transnational initiatives that film companies, operating within the parameters of national, subnational, or supranational frameworks, can undertake in order to develop a filmmaking milieu in cities that are of strategic importance for the nations in which they are situated.

Milieu-developing transnationalism is a salient feature of the cinematic case that provides the focus for my discussion here: *Advance Party*, a rule-governed, three-film collaborative endeavor involving Gillian Berrie's Glasgow-based Sigma Films[2] and Lars von Trier and Peter Aalbæk Jensen's Copenhagen-based Zentropa Productions. Drawing on interviews with producer Gillian Berrie and her assistant Anna Duffield in Scotland, and with producer Marie Gade and filmmaker Lone Scherfig in Denmark, I shall describe the motivations, as understood by some of the central players, for initiating *Advance Party* in 2002. The point is to try to grasp the participating agents' *subjective rationality*, and not necessarily to determine the accuracy of their

46

various pronouncements. I am concerned, in other words, with practitioners' agency, with the self-understandings that motivate certain transnational collaborative choices. Key questions that inform my attempt to understand the still-developing alliance between Sigma and Zentropa include the following:

1. How do the two small-nation film companies understand their transnational collaborative venture long term?

2. What makes collaboration between the two companies mutually beneficial?

3. What is the interest of working with a model involving sustained rather than one-off collaboration?

4. What is the envisaged effect of linking artistic experimentation to transnational collaboration?

5. How is the transnational project served by adopting metacultural strategies—manifestos or publicly announced rule-governed frameworks—as is the case with the *Advance Party* initiative?

My aim is to provide elements of a theoretical framework for understanding the contribution that *Advance Party* makes to both the diversification of models of transnational filmmaking and to the articulation of solutions to the problems of small-nation filmmaking. The anticipated effects of the *Advance Party* collaboration are, as we shall see, very much about transferring some of the positive features of the now thriving Danish filmmaking milieu (in Copenhagen) to Scotland (and, more specifically, Glasgow), where an appropriate milieu is deemed by Sigma to be lacking for various reasons.[3] I shall begin with a few remarks about small nations and states, and about various types of cinematic transnationalism, before considering *Advance Party* in detail.

Small Nations and States

A central claim here is that *Advance Party* was devised by film professionals who are particularly attuned to the problems of small-nation filmmaking and who prefer to try to resolve them through processes of development instead of simply avoiding them through strategies of "exit," to use Albert Hirschman's term.[4] Inasmuch as small nationhood provides a key motivation for milieu-building transnationalism in the case of *Advance Party*, it is necessary to provide some indication of what is meant by terms such as *small nation* and *small state.* The literature on small states identifies four crucial measures of size: population, territory, gross national product, and rule by non-co-nationals over a significant period of time.[5] Debates about population size inevitably focus on where to set the upper limit, with proposals ranging from Mark Bray's and Steve Packer's[6] 1.5 million to David Vital's once influential 10 to 15 million "in the case of economically advanced countries" and 20 to 30 million in the case of developing countries.[7] Viewed as having important implications for "social structure and processes" and as determining "the size of the internal market before the foreign trade factor comes into operation,"[8] population is often held to be the most important measure of size, as Björn Olafsson points out. Gross National Product (GNP) is also a decisive factor, however, inasmuch as it too has a direct bearing on infrastructure and the dynamics of internal markets. For Czech political theorist Miroslav Hroch[9] thwarted political will, in the form of rule by non-co-nationals, is the single most important determinant of small nationhood. Indeed, Hroch has been taken to task, by Ernest Gellner, for having overemphasized this particular determinant to the point of entirely overlooking others, such as geographical scale.[10]

If we turn to Scotland and Denmark, with a particular focus on the link between small nationhood and the question of viable, sustainable film industries, we note the following: with populations between 5 and 6 million, both entities have small internal markets, with language complicating access to external markets in the Danish (and at times the Scottish) case. Hroch's rule by non-co-nationals is relevant in the Scottish context, where separatist aspirations and the perceived problems on which they are based help to motivate the search for nontraditional coproduction partners outside the United Kingdom. Viewed uniquely in terms of GNP neither Scotland nor Denmark can be said to qualify for small-nation status. It is worth noting, however, that relative prosperity has meant one thing for film in Scotland and something entirely different for film in Denmark. As Duncan Petrie suggests, the €4.4 million (U.S. $6,319,759) disbursed annually by the Scottish Screen Lottery Fund between 2000 and 2005 contrasts strikingly with the almost €18 million (about U.S. $26 million) spent on state support for film in Denmark in 2003 and 2004.[11] Yet, the resulting differences at the level of infrastructure and milieu need not, as we shall see, constitute obstacles to transnational collaboration between Scottish and Danish film professionals. Indeed, the incentive for milieu-building transnationalism in small-nation contexts may to some extent derive from precisely such discrepancies.

Types of Cinematic Transnationalism

At this point the European film industry produces some 250 coproductions per year, which figure accounts for about 25 percent of the overall output.[12] In Denmark, for example, comparative figures from the 1980s and 1990s show a 600 percent increase in coproductions in the last decade of the millennium.[13] Yet there are many different ways of engaging in transnational film production, some of them considerably more interesting than others, and some of them possibly more effective than others as strategies of genuine counterglobalization. In this regard, John Hess's and Patricia Zimmermann's proposal to distinguish between "corporatist transnationalism" (which "declaw[s]," "depoliticize[s]," and "decorporalize[s]" "racial, gender, ethnic and sexual identities . . . into new, further segmented markets for the new accelerated capital growth") and "adversarial transnationalism" (which "reassert[s] the racial, gender, ethnic, sexual and national differences of multiple bodies")[14] is helpful, in part because it suggests that cinematic transnationalism is indeed a phenomenon admitting of a wide range of possible manifestations. Given the range in question, it is also clear that considerable room remains for the introduction of further types.

Drawing on my article titled "On the Plurality of Cinematic Transnationalism,"[15] let me briefly outline some production-based distinctions that will help, I hope, to shed light on the Sigma/Zentropa alliance. It should be noted that I do not see the following types as necessarily mutually exclusive:

Affinitive transnationalism: collaboration across national borders with "people like us," the perception of similarity being based in many cases on ethnicity, culture, and language, although commonality may also center on core attitudes, interests, concerns, and problems.

Milieu-building transnationalism: transnational collaboration, usually of a sustained nature, that is designed to develop capacity.

Cosmopolitan transnationalism: collaboration across borders prompted and made possible by personal transnational networks.

Epiphanic transnationalism: transnational collaboration fostered by supranational entities with an interest in funding projects that aim to make manifest supranational or regional cultural identities resting on partially intersecting national cultures.

Experimental transnationalism: collaboration across national borders resulting from the logic of attention-grabbing artistic experiments.

Globalizing transnationalism: ultra-high-budget transnational productions informed in part by Hollywood's globalizing strategies and aimed at securing at least transnational, regional audiences and ideally global audiences.[16]

Opportunistic transnationalism: collaboration motivated by a strategic relation to financial opportunities.

If we look at the statistics for Danish film from 1991 to 2000, the preference for affinitive transnationalism is clear:

Participation from other countries in Danish majors

Sweden	Norway	Germany	Finland	France	Iceland	Italy	Holland	England	U.S.
51	28	12	6	6	6	4	4	3	3

Origin of major production companies for Danish minors

Sweden	Norway	Iceland	Germany	England	Finland	France	India	Poland
25	10	4	2	1	1	1	1	1

Source: Gundelach Brandstrup and Novrup Redvall, "Breaking the Borders," in *Transnational Cinema in a Global North,* edited by Andy Nestingen and Trevor G. Elkington, 152. Detroit: Wayne State University Press, 2005. Danish Film Institute, *Facts and Figures,* 1991–2000.

The affinitive transnationalism that is apparent here involves Sweden and Norway and is clearly based on geographic proximity, on partially overlapping languages, on a strong sense of shared ethnicity and political culture, and on a long history of close interaction, not always peaceful, but shared nonetheless. While there is nothing objectionable about this kind of affinitive transnationalism, the underlying view of how the world is configured and where affinities are likely to be found has a taken-for-granted quality to it that is somewhat parochial. Coproducers involved in affinitive transnationalism in a Nordic register may be able to count on a certain comfort zone, on a homeliness that promotes understanding and thus efficiency, but the tendency to prefer members of the traditional family of nations also obscures the promise involved in other manifestations of affinitive transnationalism. Affinity need not rest only on cultural traits that common knowledge defines as more or less pervasive across entire regions, but can also arise in connection with the unexpected *discovery* of shared cultural values and common purposes embraced by individuals, small groups, and professional milieus—by producers, directors, and the companies with which they are associated, for example. The Sigma/Zentropa partnership strikes me as a good example of a purpose-driven affinitive transnationalism with cultural dimensions, and it is time now to look more closely at the nature of the relevant collaborative arrangement.

The Sigma/Zentropa Alliance

Founded in 1996 by Gillian Berrie, the Scottish filmmaker David Mackenzie, and his actor brother Alastair Mackenzie, Sigma Films describes its goals as follows on its official website: "To produce independent and internationally appealing films"; to create a "sustainable film industry in Scotland"; and to identify, nurture, and develop "creative talent in order to produce work of the highest artistic value" (www.sigmafilms.com). The idea of collaboration with Zentropa was initially proposed by Gillian Berrie at a meeting with John Archer (then CEO of Scottish Screen), Lenny Crooks, and a representative from Trust Films following a screening of Lars von Trier's *Dancer in the Dark* (Denmark etc., 2000) at the Edinburgh Film Festival.[17] That Berrie's proposal was deemed worth pursuing is not difficult to understand, for since Aalbæk Jensen and von Trier first founded Zentropa in 1992 they have pursued goals closely resembling those defined by Sigma.

Sigma and Zentropa first collaborated on David Mackenzie's feature debut, *The Last Great Wilderness* (UK/Denmark, 2002), and subsequent coproductions include Lone Scherfig's *Wilbur Wants to Kill Himself* (Denmark/UK/Sweden/France, 2002), Susanne Bier's *Brødre/Brothers* (Denmark/UK/Sweden/Norway, 2004), and Lars von Trier's *Manderlay* (Denmark/France/Sweden/Germany/UK/Netherlands, 2005). At this point, the Sigma website describes the Scottish production company as having a "close alliance with Zentropa" and as "acting as UK co-producer on their feature films" (www.sigmafilms.com). The rules governing Sigma/Zentropa coproductions are those laid down by the Department for Culture, Media and Sport (DCMS) and the European Convention on Co-Productions, but whereas the relevant guidelines allow for *one-off* collaborations, the point, claims Berrie,[18] has been to develop a lasting and open-ended relationship that encourages forms of solidarity and exchange that extend well beyond the specifics of any given coproduction.

Lone Scherfig identifies the experience of coproducing *Wilbur Wants to Kill Himself* as the basis for the creation of a genuine alliance between the two small-nation film-producing companies.[19] *Wilbur,* Scherfig points out, was intended for the exact same cast that helped to make Dogme #12, *Italiensk for begyndere/Italian for Beginners* (Denmark, 2000) an internationally recognized contemporary Danish film classic. Whereas the Dogme rules had allowed Zentropa seriously to limit the costs involved in producing *Italian for Beginners,* the success enjoyed by the film transformed the cast into stars with salary expectations well beyond what Scherfig and Zentropa could afford in connection with *Wilbur.* The decision was thus made to capitalize on the emerging relation with Sigma Films. The Danish language and cast were dropped in favor of a coproduction shot on location in Glasgow and in accordance with the rules allowing local production companies to enjoy advantageous tax breaks. Scherfig recalls the many gifts that the sudden shift away from Denmark and the Danish language entailed. Among the many positive factors, she foregrounds the pleasure involved in working with superb, yet to her entirely new, Scottish actors; the urban environment of Glasgow as a location; the sensibility of her Scottish crew; and the opportunity to make an English-language film without sacrificing the kind of control that is a feature of the director-led approach.

Scherfig's remarks evoke filmmaking practices that are shared by Scots and Danes. And a number of the other figures involved in developing the Sigma/Zentropa alliance also point to Scottish/Danish affinities. While the remarks in question may seem maudlin and unsophisticated, they do at least establish the extent to which the *perception* of shared culture figures centrally at this point in the narrative that agents participating in *Advance Party* tell themselves and others about this initiative. Berrie, for example, made the following remark to Scottish journalist Miles Fielder: "You always feel like you're with a kindred spirit when you're with a Dane. It's something to do with being on the same latitude, or the weather perhaps. There's a self-deprecating aspect to the Danish personality that's at home here. The Danes always say it's the Scots they end up with in the bar in the wee hours of the morning."[20] Marie Gade evokes the same affinities, accounting for them, not in terms of climate, but in terms rather of the properties of small nations and their characteristic mentalities: "the atmosphere, the tone, the humor are all very similar. There's that sense of being small and completely peripheral, but also somehow the absolute center of the world."[21] And Sisse Graum Jørgensen (previously Olsen), who produced both *Wilbur* and Thomas Vinterberg's *Dear Wendy* (Denmark/France/Germany/UK, 2005) says the following: "We have the same temperament, the same understated humor and more or less the same sense of order as the Scots. These kinds of soft values should absolutely not be underestimated in collaborations such as coproductions."[22]

In order to understand the origins of the strong alliance that now exists between Sigma and Zentropa, it is important to take note of some of the *imbalances* that characterize the collaborative relation, for these, quite interestingly, appear to have served as motivating factors in both Scotland and Denmark. Berrie identifies some of the inequities as follows: "In Denmark they have in excess of £25m [about U.S. $50 million] a year to put into films. They get up and they go to work and they make films every day, whereas filmmakers here get to make one film every three years, if they get to make films at all."[23] Glasgow-based filmmaker Eleanor Yule uses a similar language of contrasts to pinpoint challenges faced by the local Scottish filmmaking milieu: "When you go to Filmbyen, the film city where Zentropa and other companies are based, you see everyone helping one another out. It means you breed a more collaborative environment, but there's also the expectation that you will be making films for cinema regularly. In Scotland it feels like a lottery at every step of the process. We are not self-sufficient in the same way."[24] Zentropa, it is clear, is an attractive ally for reasons that go well beyond cultural and professional affinities. Zentropa exists within a political landscape that invests heavily in small-nation filmmaking, and Zentropa has, qua company, developed a number of highly successful strategies—many of them an ingenious mix of artistry, marketing, and networking—for coping with the obstacles that minor or peripheral cinemas face. From Sigma's perspective, part of the attraction of the Scottish-Danish alliance has to do with the sharing of cultural capital, know-how, and networks, and with gaining access to figures such as Peter Aalbæk Jensen and Lars von Trier, for whom filmmaking, among many other things, is also a form of milieu building. While many examples could be given of the two Danes' commitments, they are best evoked here in Aalbæk Jensen's blunt phrases: "In Sweden you had enormous progress with Ingmar Bergman, Jan Troell, and Bo Widerberg, but they completely forgot about the grassroots. They didn't initiate a bloody thing that could help to carry the torch forward, and this has cost them 20 to 25 years of depression, in terms of film. That's why I won't stand quietly by and watch us make the same mistake in Denmark."[25]

Interestingly, the very inequities that draw Sigma to Zentropa are also what motivate Zentropa's interest in the Scottish company. It is important to remember that Denmark used to face many of the same problems that Berrie and Yule emphasize. When I first started conducting interviews in 1997 for what would eventually become *The Danish Directors* (2001), many of the veteran filmmakers, including someone like Søren Kragh-Jacobsen (Dogme #3, *Mifunes sidste sang/Mifune,* Denmark, 1999), spoke about the difficulties involved in maintaining one's craft and expertise as a filmmaker in a system where limited resources and a commitment to distributing them fairly among all competent and promising directors meant that most filmmakers could only hope to make a film every five years or so. The now favorable situation enjoyed by Danish film is very much the result of the Danish Film Institute (DFI) CEO Henning Camre's successful bid in 1998 for a 75 percent increase in funding for film, an additional sum of approximately £40 million (nearly U.S. $80 million) over a four-year period.[26]

In discussions focusing on the strong relation between Sigma Films and Zentropa, the Danish players inevitably end up reflecting on the many ways in which the Scottish company, and the challenges it confronts, recalls an earlier and far less optimistic Danish situation. Producer Marie Gade, who has been on staff at Zentropa more or less since the beginning, insists, for example, that Sigma has the same kind of energy that characterized Zentropa when it was first established in the less favorable Danish environment of the early 1990s. For Gade the similarities between Sigma now and Zentropa then help to explain the successful Danish company's interest in the Scottish partnership: "We like the idea of trying to help Sigma Films build up a strong filmmaking milieu, of trying to get something exciting off the ground in Glasgow."[27]

A strong sense of affinity, combined with a shared commitment to film production as a form of institution building or milieu development, at least partly explains the broad-based and long-term nature of collaborative efforts between Sigma and Zentropa. An interesting example of the company's joint involvement in transnational institution building is that of the creation of Film City Glasgow in former Govan Town Hall.[28] Documents detailing plans for Film City Glasgow identify "New York's Green Street Studio and the Zentropa Studio Copenhagen" as models for this "Scottish production campus,"[29] and Berrie herself frankly admits that what she is looking for is the kind of informal corridor culture, synergy, and interaction that have come to define the Danish film town in Avedøre.[30] As far as filmmaker Lone Scherfig is concerned, the Danish Film Town's appeal for Berrie and her collaborators is easy to understand: "it's all about creating a milieu where filmmakers have lots of facilities at their disposal without having a massive production company breathing down their necks."[31] Zentropa's Marie Gade expressed considerable enthusiasm for the Govan Film Town as she recalled visits by a Scottish architect to Filmbyen in Avedøre. Gade further emphasized Zentropa's support for the Glaswegian initiative by pointing out that the Danish company aims to establish itself in the Scottish film town through the creation of postproduction facilities.

I take myself to have shown that the Sigma/Zentropa alliance rests on the subjective perception of affinities of culture and value, and on a shared commitment to the creation of viable and sustainable film milieus. Let me turn now to *Advance Party* in an attempt to show how these milieu-developing commitments can be furthered through transnational director- or producer-initiated filmmaking projects.

Advance Party

According to Gillian Berrie, *Advance Party* can be seen as an attempt to do for Scotland what Lars von Trier's rule-governed and now globalized Dogme 95 movement did for Denmark and Danish film. Following the completion of Lone Scherfig's *Wilbur Wants to Kill Himself*, Berrie contacted producer Sisse Graum Jørgensen at Zentropa about the possibility of a milieu-developing initiative that would be like Dogme 95 in key respects. Marie Gade, another prominent Zentropa producer, was brought into the conversation early on, as was Lenny Crooks from the Glasgow Film Fund. More important, however, was the enthusiastic support of von Trier, who is responsible for the basic *Advance Party* concept and for the rules by which participating filmmakers must abide. *Advance Party*, it was determined, would encompass three films by first-time feature filmmakers. All three films would be shot on location in Scotland, in no more than six weeks time, and using digital technology. Further constraints involved a budgetary ceiling of £1.2 million (U.S. $2,382,000) and use of the same set of characters, played by the same cast, across all three films. Lone Scherfig and scriptwriter/filmmaker Anders Thomas Jensen were asked to produce seven character sketches, and the *Advance Party* filmmakers—Dartford-born Andrea Arnold, Scottish Morag McKinnon, and Danish Mikkel Nørgaard—were subsequently allowed to propose two more. These nine character sketches then became the basis for the full-blown scripts the directors were to develop themselves.

The agreement between Sigma and Zentropa was that the choice of first-time directors would be shared, and that at least one of the directors would be Scottish and one Danish. Anna Duffield from Sigma Films was sent on a scouting expedition to festivals and film schools, with the intent of identifying talented directors who were managing to secure funding for short film productions, and who were gaining recognition for these cinematic efforts. Once the directors had been selected, they were all brought to Filmbyen, von Trier and Aalbæk Jensen's army barracks-turned-film town, on the outskirts of Copenhagen. Here they met with von Trier who explained the philosophy of creativity under constraint that has in fact governed his own filmmaking practice since the very beginning, although he has only recently begun to share this approach with viewers (as in the case of Dogme 95 and the collaborative film titled *De fem benspænd/ The Five Obstructions* [Denmark/Switzerland/Belgium/France, 2003]). Following their meeting at the Zentropa film town, the directors were instructed to develop their scripts and, very importantly, to agree on a cast.[32] Andrea Arnold reports that the directors opted to foreground quite different characters and thus were able to give one another considerable freedom in the choice of actors for the various lead roles.

The first *Advance Party* film, *Red Road* by Andrea Arnold, was released in 2006, and Morag McKinnon's film, with the working title *Rounding Up Donkeys,* was being shot at the time of writing and is scheduled for release in 2009. *Red Road,* the script for which was developed at the Sundance Screenwriters Lab in 2005, was included in the main competition at the Cannes Film Festival in 2006, where it ultimately won the Jury's Special Prize. The film also garnered a series of BAFTA awards in 2006: for Best Screenplay, Best Actress in a Scottish Film (Kate Dickie), Best Actor in a Scottish Film (Tony Curran), Best Director, and Best Film. And that same year *Red Road* won the Sutherland Trophy at the London Film Festival, an award honoring "the director of the most original and imaginative first feature film." This auspicious start to a collective project prompted a number of prominent figures to make public inferences about the nature and potential of Scottish film, and these statements recall those made by cultural decision makers in Denmark when Thomas Vinterberg's *Dogme #1, Festen/ The Celebration* (DK/SE) won the same award at Cannes in 1998. Patricia Ferguson, Scottish Minister for Culture, Tourism and Sport, commented as follows on *Red Road*'s success: "It is a fantastic achievement for *Red Road* to win a special jury prize at Cannes. . . . It proves that Scotland has a wealth of creative film talent with excellent writers, actors and production staff."[33] And Ken Hay, CEO of Scottish Screen, remarked that *Red Road*'s award "demonstrates that with a relatively low budget you can take on the best in the world."[34]

Writing for *Sight & Sound,* Hannah McGill describes *Red Road* as an "urban sexual revenge drama with a difference." The story focuses on Jackie Morrison (Kate Dickie), a council CCTV operative who recognizes someone from her past while monitoring the feeds from cameras surveying the notorious and imposing block of flats on Red Road in Glasgow. Clyde Henderson (Tony Curran), we learn along with Jackie, has been released early from prison on account of good behavior, and Jackie begins to stalk him. As

McGill points out, the film is "as teasingly reticent about [Jackie's] precise intentions as it is about the nature of Clyde's original offence," suggesting "a number of archetypes: stalker, spurned lover, vigilante avenger." A "staunchly minimal performance" on the part of Kate Dickie "permits each of these possibilities."[35] Jackie eventually entraps Clyde in a sexual encounter of considerable intensity, and effectively returns him to the jail cell where she believes he belongs. When a former cellmate intervenes threateningly on his behalf, Jackie explains her actions, thereby identifying the nature of Clyde's crime for the viewer, for the first time. The film concludes with Jackie achieving some measure of sympathy for Clyde, with her charges against him being dropped, and with her reconciliation with family members from whom she has been estranged since her life's tragedy occurred. While suspense generated by a mysterious crime and an equally mysterious revenge scheme creates the narrative drive in *Red Road,* an equally important involving element concerns the psychology of voyeurism and the one-way empathetic relationship at a distance that Jackie develops with the people whom she observes on a daily basis. Particularly poignant in this regard is a scene in which Jackie comes face to face with a man whose walks with his sick dog she has been following for some time. Noticing his new and clearly healthy dog, Jackie emits a spontaneous and enthusiastic "hello" that bespeaks a familiarity for which there is no shared basis, as the man's noncommittal response clearly suggests.

While there has been some reflection in film critics' writings on *Red Road* on the impact of the *Advance Party* setup on the film, there has been none of the polemicizing about whether or not the rules were actually followed that characterized the reception of the early Dogme films. One of the more insightful comments foregrounds a sense of untold stories linked to peripheral characters: "If *Red Road* sometimes seems generically jumbled, this may reflect its unusual development process. . . . Arguably, *Red Road* would be more of a forceful experience without the sense of other storylines clamoring in the wings. . . . Still, *Red Road* gains texture from the notion of a network of tangential individuals who are ceaselessly affected by the actions of its central couple."[36] A key reason for the absence of polemical debates and of the kind of attention-grabbing confessions in which Dogme filmmakers such as Vinterberg and Harmony Korine indulged has to do with an only partial disclosure of the *Advance Party* setup. The rules that preface the character descriptions are part of the *Red Road* press release, as is the character sketch of Clyde. The other character sketches have not, however, been made public and critics have not as a result been able to debate, for example, whether Jackie's father-in-law, Alfred, who makes reference to possibly hav-

Jackie (Kate Dickie) in *Red Road* (Andrea Arnold, UK/Denmark, 2006).

Jackie (Kate Dickie) in *Red Road*.

ing a malignant tumor at one point in the film but in no way appears to lie, matches the following description to a sufficient degree:

Alfred, 64

When he was young, he had great dreams and ideas about how his life would turn out. However, certain circumstances caused Alfred never to realize a single one of them and it was quite likely, that he would end his days as a bitter, disenchanted man, but he hasn't and for one simple reason: he lies.

Alfred suffers from a severe fear of dying and it worsens every time someone of his contemporaries passes on or every time he feels love for one of his close relatives. When he is really scared of dying, he behaves differently.[37]

As philosophers such as Nelson Goodman and Saul Kripke have shown,[38] rule following is no simple matter. And any attempt to determine rule abidance in relation to character sketches within a general context allowing characters either to recede into the background or to assume center stage would no doubt be a fool's game. There is thus considerable merit to the strategy of partial disclosure for which the producers and directors associated with *Advance Party* have clearly opted.

Milieu Building

Let me, by way of conclusion, return to two of my central claims: (1) *Advance Party* is an instance of transnational milieu building; and (2) *Advance Party* is an initiative designed to transfer some of the positive features of an actually thriving film milieu to a milieu that is currently underappreciated and thus struggling. When I met with Gillian Berrie in Film City Glasgow in the summer of 2006 she drew attention to the following key problems in her Scottish context:

1. The absence of a professional film school.
2. The failure on the part of Scottish Screen to train directors and producers although this institution does train four film professionals every two years.
3. The failure to recognize film as an industry.
4. The transition from short filmmaking to feature-length filmmaking as a decisive obstacle for many aspiring filmmakers.
5. The characterization of foreign coproducing partners (such as Zentropa) as "carpetbaggers," with the criticisms allegedly resulting in

changes to a leaseback system from which companies like Sigma in fact benefited enormously.

6. The decision to absorb Scottish Screen into Creative Scotland.

7. Ken Hay's decision, in his capacity as Scottish Screen CEO, to cut funding for film from £3 million to £2 million per year (approximately U.S. $6 million to U.S. $4 million).

It is, of course, possible to take issue with some of Berrie's contentions. One might, for example, point out that many noteworthy Scottish film directors have been trained at the National Film and Television School (NFTS), just outside London, the idea being that Scotland, as a unit within the United Kingdom, does in fact have a film school. Yet, it is not hard to understand why the NFTS cannot play the same role within Scotland that a Scottish film school could and would. It is worth pointing out that much of Berrie's pessimism when interviewed in the summer of 2006 had to do with the uncertainty surrounding Creative Scotland. The general sense of pessimism no doubt helps to explain Berrie's failure to invest much hope in what at the time was the newly created Screen Academy (and as of 2009 the fate of this collaborative venture between Napier University and the Edinburgh College of Art is uncertain).[39]

Faced with problems such as those identified above, many of which derive from lack of political will and underfunding, producers and directors have a number of choices. Let me mention just two of these: (1) acceptance of more or less intense, but nonetheless unending, malaise; and (2) the pursuit of artistic initiatives as an alternative to cultural policy and as a publicity- and recognition-generating device, one capable potentially of inciting political enthusiasm for film in relevant quarters, and thus of preparing the ground for the kind of comprehensive cultural policies that are the condition of possibility of thriving film milieus in small-nation contexts. Lars von Trier, it is clear, has always had a strong preference for the second option, even in a far more hospitable cultural environment. And there can be no doubt that Dogme's unexpected success, three years after it was first announced, helped then Danish Film Institute CEO Henning Camre secure the astronomical increase in funding mentioned above. Dogme 95 has also had consequences for cultural policy in Denmark. For example, even the most cursory perusal of documents pertaining to the much-touted New Danish Screen program reveals the extent to which policy makers have learned from Dogme. In some cases, in sum, director-led initiatives have the potential to function as a kind of bottom-up policy making, or at the very least as an alternative and/or complement to what is normally understood by "cultural policy."[40]

If *Advance Party* is an example of a Scottish producer refusing malaise as status quo in favor of milieu-building initiatives, then in what sense can this project be said to build capacity? Let us begin with the problem of transitions listed above. Lone Scherfig insists that whereas specific cultural policies have been developed in Denmark to facilitate the transition from short filmmaking to feature-length filmmaking, equally effective provisions have yet to be put in place in Scotland, where "there are many talented short film directors who simply cannot move on in their filmmaking careers."[41] Berrie confirms Scherfig's claim that von Trier was explicitly asked to design the Scottish/Danish project in a way that would make it a creative solution to this problem, and the result was the requirement that all participating directors should be first-time feature filmmakers. Berrie also points out that Morag McKinnon was selected, not only on the strengths of her short films, but also because she had had trouble breaking into feature filmmaking.[42]

With regard to a different problem, the absence of a professional film school culture, Scherfig's comments are once again suggestive:

At the Film School in Copenhagen there's a very high level of cooperation. We use each other a lot. We read each other's manuscripts, we ask other people to help us identify the problems with our work, and, very importantly, we ask them to help us find a *cure* for the problems. Students become all-rounders at the Film School, and everyone gets on really well for the most part. There's really not much competition. On the contrary, there's really a very strong spirit of cooperation. This is something we also wanted to give the directors as a tool. So cooperation was something the rules required.[43]

Advance Party, clearly, was to provide something resembling the congenial and supportive network that is integral to a well-functioning professional film school.

The failure to view the film sector in Scotland as a real industry requiring a certain volume, critical mass, and infrastructure is a problem to which *Advance Party* also provides the beginnings of a solution. All three films, the rules specify, are to be shot on location in Scotland, and this brings work opportunities to the region. The Scottish location requirement, for example, favors Scottish stories and thus Scottish English, which makes the choice of actors with ties to Scotland highly desirable and likely. Indeed, as Berrie remarks, with the exception of Natalie Press, whose grandparents are from Glasgow, the entire *Advance Party* cast is Scottish.

Dogme 95 taught Danish filmmakers and, just as importantly, Danish policy makers, to think of constraints linked to the realities of small-nation filmmaking as opportunities to foster creativity, rather than as debilitating and demoralizing obstacles. *Advance Party,* quite clearly, was an attempt to encourage some of the same kind of thinking about creativity and constraint in a Scottish context: Scherfig says "the aim was to unburden the directors by giving them a framework to work with. We had learnt through Dogme to interpret constraints as gifts. We wanted to give the directors some very concrete constraints, because we had learnt through Dogme that the more concrete the constraints are, the better they are able to function as a kind of 'tool.'"[44] Reflecting the realities of small-nation filmmaking, the budgetary constraint specifying a low maximal cost per film effectively minimizes the economic risks associated with feature filmmaking in order to make room, and create the conditions for, creative risks. And these creative risks are encouraged by the kind of out-of-the-box thinking that the collaborative *Advance Party* framework requires.

Whether *Advance Party* will deliver what its initiators hoped to achieve is at this point an open question. Some film critics have begun to predict, almost gleefully one might add, the project's failure (a telling example is Anthony Kaufman's article, "When the Party's Over: 'Red Road' Launches Advance Party, but Other Films Stalled").[45] At the time of writing (December 2007), Morag McKinnon, whose film was scheduled for shooting in November 2007, was experiencing delays on account of last-minute funding difficulties. It is worth noting that the *Advance Party* films are being funded one at a time, a fate with which the four Dogme brethren's projected films were initially threatened, although von Trier insisted, in an acrimonious dispute with the DFI, that lump funding for all four films was a sine qua non inasmuch as the aim was to create a *movement.* Had it not been for the visionary intervention of Bjørn Erichsen (then Head of Television, Danmarks Radio), who secured money for all four films, Dogme 95 would likely have been stillborn. There can be little doubt that the need to fund the *Advance Party* films serially has had an impact on the project's momentum, and this may well have consequences for its milieu-building potential and for its capacity to motivate policy makers to develop the Scottish film industry in the intended way. Also, while the *Advance Party* framework speaks directly to deficiencies in a given production environment, it is not clear that its rules are as effective in stimulating creativity as the ten rules that Dogme directors were required to follow. Dogme directors may have felt pressure in relation to earlier successes, but the rules were essentially neutral with regard to a director's position within an open-ended series of film productions involving rule abidance. In the case of *Advance Party,* the situation is unavoidably one of growing constraint as we move from director one through to director three. Finally, inasmuch as *Advance Party* is based on a three-film concept, it lacks the open-ended extendibility and translatability that characterized Dogme 95, and that was a crucial factor in its globalization.[46]

Yet, *Advance Party* remains an initiative that deserves the attention of film scholars, and certainly of those with an interest in transnational cinema and cultural policy. *Advance Party* outlines a compelling and potentially transferable model for cinematic transnationalism, in which various types of affinity, and a commitment to the development of viable and innovative local film milieus, become the driving force. In a world dominated by Hollywood's Global Cinema, and the reactive globalizations it has spawned, this is no small achievement.

Notes

I have profited from the helpful feedback of audiences in Edinburgh, Stirling, Glasgow, St. Andrews, London, Coventry, Norwich, Southampton, and Cardiff, and I am grateful to Martine Beugnet, Philip Drake, Christine Geraghty, Dina Iordanova, Richard Dyer, Jon Burrows, Christine Cornea, David Dunn, and Jackie Aplin for the opportunity to speak at their universities. I am particularly grateful to Philip Drake for his comments on city collaboration, to Chris Meir for his remarks about Glasgow's place within a larger UK context, and to Lynne Hibberd for generously sharing her interview with Robin MacPherson, director of the Scottish Screen Academy, with me.

1. Key scholars such as Jonathan Murray ("Scotland," 76–92) are currently examining the implications of the devolutionary process for cultural policy in Scotland, and in this regard the work of Philip Schlesinger's AHRC-funded team will no doubt be crucial.

2. Sigma Films, available at www.sigmafilms.com.

3. *Advance Party* is very much about city collaboration, between Glasgow and Copenhagen (over and against London, for example). I am grateful to Philip Drake for drawing my attention to this aspect of the project and refer the reader to his helpful article on city collaboration (Docherty et al., "Exploring the Potential Benefits of City Collaboration," 445–56).

4. Hirschman, *Exit, Voice, and Loyalty.*

5. Hjort and Petrie, "Introduction," 1–19.

6. Bray and Packer, *Education in Small States: Concepts, Challenges, and Strategies.*

7. Vital, *The Inequality of States: A Study of the Small Power in International Relations,* 8.

8. Olafsson, *Small States in the Global System: Analysis and Illustrations from the Case of Iceland,* 9.

9. Hroch, *The Social Preconditions of National Revival in Europe.*

10. Gellner, "The Coming of Nationalism and Its Interpretation: The Myths of Nation and Class," 98–145.

11. Petrie, "New Zealand," 168. Based on current exchange rates of €1, approximately equal to U.S. $1.4364 (December 2007).

12. Andersen, "Dear Europe," 16.

13. Gundelach Brandstrup and Novrup Redvall, "Breaking the Borders: Danish Coproductions in the 1990s," 141.

14. Hess and Zimmermann, "Transnational Documentaries: A Manifesto," 99.

15. Hjort, "On the Plurality of Cinematic Transnationalism."

16. See Balio, "'A Major Presence in All of the World's Important Markets': The Globalization of Hollywood in the 1990s," 58–73.

17. Gillian Berrie, interview with author, June 2006.

18. Ibid.

19. Lone Scherfig, interview with author, May 2006.

20. Miles Fielder, "There Is Nothing like a Dane."

21. Marie Gade, interview with author, June 2006.

22. Andersen, "Dear Europe," 17.

23. Fielder, "There Is Nothing like a Dane."

24. Ibid., 3

25. Jacobsen, *Uden cigar: Faderen, Sønnen og Filmkøbmanden Peter Aalbæk Jensen* (Without cigar: The father, the son, and the film merchant Peter Aalbæk Jensen, my translation), 87.

26. Here and elsewhere based on current exchange rates of £1 (pound sterling) approximately equal to U.S. $1.99 (December 2007).

27. Marie Gade, interview with author, June 2006.

28. "Govan Town Hall," available at www.glasgow.gov.uk/en/Residents/Environment/Rivers/RiverClyde/Projects/PacificQuay/GovanTownhall (accessed December 28, 2007).

29. Ibid.

30. Gillian Berrie, interview with author, June 2006.

31. Lone Scherfig, interview with author, May 2006.

32. Gillian Berrie, Anna Duffield, Marie Gade, interview with author, June 2006.

33. Cited in "'Red Road' Special Jury Prize Success at Cannes," *Regional Film and Video,* May 30, 2006, available at www.4rfv.co.uk/industrynews.asp?ID=52031 (accessed December 27, 2007), no author.

34. Sweeney, "Global Audience to Get Glimpse of Red Road."

35. McGill, "Mean Streets."

36. Ibid.

37. Document provided by Scherfig, May 2006.

38. Goodman, *Fact, Fiction, and Forecast;* Kripke, *Wittgenstein on Rules and Private Language.*

39. Hibberd, "Interview with Robin MacPherson, Director of the Screen Academy, 13 September 2007."

40. Hjort, "Denmark," 23–42.

41. Lone Scherfig, interview with author, May 2006.

42. Gillian Berrie, interview with author, June 2006.

43. Lone Scherfig, interview with author, May 2006.

44. Ibid.

45. Kaufman, "When the Party's Over: 'Red Road' Launches Advance Party, but Other Films Stalled."

46. Hjort, "The Globalisation of Dogma: The Dynamics of Metaculture and Counter-Publicity," 133–57.

Bibliography

Andersen, Jesper. "Dear Europe." *FILM* 42 (2005): 16–19.

Balio, Tino. "'A Major Presence in All of the World's Important Markets': The Globalization of Hollywood in the 1990s." In *Contemporary Hollywood Cinema,* edited by Steve Neale and Murray Smith, 58–73. London: Routledge, 1998.

Bray, Mark, and Steve Packer. *Education in Small States: Concepts, Challenges, and Strategies.* Oxford: Pergamon, 1993.

Docherty, Iain, Stuart Gulliver, and Philip Drake. "Exploring the Potential Benefits of City Collaboration." *Regional Studies* 38 (2004): 445–56.

Fielder, Miles. "There Is Nothing like a Dane." *Scotland on Sunday,* May 8, 2005. At http://scotlandonsunday.scotsman.com/review.cfm?id=494222005.

Gellner, Ernest. "The Coming of Nationalism and Its Interpretation: The Myths of Nation and Class." In *Mapping the Nation,* edited by Gopal Balakrishnan, 98–145. London: Verso, 1996.

"Govan Town Hall." At www.glasgow.gov.uk/en/Residents/Environment/Rivers/RiverClyde/Projects/PacificQuay/GovanTownhall (accessed December 28, 2007).

Gundelach Brandstrup, Pil., and Eva Novrup Redvall. "Breaking the Borders: Danish Coproductions in the 1990s." In *Transnational Cinema in a Global North,* edited by Andy Nestingen and Trevor G. Elkington, 141–63. Detroit: Wayne State University Press, 2005.

Goodman, Nelson. *Fact, Fiction, and Forecast.* Cambridge, MA: Harvard University Press, 2006.

Hess, John, and Patricia A. Zimmermann. "Transnational Documentaries: A Manifesto." In *Transnational Cinema, The Film Reader,* edited by Elizabeth Ezra and Terry Rowden, 79–108. London: Routledge, 2006.

Hibberd, Lynne. "Interview with Robin MacPherson, Director of the Screen Academy, 13 September 2007." Unpublished.

Hirschman, Albert O. *Exit, Voice, and Loyalty.* Cambridge, MA: Harvard University Press, 2006.

Hjort, Mette. "Denmark." In *The Cinema of Small Nations,* edited by Mette Hjort and Duncan Petrie, 23–42. Edinburgh: Edinburgh University Press, 2007.

———. "The Globalisation of Dogma: The Dynamics of Metaculture and Counter-Publicity." In *Purity and Provocation: Dogma 95,* edited by Hjort and Scott

MacKenzie, 133–57. London: British Film Institute, 2003.

———. "On the Plurality of Cinematic Transnationalism." In *World Cinemas, Transnational Perspectives,* edited by Kathleen Newman and Natasa Durovicova. London: Routledge/American Film Institute, 2009.

Hjort, Mette, and Duncan Petrie. "Introduction." In *The Cinema of Small Nations,* edited by Hjort and Petrie, 1–19. Edinburgh: Edinburgh University Press, 2007.

Hjort, Mette, and Ib Bondebjerg, eds. *The Danish Directors.* Bristol: Intellect Press, 2001.

Hroch, Miroslav. *The Social Preconditions of National Revival in Europe.* Cambridge: Cambridge University Press, 1985.

Jacobsen, Kirsten. *Uden cigar: Faderen, Sønnen og Filmkøbmanden Peter Aalbæk Jensen* (Without cigar: The father, the son, and the film merchant Peter Aalbæk Jensen). Copenhagen: Høst and Søn, 2001.

Kaufman, Anthony. "When the Party's Over: 'Red Road' Launches Advance Party, but Other Films Stalled." *IndieWIRE,* 11 April 2007. At www.indiewire.com/movies/2007/04/world_cinema_wh.html.

Kripke, Saul. *Wittgenstein on Rules and Private Language.* Cambridge, MA: Harvard University Press, 2007.

McGill, Hannah. "Mean Streets." *Sight & Sound,* November 2006. At www.bfi.org.uk/sightandsound/feature/49329/.

Murray, Jonathan. "Scotland." In *The Cinema of Small Nations,* edited by Mette Hjort and Duncan Petrie, 76–92. Edinburgh: Edinburgh University Press, 2007.

Olafsson, Björn. *Small States in the Global System: Analysis and Illustrations from the Case of Iceland.* Aldershot: Ashgate, 1998.

Petrie, Duncan. "New Zealand." In *The Cinema of Small Nations,* edited by Mette Hjort and Duncan Petrie, 160–76. Edinburgh: Edinburgh University Press, 2007.

"'Red Road' Special Jury Prize Success at Cannes." *Regional Film and Video,* May 30, 2006. At www.4rfv.co.uk/industrynews.asp?ID=52031.

Sweeney, Charlene. "Global Audience to Get Glimpse of Red Road." *Sunday Herald,* June 4, 2006. At http://findarticles.com/p/articles/mi_qn4156/is_20060604/ai_n16453237.

Vital, David. *The Inequality of States: A Study of the Small Power in International Relations.* Oxford: Clarendon, 1967.

Sigma Films. At www.sigmafilms.com.

Cinema in a Settler Society

Brand New Zealand

Despite the apparently bleak outlook for a pluralistic and diverse world film culture, globalization cannot simply be reduced to a new manifestation of hegemonic domination and control. Peripheral cinemas face a constant struggle to secure a visible share of their own domestic markets. They also must compete in the global arena, thus exacerbating the difficulties of sustaining small national traditions that can engage in a fundamental way with the specificity of national formations while guaranteeing alternative perspectives, stories, and representations from those produced by Hollywood and the other major players. The situation is altogether more complex, with alternative opportunities emerging that have been mobilized to the benefit of some of the smaller film-producing nations.

A good example is provided by Danish cinema and the transformation in the levels and popularity of local production in Denmark over the last ten to fifteen years. As Mette Hjort argues, this has been brought about via a combination of enlightened cultural policy on the part of the Danish government, including substantial levels of state funding and concerted artistic leadership from the preeminent figures in the industry such as Lars von Trier.[1] Hjort notes that "the New Danish Cinema is in many ways a small nation's response to globalization, an instance of globalization and a dense and complicated site for the emergence of alternatives to neo-liberal conceptions of globalization or cinematic globalization on a Hollywood model."[2] Not only are Danish films holding their own in the local market, they have also enjoyed a strong international presence at film festivals and via specialist distribution and exhibition circuits. Moreover, the Danish-initiated Dogme 95 phenomenon—described by Hjort as "a small nation's response to Hollywood style globalization"—has constituted a distinctive "brand" of international filmmaking with its rules-based "vow of chastity" and low-fi aesthetic.[3] While over two hundred productions from thirty countries have been awarded a Dogme certificate, the initiative maintains a strong association with its Danish origins.[4]

This chapter will examine another small and peripheral cinema, that of New Zealand, which has also recently enjoyed an unprecedented level of international visibility and success, if not quite on the same scale as Denmark. However, New Zealand still provides an interesting case study of a national cinema that highlights some of the opportunities and constraints deriving from the consequences of globalization within the motion picture industry.

Until the late 1970s there was no such thing as a New Zealand national cinema. Feature production had been sporadic since the silent period and only seven dramatic feature films were made between 1940 and the mid-1970s. The only regular and stable form of filmmaking in New Zealand during the period was the documentary and newsreel output of the National Film Unit, established in 1941 following a report by John Grierson. But during the 1970s an independent production sector began to emerge led by a new generation of ambitious and rebellious young filmmakers who wanted to create cinematic fictions that would tell different kinds of New Zealand stories from those churned out by the National Film Unit. This resulted in the production of a number of independently financed low-budget feature films,[5] by far the most significant of which was the political thriller *Sleeping Dogs* (1977), directed by Roger Donaldson and starring Sam Neill and the American actor Warren Oates. This privately financed production not only proved to be a great success in New Zealand, it was also distributed internationally and was the first New Zealand feature film to open in America. In addition to "doing it themselves," the nascent independent production community had also been active in a campaign to persuade the government to create a source of public support for filmmaking, which culminated in the setting up of an Interim Film Commission in 1977, paving the way for the establishment of a permanent body, the New Zealand Film Commission (NZFC), the following year.[6] With an initial modest fund of NZ$640,000 (U.S. $480,000),[7] the NZFC provided the resources by which a moderate but bona fide New Zealand national cinema could become a reality, with an average of four or five features a year being supported. Three decades on, the number of films being produced remains fairly constant, although there is substantially more money in the pot—in 2005/6 the New Zealand Film Commission invested a record NZ$17.4 million (U.S. $13,050,000) in ten feature projects, in addition to significant levels of support for feature film development and short film production.

While creating a national cinema, the NZFC has been less successful in nurturing a sustainable film industry. As a result New Zealand cinema has remained small, fragile, and almost totally dependent on state support. There have been two periods when significant alternative sources of finance have been tapped: in the early 1980s tax shelter opportunities attracted significant levels of investment, substantially boosting the number of films being made before the loophole was closed in 1984. The second boom period has occurred since 2000, stimulated by various government initiatives to attract offshore productions and coproducing partners for New Zealand films and leading to more medium- and high-budget productions being made. But cultivating overseas markets for New Zealand films has remained an extremely difficult proposition, and relatively few of the two hundred plus films produced over the last thirty years have enjoyed a significant international profile. Moreover, opportunities to develop careers in the New Zealand industry have remained heavily constrained, and so a pattern was quickly established whereby local filmmakers who demonstrated any significant talent were quickly lured overseas. The pattern was already being set by the mid-1980s with the departure of Roger Donaldson, Geoff Murphy, and Sam Pillsbury to Los Angeles and subsequently continued with the likes of Vincent Ward, Jane Campion, Lee Tamahori, and Niki Caro, while others such as Andrew Adamson, Martin Campbell, and Andrew Niccol (*Gattaca,* 1997) have made their reputations entirely outside New Zealand and are primarily recognized as Hollywood directors. Indeed the only kiwi filmmaker of major international stature to resist the temptation to emigrate has been Peter Jackson. Rather, he has achieved the remarkable feat of getting Hollywood to come to him, beginning with *The Frighteners* in 1996, produced by Robert Zemeckis for Universal, and followed by the even more substantial *The Lord of the Rings* trilogy and *King Kong,* produced for New Line Cinema and Universal respectively.

New Zealand cinema's ongoing negotiation of the local and the global is bound up with the integration of cultural and economic imperatives. Domestic films have sought to play a major role in the cultivation and projection of a national culture while at the same time actively seeking to secure a presence in the global marketplace. If the former priority represents the traditional justification for the public funding that has underpinned New Zealand cinema since the creation of the NZFC, the latter is now also a key desired outcome of government *investment* (as opposed to subsidy) in a sector now designated as one of New Zealand's major creative industries. This intertwining of the cultural and the economic, the local and the global is clearly articulated in the following statement included in a 2004 press release from Prime Minister Helen Clark announcing a NZ$10 million (U.S. $7.5 million) increase in funding for the NZFC: "Film and television make a significant contribution to New Zealand's economy and export earnings, as well as being very powerful media through which we express our national identity and assert our unique brand."[8] Since coming to power in 1999, Helen Clark's Labour-led government has been an enthusiastic supporter of the nation's screen industries, reinforced by the fact that Clark also held the post of Minister for Culture, which provides the funding for the NZFC.

National Cinema in a Settler Society

The relationship between nation building and global trade is a direct consequence of New Zealand's peripheral location and historical legacy as a settler nation. While the first European contact occurred in 1642 when the Dutchman Abel Tasman sighted and then briefly landed on the South Island, it was the arrival of James Cook in 1769 and the charting of the islands that paved the way for later British settlement. New Zealand became a British sovereign colony in 1840 with the signing of the Treaty of Waitangi by representatives of the Crown and some of the Maori tribes. The process of settlement subsequently intensified with the British population increasing from around 2,000 in 1839 to 250,000 by 1870. During the same time the number of indigenous Maori (who had originally arrived from Polynesia around the end of the first millennium) declined from an estimated 70,000 to 48,000, primarily due to disease. The 1860s had witnessed concerted attempts by Maori to resist the onward rush of appropriation of tribal land by the settlers, much of it in direct contravention of the Treaty that had guaranteed Maori rights in return for British sovereignty, but in the end they were outgunned and outnumbered. In 1907 New Zealand became an independent dominion, but the strong cultural and economic connection to Britain continued to such an extent that historian James Belich has identified New Zealand's prevailing sense of identity as a kind of "Better Britain" that "maintained that New Zealanders were even more loyal and closely linked to Old Britain than other neo-Britains, but also that they were in some respects superior to Old Britons. The self-image of New Zealanders asserted greater egalitarianism, ingenuity and self-reliance than Old Britons. The collective identity asserted New Zealandness and Britishness, with an assumption of compatibility that it required no stating."[9]

This close identification with the imperial mother country was also underpinned by economic dependency, with 50 percent of New Zealand's largely agricultural exports bound for the UK market. Then, in the 1970s, Britain's decision to join the European common market began to unravel, which was to have a devastating effect on the New Zealand economy. This in turn paved the way for the next great shock, which occurred a decade later when David Lange's Labour government embarked on a wholesale policy of economic liberalization, deregulation, and a considerable reduction of the public sector through the selling off of public assets and the curtailing of subsidies. This transformed almost overnight what had been one of the most state-centralized economies in the capitalist world into one of the most market-dependent, aggressively opening up New Zealand to the forces of economic neoliberalism that came to underpin globalization.

The reorientation of dependency away from Britain and toward the rest of the world entailed the forging of a new sense of cultural identity that rejected the neocolonial mindset. During the interwar period New Zealand had experienced a surge of cultural nationalism, reflected particularly in literature and painting, in terms of an oppositional and left wing search for local meaning and specificity.[10] But this process assumed a far greater significance from the 1970s onward as means of establishing a national identity distinct from the old neocolonial mindset.[11] The primary drivers of this were the members of the New Zealand counterculture, the generation of baby boomers who took their lead from the radicals of the protest movements in the United States and the United Kingdom. Their opposition to the old establishment, while espousing greater personal freedoms and identity politics, was also inextricably linked to this broader shift away from the patrician ideology of Better Britain and toward a new sense of an independent and distinct *New Zealandness.* Just one of the direct manifestations of this within the cultural sphere was the demand for a New Zealand national cinema underpinned by state support, a direct acknowledgment of the medium's power not only to reflect New Zealanders back to themselves but also to project this identity outward to the rest of the world.

Alongside this shift, there was an ongoing intensification of political activity on the part of the indigenous Maori for greater recognition of their own claims and grievances. Maori political activism increased during the 1970s and led to some significant gains, including the establishment of the Waitangi Tribunal in 1975 as a means by which land rights could be settled. Ten years later the Tribunal had its remit backdated to 1840, enshrining in the process a constitutional recognition of Maori rights and criticisms. Progress was also being made on the cultural front with a revival in the Maori language, *te reo,* and the development of Maori schools, Maori radio, and, by 2004, the introduction of a Maori television channel. In some respects the Maori revival has assisted New Zealand cultural nationalism in the creation of a notion of biculturalism or partnership. In its benign form, the Maori presence also served to provide *brand New Zealand* with a unique selling point, differentiating it from other Anglo-centric settler nations such as Australia and Canada. Dissenting voices from within Maoridom have regarded this as a new form of benevolent paternalism that may pay lip service to the idea of partnership while simultaneously maintaining the existing unequal power relations that continue to serve the interests of Pakeha (New Zealanders of European descent). Indeed, the foremost articulation of New Zealand history from a Maori perspective by Ranginui Walker is appropriately titled *Struggle without End.*[12] The Maori challenge has also served to complicate and even unsettle the decolonializing discourse of cultural nationalism propagated by Pakeha New Zealanders.[13]

Cultural difference and diversity in New Zealand, however, extends beyond the scenario of biculturalism. The ushering in of neoliberalism also had ramifications for culture as well as economics, the most tangible impact being an increase in immigration from Polynesia, Asia and South Africa as well as other immigrants who continue to arrive from the United Kingdom and Europe. This migratory dynamics has radically transformed the composition of the national population. In 1986, of a population of 3,310,000 just over 81 percent were of European origin, 12.6 percent were Maori, and 6.3 percent others—mainly Chinese, Indian, and Pacific Islanders. The 2006 census indicated that of a total national population of just over 4,143,000, 67.6 percent of the population were of European origin, 14.6 percent were Maori, 9.2 percent Asian, and 6.9 percent were from the Pacific. In Auckland, the major urban center, 56.5 percent were European, 18.9 percent Asian, 14.4 percent Pacific, and 11.1 percent Maori. The increased mobility of people has contributed to both inflows and outflows of population with the result that 23 percent of present-day New Zealanders were born overseas, while around 10 percent of those who were born in New Zealand are currently living elsewhere in the world (mainly Australia and the United Kingdom). This changing composition—with major increases in both the Asian and Pacific Island populations in New Zealand—and the creation of a much more multicultural New Zealand (Auckland in particular) has profoundly affected the discourse on cultural identity and cultural nationalism. While for some this diversity renders meaningless any sense of a unitary national culture, for others it confirms the importance of nation-building in providing a sense of commonality among a diverse population.

Consequently, the articulation of identity provides the basis for a distinctive national branding of New Zealand goods in the global market, from agricultural produce and wine to films and television programs. The support of the NZFC ensures that cinema continues to provide the means by which New Zealand stories and New Zealand images can circulate at home and abroad. The creation of a new NZ$22 million (U.S. $16.5 million) Film Fund in 2000 has stimulated a small but significant number of medium-budget coproductions that are primarily New Zealand films with strong international elements such as financial deals and creative talent. These are epitomized by films like *Whale Rider* (Niki Caro, 2003), *Perfect Strangers* (Gaylene Preston, 2004), *The World's Fastest Indian* (Roger Donaldson, 2005), *River Queen* (Vincent Ward, 2006), *Perfect Creature* (Glenn Standring, 2007) and *The Ferryman* (Chris Graham, 2007). Offshore production has also been strongly encouraged, most notably via the NZFC-administered Large Budget Production Grant Scheme, which provides an automatic subsidy of 12.5 percent of production spend in New Zealand where that spend is NZ$15 million (U.S. $11,250,000) or over, effectively ensuring that only overseas (primarily Hollywood) financed productions can benefit from this initiative.[14] Such enthusiastic participation in "the new international division of cultural labour"[15] also indicates the how the "third way" policies of Helen Clark's government also embraced the neoliberal priorities of globalization.

Branding and Representation

While the relationship between national identity and cinematic fictions is necessarily complex, the connections between New Zealand cinema and some of the major tropes of the shifting identity discourses noted above are very apparent. The most resonant statement of the cultural specificity of New Zealand cinema arguably remains Sam Neill and Judy Rymer's controversial identification of "a cinema of unease" articulated in their 1995 documentary.[16] The film depicts a rather dysfunctional national culture marked by social conformity, Puritanism, fear, insanity, and violence, which has in turn generated a cinema offering a dark and troubled reflection with a central trope being the destructive force of the landscape. *A Cinema of Unease* was vociferously criticized within New Zealand as overreliant on the discourse of cultural nationalism that emerged in the interwar period. This discourse was regarded as too reliant on masculine narratives of isolation, loneliness, and struggle, and therefore not particularly appropriate for understanding the diversity of contemporary New Zealand film culture. While such criticisms are well founded, they do not entirely displace Neill and Rymer's central argument in that there clearly remains a brooding presence in the national cinematic imaginary, from *The Piano* (Jane Campion, 1993) and *Heavenly Creatures* (Peter Jackson, 1994) to more recent productions like *Rain* (Christine Jeffs, 2002) and *In My Father's Den* (Brad McGann, 2004).

However, this can be more effectively examined not as a critique of colonial subservience but rather as a symptom of a deeper sense of settler unease that has been provoked by the cultural and political gains of Maori since the 1970s. In one of the most insightful and provocative analyses of New Zealand cinema, Martin Blythe foregrounds the dialectic between integration and segregation that has marked the relationship between Pakeha and Maori, colonizer and colonized. Drawing on the radical psychiatry of Gregory Bateson and R. D. Laing, Blythe characterizes this in terms of a double bind that creates a no-win situation for the weaker partner in an unequal power relationship:

On one hand, the Maori are declared to be "New Zealanders" by virtue of the Waitangi Treaty of 1840 ("You are New Zealanders and British subjects, titled to all the benefits which follow from that"). On the other, "New Zealand" is defined along British (Pakeha) lines ("You are Maori, you are different and we don't necessarily want what you represent"). And the second always comes attached to the first—a kind of double play which oscillates between annexation (assertion of nationalism) on the one hand, and exclusion (denial of biculturalism) on the other.[17]

While Blythe does not use the term, *unease* remains a haunting presence in the scenario, serving to undermine the project of a cultural nationalism seeking reassurance in the construction of a stable and durable identity. An alternative interpretation of the problem is provided by Stephen Turner in his astute and provocative questioning of New Zealand's history in which "the melancholy of dislocation is particularly acute."[18] This is partly a consequence of geography, of distance and isolation, but it has also led to forms of amnesia or covering up of the trauma of the process of settlement.

Rather than seeing themselves as immigrants, settlers reconstruct their identity as indigenous, albeit distinct from the Maori. For Turner, the trauma continues to lie within the "acculturated body of the settler." Consequently, the current obsession with building New Zealand's national identity is not simply a response to a changing and diversifying population; it is also a palpable symptom of settler anxiety. New Zealand cinema therefore, like the country's literature, is stuck in a quest for foundational narratives, or affirming the fundamental unease of settlement, as articulated by Turner in terms of the concept of "broken history": "the history of the place, considered as singular, continuous, now unified, the foundation therefore of identity and nationhood, is *broken*. The idea of one history/nation/people flies in the face of this historical discontinuity, making the attendant narrative a rickety footbridge thrown over an abyss."[19] Two recent films that reveal the extent of this identity crisis, albeit from a kind of Jekyll and Hyde perspective, are *In My Father's Den* and *The World's Fastest Indian. In My Father's Den,* adapted from Maurice Gee's novel by Brad McGann, is a bleak tale of alienation and repression that updates the "Cinema of Unease" idea.[20] It tells the story of a New Zealander, Paul Prior (Matthew Macfadyen), an emotionally damaged young man who returns to his South Island home after a seventeen-year absence, ostensibly to attend the funeral of his father but ultimately to confront the painful ghosts of the past. We eventually discover that Paul left home after witnessing his father having sex with his girlfriend in his secret den (which the young Paul had regarded as a place of magic and wonder) and his mother's subsequent suicide, a traumatic memory he had repressed. But the family horror is compounded by his relationship with a young girl, Celia (Emily Barclay), who he thinks may be his daughter but is ultimately revealed to have been sired by Paul's own father. Halfway through the film Celia disappears, and the mood turns even darker as the narrative moves toward the final revelations, including the discovery that Celia has been accidentally killed after a confrontation with Paul's brother Andrew and his wife.

In total contrast, *The World's Fastest Indian* is a warmhearted celebration of local hero Burt Munro, who at the age of sixty-seven set a new world speed record at Bonneville Flats, Utah on his forty-year-old Indian Scout motorcycle, a machine that he had modified in his own idiosyncratic and resourceful way. Burt Munro (Anthony Hopkins) is an unlikely hero, a resourceful "kiwi" who despite his age, deafness, and angina, fulfills his dream by traveling out into the world, and charming those he meets with his honesty, humanity, and childlike innocence. Although considered an eccentric nuisance by his neighbors, Burt ultimately inspires universal goodwill by winning over the hearts and minds of everyone he comes in contact with, from the local bike gang in Invercargill, to assorted American customs personnel, police officers, and the racing officials at Bonneville who are persuaded to bend the rules after initially declaring Burt's Scout unfit to run. Burt is also allowed two love interests with women of his own age: the New Zealander Fran (Annie Whittle) and the American Ada (Dianne Ladd), while his acceptance of Tina, the large African American transvestite who helps him when he arrives in Los Angeles, underscores his nonjudgmental approach to his fellow human beings. This, in conjunction with his no-nonsense resourcefulness (his bike features homemade pistons and racing tires—which Burt modifies by simply cutting off the tread with a carving knife) and charming naïveté identify him as a "kiwi," or New Zealander, something he continually reasserts during his encounters in California and Utah.

In My Father's Den, on the one hand, allegorizes the dark trauma and repression of the settler experience through its focus on family dysfunction, the isolation of the community (Celia's desire to escape and discover the world echoes Paul's own earlier dreams), and the ambivalent response to the local boy whose success (as a war photographer) is difficult to accommodate. Paul is also quizzed a number of times on the "pommie accent" he has acquired that marks him as "different." The bleak ending reconfirms a sense of the impossibility of "home" for Paul. While the temporal manipulations of the narrative have the film ending with the moment when Paul says goodbye to Celia for the last time, his final act is to burn down his father's den.

The World's Fastest Indian, on the other hand, can be read as a kind of idealized overcompensation. For if Pakeha identity is epitomized by Burt Munro, then this construction of national identity in such unremittingly positive terms serves to erase a past scarred by the uncompromising and brutal displacement of others. Burt's virtues are part and parcel of his "kiwi" identity, he is a "salt-of-the-earth" character, and that earth is the contested land of New Zealand. Placing this story in the 1960s also conveniently locates it in a period that precedes the Maori revival, which forced a new confrontation with the inconvenient facts of history. But the figure of the indigene still makes an appearance: During his journey from Los Angeles to Utah, Burt meets Jake, an old Indian who invites him to spend the night at his rudimentary trailer in the desert. In the morning, Jake presents Burt with a pendant for good luck, forging a bond of friendship between settler and native devoid of the usual complications of contestation over shared territory.

In My Father's Den was made as an official NZ/UK coproduction and has been released in nineteen countries. It also picked up a number of awards at international film festivals in the United Kingdom, France, Spain, Canada, and China. *The World's Fastest Indian* was supported by the New Zealand Film Fund and had Japanese investment. While less successful on the international awards front the film opened theatrically in twenty-nine countries. Both films proved popular at the local box office, *In My Father's Den* made NZ$1.5 million (U.S. $1,125,000) and is currently the eighth highest grossing local film at the New Zealand box office, while *The World's Fastest*

Indian earned more than NZ$7 million (U.S. $5,250,000), making it the most successful local film of all time in the home market.

The uneasy presence of Maori (as seen from a Pakeha perspective) in current New Zealand cinema can also be examined via two other contrasting productions, *Whale Rider,* Niki Caro's adaptation of the novel by acclaimed writer Witi Ihimaera, and *River Queen* (2006), Vincent Ward's ambitious tale of colonial confrontation set in the 1860s.

Whale Rider features an all Maori cast and tells the story of a young girl's struggle to achieve her destiny as the future leader of her tribe against the formidable opposition of her grandfather who refuses to acknowledge her birthright on the grounds of gender. Encouraged by her grandmother, Pai prepares to fulfill her destiny, which is confirmed when she climbs onto the back of a beached bull whale and rides out to sea. The plot is rooted in indigenous folklore in that Pai is revealed to be the descendant of Paikia who, according to the legend, had arrived in Whangara—a village on the East Cape of New Zealand's North Island and the location for the film—on the back of a whale.

Despite its huge success at home and abroad, *Whale Rider* generated a great deal of controversy in New Zealand over its identity as a "Maori film." Some commentators argued that it represents an exemplary model of bicultural cooperation. Others, including filmmaker Barry Barclay, suggested that the specificity of Maori culture was sidelined in the construction of an outsider's view.[21] Certainly, as a Maori story *Whale Rider* does not threaten settler hegemony, the community seems untouched by the history and consequences of settlement. Consequently, the film is a cultural product that has been comfortably co-opted into "Brand New Zealand." This is reinforced by a crowd-pleasing plot and reliance on, as Claire Murdoch puts it, certain familiar Western narrative and filmic tropes from *The Lion King* to *Harry Potter* to the story of Christ: "the nationally representative Maori and the internationally available New Zealand . . . are as closely enmeshed in *Whale Rider* as the jags and plummetings and reincarnations of its triumphal plot. They are part of what the film tells and part of what the nationalistic discourse celebrates."[22] *River Queen,* in contrast, directly confronts the history of settlement, the first New Zealand feature to do so since Geoff Murphy's *Utu* in 1983. It tells the story of a young Irish woman's search for her son, set against a fictionalized version of the campaign of Maori chief Titokowaru against the colonizers in Southern Taranaki in the 1860s. Sarah O'Brien's (Samantha Morton) son, Boy, is the result of a love affair with a young Maori who subsequently dies of influenza. The child is taken upriver by his grandfather, Old Rangi (Wi Kuki Kaa) as punishment after Sarah's father defiles sacred Maori ground. After witnessing the wanton destruction of a village and the killing of Rangi by the ruthless Major Baines, Sarah is reunited with Boy when she is taken upriver by a Maori scout, Wiremu, later revealed to be the brother of Sarah's dead lover, to treat the ill warrior, Te Kai Po. Gradually, Sarah becomes caught between two worlds, two cultures, and two identities. Boy refuses to come back downriver with her, claiming that he wishes to stay with "his people." Sickened by the brutality of settlers, Sarah asks Wiremu to tattoo a traditional Maori moko on her chin, culminating in a symbolic rebaptism in the river. Although shot while bathing, Sarah survives. The coda of *River Queen* depicts the new hybrid family (including an adult Boy) living peacefully in a small cottage by the sea. While both confronting the trauma of settlement and positing an alternative kind of melding (melting?) of cultures in which it is the settler who assimilates into the "host culture," the outcome of this cinematic narrative runs counter to the outcome of this key period in New Zealand's recorded history. Despite his earlier military success against the settlers, based on sophisticated military tactics, Te Kai Po decides to withdraw his forces in the second battle and effectively disappear from sight, allowing the colonists to consolidate their dominance over the entire country. Consequently, *River Queen* wrestles with the dilemmas of settlement, but all it can put forward as a kind of counter history is the integrated hybrid family. Sarah's Irishness (Britain's geographically closest colony) is crucial here also as she can, like Wiremu, be positioned as a victim of British imperialism, here transplanted to the most remote colony.

A New Zealand/German coproduction, *Whale Rider* is currently the third-highest grossing local production in the home market, where it made NZ$6.4 million (U.S. $4.8 million). It was also distributed successfully around the world, screening theatrically in more than forty countries, winning numerous awards, and earning an Oscar nomination for Keisha Castle Hughes. *River Queen* has been less conspicuously successful. While it also enjoyed a significant profile at home—grossing over NZ$1 million (U.S. $750,000), it has to date screened theatrically in only seven countries.

All four of these features were effectively international coproductions: *In My Father's Den* and *River Queen* with the United Kingdom, *Whale Rider* with Germany, and *The World's Fastest Indian* with the United States and Australia, and all but *In My Father's Den* were supported by the Film Fund. In this way they all contain elements oriented toward an international market, including casting (the leads of all but *Whale Rider* are British or American), plot elements (much of *The World's Fastest Indian* takes place in the United

States), or known directors (Roger Donaldson and Vincent Ward). Ironically the most risky of the four from the point of view of such recognizable elements, *Whale Rider,* proved to be the most successful internationally.

As I have noted elsewhere, one consequence of the raft of government initiatives to support film in New Zealand has been the creation of a national cinema comprised of distinctive overlapping spheres of production that in turn can be related to the tripartite system articulated by the "Third Cinema question."[23] In this model First Cinema refers to the commercial mainstream of Hollywood and its imitators, Second Cinema to auteur or art cinema, and Third Cinema to a more overtly oppositional cinema informed by anti-imperialist struggle and a commitment to alternative production practices. In the New Zealand context First Cinema relates to the domain of runaway and offshore production, including Hollywood-financed films that have retained a connection to New Zealand through the involvement of local creative talent, such as *The Lord of the Rings* and *King Kong.* The body of work supported by the NZFC since its inception can be clearly categorized as Second Cinema, although this is a flexible term that also embraces genre-driven work that aspires to a cut-price version of Hollywood. But the appropriateness of the category Third Cinema has also been challenged in the context of the struggles of first peoples by Barry Barclay who has advocated a new category of Fourth Cinema as an expression of indigenous cultures. Barclay argues that "First, Second and Third Cinemas are all cinemas of the modern Nation State—from the indigenous place of standing they are all invader cinemas."[24] Therefore, Fourth Cinema can be constituted as a small category comprising six major works by Maori: Barry Barclay's features *Ngati* (1987), *Te Rua* (1991), and *The Feathers of Peace* (2000); *Mauri* (1988) by Merata Mita; Lee Tamahori's highly successful *Once Were Warriors* (1994), and Don Selwyn's *Te Tangata Whai Rawa o Weniti/The Maori Merchant of Venice* (2002). What is notable here is that neither *Whale Rider* nor *River Queen* is included in this category, pronouncing them external perspectives on indigenous culture, rendered more palatable for the international marketplace.

However, all three categories of filmmaking as applied to New Zealand production have a global dimension: from the high exposure and mass distribution of the Hollywood machine, the film festivals and more specialized circulation of art cinema, to the equally distinctive international networks, and seasons or exhibitions dedicated to indigenous cinemas. Consequently, if First Cinema in the New Zealand context reflects the consequences of the New International Division of Cultural Labour, as defined by Miller and colleagues,[25] then Second Cinema is Pakeha-dominated and central to the ongoing debates about national identity, and Fourth Cinema constitutes the indigenous response to settler hegemony.

Brand New Zealand

While representations of Pakeha and to a lesser extent Maori served to distinguish New Zealand cinema, the Pacific Island presence is also beginning to be recognized with Auckland-based features such as *Sione's Wedding* (Chris Graham, 2006), built on the comic talents of the Naked Samoans and *No. 2* (2005), Toa Fraser's big-screen adaptation of his stage play about a Fijian New Zealand family gathering. But even here globalized forms of culture play a key role. *Sione's Wedding,* for example, relies heavily on the generic conventions of comedy and a soundtrack featuring top local hip-hop and R&B artists for its appeal, while the formidable Fijian matriarch at the center of *No. 2* is played by African American actress Ruby Dee.

In a more internationally oriented production environment encouraged by both funding initiatives and the success of Peter Jackson, New Zealand filmmakers appear to be drawing on the formulas of Hollywood with greater enthusiasm than ever, albeit often with a local twist. And befitting a national cinema with a penchant for the darker side, horror has enjoyed a particularly high profile in recent years and is currently flavor of the month with 2007 seeing the release of *Black Sheep* (Jonathan King), *Perfect Creature* (Glenn Standring), *The Ferryman* (Chris Graham), and *The Tattooist* (Peter Burger), the last with a strong Samoan cultural connection. While this can clearly be read as a concerted attempt to boost the international marketability of New Zealand films, it has arguably worked against the development of more marginal and culturally difficult work. In this light it is instructive to note that *Eagle versus Shark* (2007), the first feature by Taika Waititi, moves away from the more overtly Maori subject matter of his acclaimed short films—the Oscar-nominated *Two Cars, One Night* (2003) and *Tama Tu* (2005)—in favor of the self-consciously quirky comedy of indie filmmakers like Jared Hess and Michel Gondry. What Waititi has conspicuously not done is follow in the footsteps of Barry Barclay, Merata Mita, and Don Selwyn by making a "Maori" film. While this may be prompted by a desire to maximize the opportunities offered to an emerging young filmmaker with the desire to reach an international audience, it also underlines how globalization simultaneously craves variety and difference as consumer choices while constraining the ways in which these can be expressed in terms of cultural specificity or antagonism. What we get instead is a reinforcement of the ideology of the "national brand" where the offbeat quirkiness of *Eagle versus Shark* can sit comfortably alongside the idealism of *The World's Fastest Indian,* the native charm of *Whale Rider,* or even the brooding anguish of *In My Father's Den.*

The emphasis on the national brand may reflect a concerted effort to negotiate the complexities of local and global and be another small and peripheral nation's attempt to adapt in appropriate and creative ways to new opportunities within the sphere of international cinema. But it also raises real concerns about how effectively the moving image can engage with the underlying complex cultural issues that continue to define and trouble New Zealand as a rapidly changing nation.

Notes

1. Hjort, "Denmark," 23–42.
2. Hjort, *Small Nation, Global Cinema: The New Danish Cinema,* 8–9.
3. Ibid., 36.
4. From the official Dogme 95 website. Available at www.dogme95.dk/menu/menuset.htm (accessed December 19, 2007).
5. These included the experimental *Test Pictures: Eleven Vignettes from a Marriage* (Geoff Steven, 1975); *Landfall* (Paul Maunder, 1977), produced under the auspices of the National Film Unit two years earlier; the narrative documentary *Off the Edge* (Mike Frith, 1977); and *Wild Man* (Geoff Murphy, 1977), produced off the back of a television series.
6. Waller, "The New Zealand Film Commission: Promoting an Industry, Forging a National Identity," 243–63.
7. Based on current exchange rates of NZ$1 approximately equal to U.S. $0.75 (December 2007).
8. Boost for New Zealand Screen Production—Media Statement from Rt. Hon. Helen Clark, Minister for Arts, Culture and Heritage and Hon Judith Tizard, Associate Minister for Arts, Culture and Heritage—November 10, 2003. At www.med.govt.nz/templates/Page____659.aspx (accessed December 19, 2007).
9. Belich, *Paradise Reforged: A History of the New Zealanders from the 1880s to the Year 2000,* 78.
10. This is discussed in detail by Keith Sinclair, in *A Destiny Apart: New Zealand's Search for National Identity.*
11. Although Bruce Jesson has argued that even by the late 1990s the British cultural imprint remained strong in New Zealand, thus inhibiting the growth of Republican sentiment. And to this day the British Monarch remains the New Zealand Head of State. Jesson, *To Build a Nation: Collected Writings, 1975–99.*
12. Walker, *Ka Whawhai Tonu Matou/Struggle without End.*
13. This was particularly notable in 2004 with the Maori claims to customary title over the Foreshore and Seabed, leading to a campaign that saw the biggest protest march since the 1970s and the formation of a new Maori political party.

14. In July 2007 the New Zealand government increased the grant to 15 percent of New Zealand expenditure and made it more accessible to a wider range of productions. The primary beneficiaries of the scheme have been offshore-financed productions like *King Kong* and *The Chronicles of Narnia: The Lion the Witch and the Wardrobe,* which received grants of NZ$48.6 million (U.S. $36,450,000) and NZ$18 million (U.S. $13.5 million) respectively.

15. Miller et al., *Global Hollywood 2,* 2005.

16. Sam Neill and Judy Rymer, *A Cinema of Unease* (1995), produced by the British Film Institute for their Centenary of Cinema series.

17. Blythe, *Naming the Other: Images of the Maori in New Zealand Film and Television,* 6–8.

18. Turner, "Settlement as Forgetting," 22.

19. Turner, "Being Colonial/Colonial Being," 63.

20. Petrie, "From the Cinema of Poetry to the Cinema of Unease: Brad McGann's *In My Father's Den,*" 2–8.

21. The case against *Whale Rider* in this regard is elaborated by Kirsty Bennett, in "Fourth Cinema and the Politics of Staring," 19–23.

22. Murdoch, "Holy Sea Cow," 104.

23. Petrie, "New Zealand," 160–76.

24. Barclay, "Celebrating Fourth Cinema," 10.

25. Miller et al., *Global Hollywood 2.*

Bibliography

Barclay, Barry. "Celebrating Fourth Cinema." *Illusions* 35 (Winter 2003): 10.

Belich, James. *Paradise Reforged: A History of the New Zealanders from the 1880s to the Year 2000.* Auckland: Allen Lane, 2001.

Bennett, Kirsty. "Fourth Cinema and the Politics of Staring." *Illusions* 38 (Winter 2006): 19–23.

Blythe, Martin. *Naming the Other: Images of the Maori in New Zealand Film and Television.* Metuchen, NJ: Scarecrow Press, 1994.

Dogma 95. At www.dogme95.dk/menu/menuset.htm.

Hjort, Mette. *Small Nation, Global Cinema: The New Danish Cinema.* Minneapolis: University of Minnesota Press, 2005.

———. "Denmark." In *The Cinema of Small Nations,* edited by Mette Hjort and Duncan Petrie, 23–42. Edinburgh: Edinburgh University Press, 2007.

Jesson, Bruce. *To Build a Nation: Collected Writings, 1975–1999.* Auckland: Penguin, 2005.

Miller, Toby, Nitin Govill, John McMurria, Richard Maxwell, and Ting Wang. *Global Hollywood 2.* London: British Film Institute, 2005.

Ministry of Economic Development. "Boost for New Zealand Screen Production—Media Statement from Rt. Hon. Helen Clark, Minister for Arts, Culture and Heritage and Hon Judith Tizard, Associate Minister for Arts, Culture and Heritage—10 November 2003." At www.med.govt.nz/templates/Page_659.aspx

(accessed December 18, 2007).

Murdoch, Claire. "Holy Sea Cow." *Landfall* 206 (November 2003): 97–105.

Petrie, Duncan. "From the Cinema of Poetry to the Cinema of Unease: Brad Mc-Gann's *In My Father's Den.*" *Illusions* 37 (Winter 2005): 2–8.

———. "New Zealand." In *The Cinema of Small Nations,* edited by Mette Hjort and Duncan Petrie, 160–76. Edinburgh: Edinburgh University Press, 2007.

Sinclair, Keith. *A Destiny Apart: New Zealand's Search for National Identity.* Wellington: Allen and Unwin, 1986.

Turner, Stephen. "Being Colonial/Colonial Being." *Journal of New Zealand Literature* 20 (2002): 40–63.

———. "Settlement as Forgetting." In *Quicksands: Foundational Histories in Australia and Aotearoa New Zealand,* edited by Klaus Neumann, Nicholas Thomas, and Hilary Ericksen, 20–38. Sydney: University of New South Wales Press, 1999.

Walker, Ranginui. *Ka Whawhai Tonu Matou/Struggle without End.* Auckland: Penguin, 1990. Revised edition published in 2004.

Waller, Gregory A. "The New Zealand Film Commission: Promoting an Industry, Forging a National Identity." *Historical Journal of Film, Radio, and Television* 16, no. 2 (1996): 243–63.

Peripheral Visions

Blak Screens and Cultural Citizenship

> In May 2006, I was standing dumbfounded in the foyer of the Sydney Opera House, watching a huge crowd snaking out the door . . . to see the Message Sticks Indigenous Film Festival and there were twice as many people as seats available. . . . Why is it that Indigenous film has been so well received in Australia and on the world stage? What is it that makes the work distinctive and sets it apart?
>
> —Sally Riley (Wiradjiri), manager, Indigenous Branch, Australian Film Commission

The questions framed by Sally Riley[1]—filmmaker, dramaturge, and advocate for the development of filmmaking by Indigenous Australians—are precisely the ones I want to address. What has enabled the emergence of such vibrant filmmaking across many genres—and in particular the development of feature films—in what one might think of as the periphery's periphery? Aboriginal people comprise only about 2 percent of the population of Australia, a small nation that is itself seen as being "off-center."[2] Given this kind of cultural location, how is it that Australia's Indigenous media makers—particularly those oriented toward feature filmmaking—have managed to attract the attention and support of the wider Indigenous community, as well as non-Indigenous communities at home and abroad?[3]

Research into how the "media worlds"[4] of Indigenous feature filmmaking came into being in Australia is part of the broader project of the burgeoning work in the ethnography of media, which turns the analytic lens on the production, circulation, and consumption of media in a variety of locales. Indigenous filmmaking in any part of the world raises important questions about the role of media in the discursive evolution of diversity. In Australia, such work contributes to the expanding (if contested) understanding of Australia as a culturally diverse nation. It offers alternative accountings to those presented by unified national narratives and it also demonstrates the value of analysis that takes into account the offscreen cultural and political labor of Aboriginal activists and their fellow travelers whose efforts at gaining a space in this cultural arena have made this work possible.

More broadly, the study of Indigenous media is part of the broader discussions regarding how contemporary settler states and their citizens negotiate diversity—what some call *cultural citizenship*—a topic that has gained considerable currency over the last decade, but which gives only occasional attention to media, despite the foundational work of Benedict Anderson[5] in clarifying the role of print media in the formation of modern nations.[6] As an exception to that tendency, Australian media theorist John Hartley has argued in his work on this topic that "the evolution of new forms of citizenship is matched by post-broadcast forms of television, in which audiences can be seen as organized around choice, affinity, and the production as well as consumption of media. These developments have powerful implications for the way nations are narrated in broadcast television . . . Indigeneity points the way to new notions of nation and television."[7] Hartley's work points to the critically important role that Aboriginal media have played in Australia over the last two decades in the creation of an Indigenous public sphere.[8] His deployment of Jürgen Habermas's language to capture how media made by and about Indigenous people has created a new space of representation for their concerns has a colloquial counterpart: the term *Blak screens,* used in the title of this article. I draw on its use in the title Blak Screens/Blak Sounds, given to the inaugural (and now annual) 2001 Message Sticks Festival of Indigenous film and music held at the Sydney Opera House. The use of the Aboriginal English *Blak* takes up a term of pride and assertion of cultural identity, marked by its orthographic change from Black to Blak, which emerged along with the Aboriginal activism of the 1970s—a period in which symbolic politics borrowed heavily from the language, strategies, and tactics deployed by the U.S. Black Power movement. To associate Blak with the term *screens* in this context inverts the usual association of the idea of the *black screen* in film or television as blank (and in this case devoid of Indigenously authored stories and images), and rather claims it as Blak, or proudly Aboriginal, now that Indigenous directors are creating their own work. The development of Indigenous filmmaking in Australia, which is the central concern of this chapter, has been a two-decade-long effort on the part of Indigenous media activists to reverse that erasure of Aboriginal subjects in public life (what we might call the blank screen) through their cultural labor, by making representations about Blak lives visible and audible on the film and television screens of Australia and beyond.

Indigenous media in Australia's national film and television industries have contributed to the ongoing process of narrative accrual[9] through which an Australian national imaginary is produced, contested, and transformed. This argument about the place of national cinema in the imagined community of Australia has been central to the work of Australian media scholars and public intellectuals over the last two decades.[10] Most recently, it was reframed by Felicity Collins and Therese Davis in *Australian Cinema after Mabo,* who argue that the 1992 Mabo decision, which supported Indigenous claims to land and recognition by overturning Australia's founding doctrine of *terra nullius* (which asserted that the continent was empty land when the British settlers arrived in the eighteenth century, despite the presence of Aboriginal people) irreversibly destabilized the way in which Australians relate not only to the land but also to their colonial heritage, a paradigm shift, they conclude, that shaped the new antipodean films following that judicial landmark.

Using the central image of backtracking, Collins and Davis suggest that in the narrative drive of a range of films made during the last decade—including a number of works examining Indigenous/settler relations by Euro-Australian directors, such as *The Tracker* (Rolf de Heer, 2002) and *Rabbit-Proof Fence* (Phillip Noyce, 2002), as well as by Aboriginal directors such as *Radiance* (Rachel Perkins, 1998), *One Night the Moon* (Rachel Perkins, 2001), and *Beneath Clouds* (Ivan Sen, 2001)—there is a renewed and more complex exploration of Australia's past. These works backtrack through the nation's history not in triumphalist terms, but in ways that address the legacies of grief and violence wrought by settler colonialism, a significant transformation in the country's sense of its own legacies, and a recognition that it matters whose stories are told and by whom.

Books such as *Australian Cinema after Mabo* offer an occasion to think about Australia's film industry, a privileged arena of national visual culture, within the context of the country's cultural politics. Is a term such as *the post-Mabo era* merely symptomatic of a changed sensibility in the kinds of stories told or does it index a transformed recognition of who is authorized to tell these stories? What does such periodization mean in the crucial offscreen world on which a complex form of cultural production like filmmaking depends? Collins and Davis provide important discussions of shifts in cultural policy and the critical role played by certain key producers that helped bring at least some of this work into being. Here I want to underscore the crucial role played by Aboriginal cultural activists and their fellow travelers who pushed to get support for the programs and resources necessary to create the kind of films that are expanding, if not transforming, Australian national cinema.

Indigenous filmmakers hoping to enter into feature filmmaking face a far more complex and costly field of cultural production than those who started the 1980s outback experiments in small-scale video. The histories of initiatives to develop Indigenous feature film, launched in a systematic way a decade ago, are instructive not only for understanding the Australian case but also for recognizing more broadly the capacity of peripheral cinemas to offer fresh perspectives on the problematic dimensions of multicultural arts policies; in particular, the impact of culturally bounded categories of support for this form of Indigenous cultural production. Are new arenas emerging for cross-cultural recognition beyond the screenings of the films themselves? Furthermore, it is important to think about other offscreen dimensions of this work, and ask whether the post-Mabo framing is the most significant way to understand what is shaping these works as, increasingly, they circulate beyond Australia, implicating such work in broader trade relations and political economies in which culture is progressively caught up.

Debates about Australia's cinema industry and its value have been key in considering the nation's place in a global economy. In particular, questions have been raised about the consequences of the Australia-U.S. Free Trade Agreement (signed February 8, 2004) for what the Department of Foreign Affairs and Trade calls "the audiovisual sector," which raised industrywide anxieties that this agreement will facilitate the displacing of Australian media by American products. These changing global trade relations are crucially reframing national debates about what can be seen on Australian screens, while also resituating the place of Indigenous Australians not only in the national narrative but also as icons of Australia on the world stage. I would argue that the cultural capital available to Australia's Indigenous filmmakers through the international circulation of their media work at prestigious film festivals and media markets, from Cannes, to Sundance, to Toronto, has given added value to their claims to cultural citizenship—they increasingly find themselves serving as representatives of their own communities and also (somewhat ironically) of Australia.

The Emergence of Indigenous Features

In 1998, the feature film *Radiance,* which focused on the lives of three Indigenous Australian sisters and directed by Australian Aboriginal filmmaker

Rachel Perkins (Arrernte/Kalkadoon), was released to considerable domestic acclaim. It circulated successfully to major film festivals, garnering nine major awards and securing recognition for Perkins as an independent director to be reckoned with in the evolution of Australian national cinema, and as an Indigenous cultural activist. The critical success of her first feature film, as well as later films by Perkins (*One Night the Moon*) and Indigenous director Ivan Sen (*Beneath Clouds*), marked an irreversible change in the recognition of Australian Indigenous media, which had not been expected to move from remote communities in the outback to the world stage in so short a time. This unexpected transformation was effectively captured in the title From Sand to Celluloid, given to the pioneering 1996 program of short fiction films by Indigenous directors, made through a training program organized by the Indigenous Unit of the Australian Film Commission (AFC).[11]

In the 1980s, the first incarnation of Indigenous media in small format analog video made in traditional communities suggested utopian possibilities for a radical alternative to Western practices, as supporters of this experiment in Aboriginal television claimed at the time.[12] This new form of Indigenous cultural expression in remote communities was simultaneously celebrated and kept at a relatively safe distance from mainstream Australian media. A decade later, the emergence of Indigenous feature films offered a different kind of intervention, creating new sites for the broader recognition of the cultural citizenship of a range of Indigenous Australians, from remote settlements to urban neighborhoods. These *first features*[13] speak of other, multiple legacies of settler colonialism that have shaped Aboriginal lives but that are less clearly marked in public discourse. These works reject an easy division between remote, traditional people and deracinated urban Aboriginals. They offer alternative and complex accounts of alternative subjectivities, and draw on a broader range of Indigenous experience than the depleted repertoire of longstanding stereotypes of "the Aboriginal." This is particularly true for a sector whose experience has been rendered largely invisible in the Australian imaginary: mixed race, urban and rural Indigenous subjects, historically removed from contact with their traditional forebears, those for whom history—until quite recently—and the reflective screens of public media have been, so to speak, black.

There is some irony in the fact that the first works coming out of these projects entered into public circulation in 1996, the year in which John Howard's election as prime minister definitively marked a decade-long rightward shift in Australian political culture.[14] Given this background, it is particularly relevant to ask whether these films have achieved a level of recog-

Ivan Sen (Gamiloroi), director of *Beneath Clouds* (2001). Photo by Charmaine Jackson-John.

nition one might expect from both black and white audiences, or whether they remain a kind of promissory note toward fuller development of such work, in part due to the difficulty of placing Indigenous filmmaking in the recognized categories of what has come to be known as world cinema. Such recognition, of course, is crucially important in a national film industry that is constantly hoping to overcome its peripheral status, and which depends heavily on governmentally supported programs.

Since the mid-1990s, Indigenous filmmakers and their works are regularly sent to the world's most prestigious film festivals as representative of Australia's current talent. In 2005, the Indigenous Branch of the Australian Film Commission had a budget from the government of approximately AU$1.5 million. This money is spread across a number of initiatives and is not enough to fund even a single feature film. Nonetheless, the judicious use of these funds to expand the training and opportunity structure for Indigenous filmmakers has been remarkably effective in creating a space in Australian cinema—including feature filmmaking—for work being produced by Indigenous directors. It is also important to recognize the offscreen cultural labor of Aboriginal activists in Australia and elsewhere that helped to support these new forms of cultural production and circulation. Such labor has been crucial in creating cultural, creative, and institutional spaces for the work of fiction and feature filmmakers that was unimaginable two decades ago.

From Sand to Celluloid: The Space of Collaboration

> In the past our grandmothers and grandfathers told us stories
> in the sand, and the winds came and buried these stories.
> Now, we are telling our stories again, but this time in cellu-
> loid; never again will the winds of time take that away from
> us.
>
> —From the dust jacket of the first title in the From Sand
> to Celluloid series (1996)

One might trace the roots of Indigenous feature films to the 1980s eruption in Indigenous cultural activism that demanded greater media presence for urban Aboriginals.[15] It was not until 1988, during Australia's bicentenary, that Aboriginal activists—whose protests were organized around what they aptly renamed Invasion Day—insisted that there be a regular Indigenous presence on national television, as one of a number of demands they presented in a range of areas. In response to these protests, Indigenous Units were established at Australia's two public-sector broadcasters headquartered in Sydney: The Indigenous Programs Unit was created at the ABC while the multicultural alternative station, SBS (Special Broadcasting Service) set up its own Aboriginal Television Unit. They became important first sites within mainstream national television for the training and development of urban Indigenous producers who had the opportunity to create and produce a range of programs within the paradigm of public sector television.[16]

Four years after the inauguration of these units, a report commissioned by the Australian Film Commission[17] urged that the AFC establish an Aboriginal Program, "to develop strategies to proactively engage Indigenous Australians in the film and television industry."[18] In response to that recommendation, 1993 brought about the launch of what became known as the Indigenous Branch of the AFC. Its founding director, Wal Saunders (Gunditj-Marra), a longtime Aboriginal activist and media producer, saw his mandate as twofold: (1) *promoting* Australia's Indigenous media work internationally as part of the nation's cultural export; and (2) *creating* new kinds of Indigenous media, filmmaking that could be considered part of Australian cinema, arguably the nation's most prestigious arena of both creative media arts and culture industries. Saunders hoped to broaden the focus of Australia's innovative if sometimes uneven experiments with Indigenous media in remote communities by putting in place structures that would help support the development of new cohorts of Aboriginal filmmakers. The core of Indigenous cultural activists, who had been working in theater, film, and in the Indigenous units at the ABC and SBS since 1988, had developed significant storytelling capacities in different types of media. Correctly anticipating that they could build on this background, Saunders worked with the Indigenous director and producer Rachel Perkins to expand the remit of the Indigenous Branch of the AFC by creating a series of programs to train Aboriginal filmmakers in fiction and feature film genres. To accomplish this, Saunders and Perkins developed innovative training initiatives that established an enduring model by drawing in some of the country's top film professionals to work with fledgling Indigenous filmmakers as they refined their directing, writing, and editing skills, initially through short projects. Seasoned producers and directors with longstanding experience in filmmaking and with Aboriginal cultural projects were brought on to "fast track" Indigenous directors in a way that encouraged the particularity of their vision as they helped Aboriginal directors refine their sensibilities. To this day, every filmmaker works with a well-established professional mentor (usually a director or screenwriter) until scripts are ready to be shot.[19]

Much of this collaborative method for training Indigenous filmmakers was built with the support of two key state-supported institutions: (1) the national Australian Film, Television, and Radio School (AFTRS), located just outside of Sydney, established an Indigenous Program Initiative (IPI) in 1994 designed to cultivate the creative and technical skills of Indigenous Australians already working in the film, broadcasting, and new media industries; and (2) the Special Broadcasting Service's film production wing, SBS Independent (SBSi), which has provided financial support for these projects as well as a highly visible venue for screening completed works. Drawing on these collaborations, which provided professional mentors, equipment, and other resources, Saunders was able to launch a pilot drama initiative, the aforementioned series From Sand to Celluloid (1996). This project, which resulted in six short fiction films by Indigenous directors, was remarkably successful.[20] The series was broadcast on Australia's ABC-TV and on SBS-TV and screened in cinemas across Australia in a national tour. One participant described the premiere screening of this work at Sydney's prominent Chauvel Cinema as "a revelation. It felt like being part of a history-making event."[21] A second initiative, based on the success of the first, titled Shifting Sands: From Sand to Celluloid Continued, was completed in 1998. These short film projects gave a significant opportunity for the further development of Indigenous filmmakers, almost all of whom went on to make longer, award-winning works, and four of whom are currently in development on feature films. Thus, these relatively modest projects succeeded precisely as intended by supporting the development of new filmmakers as well as the (now) more experienced ones. The commitment to intensive mentoring and workshops established from the outset was key to the success of these programs.

The goal had been to develop broad support to cultivate Indigenous filmmaking talent with the kinds of resources that had been made available to other Australian filmmakers. As one of the nation's more recognized forms of cultural export, the film industry had established, by the 1980s, a distinctive profile ranging from the quirky and irreverent on the one hand to works drawing on the long tradition of the eerily beautiful outback landscape as a site for the Australian uncanny on the other. By the time Saunders left the Australian Film Commission in 1999, he had helped to build up "a body of work that has won acclaim both locally and internationally and . . . resulted in the development of a pool of Indigenous filmmakers who have benefited from ongoing production and development investment as well as professional development support."[22] But clearly, it was more than simply training new talent in the interests of diversifying professional fields in a multicultural society and going beyond changing the kinds of stories that were being told. It was about changing the script, so to speak, regarding who is entitled to tell the stories of Aboriginal Australian lives at the scale of the feature film.

In 2000, Indigenous stage director and filmmaker Sally Riley (Wiradjuri) took over as manager of the Indigenous Branch, bringing her rich background in theater and filmmaking to this position. A strong supporter of the methods established by Saunders for developing Indigenous talent, Riley was also aware of the potential hazards of ghettoization that might come to haunt programs set up to support Indigenous work, on the one hand, but whose funding structures might not be sufficient to subsidize work at the scale that feature filmmaking requires, on the other. Such structures for Indigenous media funding—what counterparts in Canada have dubbed "media reservations"—can, ironically, make it difficult for Aboriginal filmmakers to get the support they need for the bigger projects imagined when the Indigenous Branch was first put in place in the mid-1990s. Fortunately, the Australian media industry has responded positively, increasing its support for and access to low-budget production funds for what is clearly one of the more original and exciting dimensions of new Australian filmmaking.

Since her arrival, Riley has inaugurated key programs to help bring this work to the next level of development. In 2003, a project titled Fifty/Fifty supported two fifty-minute films by more experienced directors: *Cold Turkey*, and *Queen of Hearts*. Long Black, launched in 2005, is supporting feature-length projects by seasoned Indigenous filmmakers through intensive workshops, most recently (2007) with senior Indigenous directors such as Merata Mita (Maori) and Nils Gaup (Sami). At the same time, in order to continue nurturing new talent, new short films are continually being developed. In 2009, the festival opened with veteran Warwick Thornton's new feature film, *Samson and Delilah,* prior to its showcase at the Cannes Film Festival, along with seven ten-minute shorts from the New Blak series, listed as world premieres by new Australian directors for the May 2009 Message Sticks Indigenous Film Festival at the Sydney Opera House.[23] While Indigenous directors are supportive of their stories being told well and sympathetically in any venue, there is still frustration that capital for feature films—outside of the programs described here—is far easier to mobilize for Euro-Australian directors than Indigenous ones; thus, it is not just claiming the right to be able to tell Indigenous stories in this genre, but gaining the support they need to be the authors of those stories.

These concerns—related to issues of cultural citizenship, free expression, the entitlement to speak on one's history, and the implications of cultural compartmentalization of support—have been central to the Indigenous cultural activists who mobilized the political and cultural capacity to develop new initiatives for self-determined representations of Aboriginal lives. Indeed, Aboriginal anthropologist and activist Marcia Langton commented on the potential impact of policing the boundaries of Indigenous cultural production that, "to demand complete control of all representation, as some Aboriginal people naively do, is to demand censorship, to deny the communication which none of us can prevent."[24] Rather than operating in an exclusively Indigenous space—as if such a thing existed—the work of Indigenous filmmakers is characterized by forms of collaboration with a range of players from both Indigenous and non-Indigenous backgrounds, but in which their stories are the dominant focus along with creative and artistic control.[25]

Collaborative practice is especially important for the filmmaking initiatives that began in the mid-1990s. Since then, they have become an important base for a small and talented group of young mostly urban Aboriginal cultural activists to forge a cohort and gain the professional experience and entrée that is placing them and their work onto national and international stages. The Indigenous filmmakers identified with this movement—and the films they have made, from shorts to features—represent a wide range of backgrounds, from those living in cities such as Sydney and Melbourne to inhabitants of rural and remote Australia.[26] Collectively, they recognize the potential their work has to change the way that Aboriginal realities are understood by the wider Australian public and international audiences. But to do so through the social practice of filmmaking requires ongoing access to the resources and professional opportunities that fuel Australia's film culture. Increasingly, as some of these players move to feature film work, one of the questions they face is whether they need to move outside the "Indigenous box."

Black to "Blak": Rachel Perkins

A clear objective that shaped the work of first generation of the 1990s Indigenous filmmakers was to change black screens to "Blak" screens, a shift from cultural absence to the creation of a self-determined sense of cultural identification and storytelling. If anyone has served as a role model in this process, it is Rachel Perkins, not only a talented producer and director but also a tireless advocate for expanding the development of Indigenous media; she is especially effective in bridging the interests of remote and urban Aboriginal people. Her career parallels the development of Indigenous media in Australia as it moved beyond the outback experiments to the world of feature filmmaking. Her success, and that of others who followed a similar path and who now collaborate regularly, is testimony to the potential value of these programs in helping develop what we might consider a cohort effect—the creation of a group whose work and relationships create synergy and influence. They have the capacity to reshape institutions and cultural worlds, and to provide forms of mediation in which Aboriginal people are active cultural players in representing their lives on the nation's film and television screens.

Perkins also exemplifies those most active in the Indigenous media scene today: a generation of cultural activists who grew up with new political possibilities. While the struggle for Aboriginal civil rights was already a social fact, the world of available cultural spaces was not so easily changed. The mass audience was still "significantly racist," and the mainstream still holds "conventional monocultural views of nation and national identity."[27]

In 1988, Perkins (at age eighteen) left Canberra for Alice Springs, where she trained with the Central Australian Aboriginal Media Association, one of the foundational Indigenous media associations serving remote Australian communities from four language groups, including the Arrernte, her father's people. Three years later, she moved to Sydney to become executive producer with the three-year-old Indigenous Programs Unit at SBS-TV. While there, she developed a number of initiatives, including the award-winning *Blood Brothers* (1993). The latter is a series of four documentaries, each featuring a prominent Aboriginal man. It includes *Freedom Ride* (1992), which she directed. The film is a history of the freedom rides that helped launch the

Rachel Perkins (Arrernte/Kalkadoon), director of *Radiance* (1998), *One Night the Moon* (2001). Photo by Australian Film Commission.

Aboriginal civil rights movement told through the story of one of its key leaders, her father Charlie Perkins.

In 1993, she formed her own company, Blackfella Films, through which she worked with Wal Saunders to help create the AFC's enduringly successful Indigenous Drama Initiative, described earlier. She became the first Indigenous participant in the AFTRS Producing Program and served as a producer for Warwick Thornton's *Payback* (1996), one of the six films in the series From Sand to Celluloid. From 1996 to 1998, Perkins worked as executive producer of the ABC's Indigenous Programs Unit, where she commissioned fifteen documentaries and created an Indigenous music series, Songlines. She also developed a wide range of collaborations with Indigenous and non-Indigenous media makers. Thus, by the time she left that position to direct her first feature film, *Radiance* (1998), she had over ten years of experience producing and directing different genres, thanks to the offscreen opportunities for Indigenous media created in response to activist demands and actions.

The film, adapted from the play *Radiance* by Euro-Australian playwright Louis Nowra, focuses on an incendiary reunion of three Aboriginal sisters who have had different life trajectories and who come together for the first time in years after the death of their mother, a context in which many previously unspoken complex secrets are revealed.

In Australia, *Radiance* was a clear success on the festival circuit[28]; it won a range of awards and played at international festivals. Right on the heels

The actress Rachael Maza, as Cressy in *Radiance* (1998). Photo by Australian Film Commission.

of *Radiance,* Perkins began working on the musical drama *One Night the Moon,* inspired by the documentary *Black Tracker* (1997), about the famous Aboriginal Tracker Riley whose extraordinary tracking skills and services to the Australian Police had earned him a King's Medal.[29]

The film is set in the Australian outback of the 1930s. Against the advice of the local police, a family of racist white settlers rejects the tracker's services to help locate their missing daughter, an act that proves fatal to the child. Much later, the mother goes to the Aboriginal tracker who is able to find the child's body despite the effacement of evidence and the passage of time. Thus, by retelling a classic Australian narrative from an Indigenous point of view, the film enacts both the senseless tragedies of racism and the possibilities of collaboration and reconciliation.

The unusual approach of the film—there is almost no spoken dialogue, and the original musical score and lyrics are used to signify the characters inner thoughts—was catalyzed by a singular funding initiative, Music Drama Television (mdTV), meant to bring Australian performing arts to the screen through innovative music dramas. The exquisite cinematography by Kim Batterham effectively evokes the sensibility of the 1930s Australian bush. The film was shot in Australia's Flinders Ranges, and processed using a bleaching process that takes out some of the color, especially pink, but emphasizes contrast, thus heightening the mythic style, removing it from a sense of the everyday. The allegorical sensibility of the film is enhanced by the spare landscape, gestural acting, and folk operatic score, composed and performed by some of Australia's most gifted and well-known musicians and actors. Perkins saw the film as an opportunity to "talk about a loss that didn't need to be, so it's a small story, but one that has meaning for us all"—a statement she made when introducing the film at its debut screening in 2001 at the opening night of Blak Screen/Blak Sounds, part of the inaugural Message Sticks Festival that covers a broad sweep of Indigenous life in Australia. The festival, now an annual event, was held at the Sydney Opera House's Playhouse, the first time this elite venue hosted films by Aboriginal directors.

Although *One Night the Moon* was made for television with no planned theatrical release, the film went on to enter the official selection of some of the world's most prestigious film festivals. Since then, Perkins has been working on a number of projects—she was coartistic director of the Yeperenye Festival (2001) when 20,000 Australians converged in Alice Springs for the largest Indigenous Centenary of Federation ever held, and in 2002, was the convener of the first National Indigenous Film and Television Conference. Since 2006 and 2007, she has programmed the Message Sticks Festival with Indigenous colleague Darren Dale (Bundjalung). They also produced *First Australians,* an extraordinary seven-part documentary series for Australian television (SBS I) focusing on the history of Australia from an Indigenous perspective; she directed four of the episodes, while Beck Cole (Yawaru/Djarbera-Djarbera) directed three. The series' launch in October 2008 had a remarkable impact across the nation, with praiseworthy and lengthy coverage in the mainstream press. The words of one writer in *The Age* were typical of the critical reception; the series was hailed as "one of the most significant documentary series in the history of Australian television. For the first time, the story of Aboriginal Australia has been condensed into a coherent narrative that begins with the mythological birth of humanity on this continent."[30]

As testimony to the widespread respect she commands, Perkins has taken on prominent roles in Australia's leading mainstream film organizations as well as Indigenous media organizations.[31] Perkins has also been a presence at the Sundance Film Festival, where she served as a mentor in screenwriting labs for emerging Indigenous filmmakers from all over the world, part of the Native Forum that Sundance has supported for a number of years. She also took the opportunity to meet and connect with other Indigenous directors, such as Merata Mita (Maori), and Randy Redroad (Cherokee). The Native Forum, which originally focused on nurturing Native American filmmaking when it began in the 1980s, has expanded to include Indigenous filmmakers from around the world and has created labs for the development of their work, an initiative currently spearheaded by N. Bird Runningwater.[32]

Peripheral Visions

While the value of such developments cannot be underestimated, the crucial forms of support for this work are still fundamentally national. It is reasonable to ask about the fate of continued funding for Indigenous media makers in Australia given an array of concerns directed against Indigenous Australians, including what some Australians see as an ongoing backlash against policies supporting Aboriginal self-determination, particularly when Australia was under the leadership of the politically conservative John Howard from 1996 to 2006. Of course, the situation is more hopeful since the election of the Labor Party Prime Minister Kevin Rudd in November 2007, in what some pundits have called a "Ruddslide," a sensibility that was strengthened by his historic apology to Australia's Indigenous citizens on February 13, 2008.[33] When I asked whether these political ups and downs put the support of Indigenous media at risk, Sara Hourez, manager of Indigenous Programs at AFTRS, explained that at least in her institution the longstanding support of such initiatives could be attributed to the school's director, Malcolm Long. However, she turned to the impact of globalization on the nation's culture industries. Australian filmmaking itself may be overwhelmed by the Free Trade Agreement with the United States discussed earlier, a relation that many fear will displace Australian-produced media from the nation's screens, which in turn could diminish the opportunities for those working in Australia's media sector. Ironically, then, the possibilities opened for Australia's Aboriginal filmmakers through the international networks of Indigenous cultural activists established via film festivals and other forms of offscreen culture making,[34] at home and abroad, may be threatened by the encroachments of other circuits of global trade in which such forms of localized cultural production find themselves increasingly at risk. Still, key funding structures such as the Australian Film Commission have not only increased support for the Indigenous Branch, but are also working to get more Indigenous staff in place across the organization and beyond.[35] The last few years of success by Indigenous directors, cinematographers, scriptwriters, and others means there are now people to take up such positions, testimony to the resilience of the offscreen structures supporting the cultural, narrative, and social development of such work. All of this has contributed to the strength of the cohort of Aboriginal filmmakers that has grown over the last decade, along with the density of the broad web of collaborations within and beyond Australia.

Their *peripheral visions* enable us to see and hear not only their stories, but also to recognize the offscreen lives of Indigenous people and movements that extend far beyond the range of a conventional central gaze, enabling the comprehension of a much broader sense of the world. That vision is both what we see and hear onscreen, as well as the vitality of the social networks established throughout the world among Indigenous filmmakers with a shared vision, who are starting to identify themselves as part of a world cinema, drawing attention to an Indigenous periphery that bends the boundaries of the national and the very categories of cinema itself.

Notes

Many thanks to Dina Iordanova for her careful work and fine editorial judgment, and to both Dina and Belén Vidal for their patience. This chapter, revised from a piece titled "Blak Screens and Cultural Citizenship," published in 2005 in a special issue of *Visual Anthropology Review:* 80–97, is based on ongoing research that began in 1988 in Australia, and has continued in many locations including New York City; the work has been funded by fellowships and grants from New York University and the Guggenheim and Macarthur foundations. I am indebted to a number of people for ongoing conversations that have informed this paper, in particular Rachel Perkins, Sally Riley, Wal Saunders, Sara Hourez, and Graeme Isaac. As always, I am grateful to Fred Myers for his thoughtful comments and to Françoise Dussart for the initial provocation to write it.

1. Riley, "Revolutions: The AFC Indigenous Branch," 2.

2. The usual figure for numbers of Indigenous Australians is 2 percent and more recently 2.5 percent, as more and more people have discovered and come to identify with their Indigenous heritage.

3. Riley, "Revolutions: The AFC Indigenous Branch," 2.

4. Ginsburg, Abu-Lughod, and Larkin, "Introduction," in *Media Worlds: Anthropology on New Terrain.*

5. Anderson, *Imagined Communities: Reflections on the Origins and Spread of Nationalism,* 2nd ed.

6. The term *cultural citizenship* has several intellectual genealogies: All include the well-respected work of British sociologist T. H. Marshall, who divided citizenship rights into three categories: civil, political, and social (1950); Iris Young's notion of "differentiated citizenship" (1990); and the work of political philosopher Will Kymlicka (1995), who argues that in liberal democracies, citizenship is not just a legal status but also an expression of one's membership in a political community, an identity that must be accommodated within liberal democracies. Australian studies include the work of Alastair Davidson (1997), who argues that the 1992 Mabo decision amounted to a paradigm shift in the possibilities of citizenship for Indigenous people. Nicholas Peterson and Will Sanders (1998) argue that the recognition of Indigenous rights becomes pursuit of equal rights at a more sophisticated level. Paul Havemann (1999) argues that new notions of citizenship, stressing collective rights to self-determination, and the need for states to recognize cultural diversity and plu-

ralism, are displacing earlier notions of citizenship based on concepts of equal rights that assume homogeneous identity. John Chesterman and political scientist Brian Galligan (1997) argue that Indigenous rights should have a special status as claims to land and nationhood distinguish their positions from liberal notions of citizenship. Elizabeth Povinelli (2002) critiques Australian liberal multiculturalism as a form of governmentality that idealizes certain customary ways of being an Indigenous subject to the detriment of others.

7. Hartley, "Television, Nation, and Indigenous Media," 7–25.

8. Hartley and McKee, *The Indigenous Public Sphere: The Reporting and Reception of Aboriginal Issues in the Australian Media.*

9. Atwood, ed., *In the Age of Mabo: History, Aborigines, and Australia.*

10. Dermody and Jacka, *Screening of Australia: Anatomy of a National Cinema;* O'Regan, *Australian National Cinema.*

11. Two other features by Indigenous directors preceded these: *Jindalee Lady* (1992) by Brian Syron, which was never picked up by a distributor; and the experimental work *Bedevil* (1993) by Tracey Moffat, an artist whose photography and film work have earned her a well-deserved international reputation. Inspired by ghost stories she heard as a child within her extended Aboriginal and Irish Australian families, the film is a trilogy in which characters are haunted by the past and bewitched by memories, set in highly stylized, hyperreal, Australian landscapes.

12. Michaels, *Aboriginal Invention of Television in Central Australia, 1982–86.*

13. I take this term from First Nations/First Features, a showcase of world Indigenous feature film that I co-curated in May 2005, and which screened at the Museum of Modern Art in New York, and the National Museum of the American Indian in Washington, DC. Available at www.firstnationsfirstfeatures.org (accessed May 1, 2007).

14. In November 2007, after more than a decade in power, John Howard and the right-wing Liberal Party lost to the center-left Australian Labor Party led by now Prime Minister Kevin Rudd.

15. For other accounts of factors contributing to this development, see Bostock, "Indigenous Screen Culture: A Personal Experience," 7–12.

16. Ginsburg, "Station Identification: The Aboriginal Programs Unit of the Australian Broadcasting Corporation," 92–97.

17. McPherson and Pope, *Promoting Indigenous Involvement in the Film and Television Industry.*

18. For more information on this report, see www.afc.gov.au/funding/indigenous/default.aspx (accessed January 5, 2008).

19. Later series supported longer (twenty-six-minute) formats, included *Crossing Tracks* (1999) (with works by Richard Frankland [*Harry's War*], Ivan Sen [*Wind*], and Rima Tamou [*Saturday Night, Sunday Morning*]); and *On Wheels* (2000) (with Catriona McKenzie [*Road*], Ivan Sen [*Dust*], and Sally Riley [*Confessions of a Head Hunter*]). In 2002 the series Dreaming in Motion supported five short films for new filmmakers.

20. Of course, now, less than a decade later, *celluloid* already seems dated given the rapidity with which terms such as *the digital age* have transformed the way we

imagine the materiality and distribution of media forms. For further discussion of this point, see Ginsburg, "The Unwired Side of the Digital Divide."

21. Riley, "Revolutions: The AFC Indigenous Branch," 2.

22. Australian Film Commission, "The Shifting Sands Continue," 1.

23. For more information on these films and the festival, see www.sydneyopera-house.com/About/Program_Message_Sticks.aspx (accessed May 4, 2009).

24. Langton, *"Well, I Heard It on the Radio and I Saw It on the Television,"* 10.

25. Australian film historian Tom O'Regan, writing about the early stages of this work, argued that "collaboration means here a more central bargaining position for Aboriginal and Islanders in the shaping of film meaning. It is the middle position between complete control and no control. In a sense it is also necessary, because structurally an Indigenous cinema is limited by its relatively small population base of 1.5 per cent [*sic*] of the Australian population and a chronically disadvantaged and dependent condition." O'Regan, *Australian National Cinema,* 278.

26. I estimate that this group is about one hundred people, based on those I have been in touch with during the course of my research and other indicators. The 2003 listing of Indigenous graduates of Australian Film, Television, and Radio School (AF-TRS) provides another helpful measure (see Hourez, ed., *Indigenous Voices: Celebrating the Journeys of Australian Film, Television, and Radio School Graduates*). Twenty out of the forty-three entries in the booklet include many of the most active names in Indigenous media making outside of more traditional remote communities. Using the Black Book, an online directory for Indigenous artists and media makers (with the slogan "it's taken sixty thousand years but finally the portal to indigenous media and the arts in Australia is here"), there are 163 listings in response to a search with the keyword media; approximately seventy of those listings are remote community organizations. See also www.theblackbook.com.au (accessed January 6, 2008).

27. O'Regan, *Australian National Cinema,* 331.

28. *Radiance* was produced and developed in association with the AFC, the NSW Film and TV Office, the Premium Movie Partnership for Showtime Australia, and Andyinc Pty Ltd, Joanna Baevski, and Michael Myer.

29. The documentary was directed by the late Michael Riley, a talented Indigenous photographer and filmmaker, who was Tracker Riley's grandson.

30. Sacha Molitorisz, "The Story of Black Australia." *The Age.* October 9, 2008, at www.theage.com.au/articles/2008/10/08/1223145363254.html (accessed May 2, 2009). The commentary on the series' website, www.sbs.com.au/firstaustralians/, is uniformly positive, with many people posting comments as to how little they knew of Australia's black history. At www.sbs.com.au/firstaustralians/ (accessed May 2, 2009).

31. These appointments include commissioner to the board of the AFC; a member of the Governing Council of AFTRS; a member of ScreenSound Australia, the National Screen and Sound Archive's Interim Advisory Committee; former Chair of Film and Television of the National Indigenous Media Association of Australia (now the National Indigenous Communications Association of Australia); and founding Chair of Indigenous Screen Australia.

32. Due to concerns raised offscreen by Indigenous directors, since 2004 their

work is no longer contained in a separate stream from the Sundance festival's general competition, but is part of World Cinema (although a Native Forum endures). This marks a kind of coming of age of Indigenous cinema from Australia and elsewhere. As it finds a place for itself outside the national frameworks that have contained it to date, this work takes its place, on its own terms, on the world stage.

33. For example, in May 2004, the government used revelations about corrupt Aboriginal leadership to abolish Aboriginal and Torres Straits Islanders Commission (ATSIC), the Indigenous-run bureaucracy through which most funds were distributed to communities and projects over the last ten years.

34. Myers, *Painting Culture: The Making of an Aboriginal High Art.*

35. Gallasch, "Australian Indigenous Film: A Community of Makers," 13–21.

Bibliography

Australian Film Commission. "The Shifting Sands Continue." *Australian Film CommissionNews,* 170–71, March/April 1998, 1.

Anderson, Benedict. *Imagined Communities: Reflections on the Origins and Spread of Nationalism.* 2nd ed. London: Verso, 1991.

Atwood, Bain, ed. *In the Age of Mabo: History, Aborigines, and Australia.* Sydney: Allen and Unwin, 1996.

Bostock, Lester. "Indigenous Screen Culture: A Personal Experience." In *Dreaming in Motion: Celebrating Australia's Indigenous Filmmakers,* edited by Keith Gallasch, 7–12. Sidney: Australian Film Commission, 2007.

Chesterman, John, and Brian Galligan. *Citizens without Rights: Aborigines and Australian Citizenship.* Cambridge: Cambridge University Press, 1997.

Collins, Felicity, and Therese Davis. *Australian Cinema after Mabo.* Melbourne: Cambridge University Press, 2004.

Davidson, Alastair. *From Subject to Citizen: Australian Citizenship in the 20th Century.* Cambridge: Cambridge University Press, 1992.

Dermody, Susan, and Elizabeth Jacka. *Screening of Australia: Anatomy of a National Cinema.* Sydney: Currency Press, 1988.

Gallasch, Keith. "Australian Indigenous Film: A Community of Makers." In *Dreaming in Motion: Celebrating Australia's Indigenous Filmmakers,* edited by Keith Gallasch, 13–21. Sidney: Australian Film Commission, 2007.

Ginsburg, Faye. "Aboriginal Media and the Australian Imaginary." *Public Culture* 5, no. 2 (1993): 557–78. Special issue on television edited by L. Abu-Lughod.

———. "Blak Screens and Cultural Citizenship." *Visual Anthropology Review* 21, nos. 1–2 (2005): 80–97.

———. "Station Identification: The Aboriginal Programs Unit of the Australian Broadcasting Corporation." *Visual Anthropology Review* 9, no. 2 (1993): 92–97.

———. "The Unwired Side of the Digital Divide." *Flow: A Critical Forum on Television and Media Culture.* At http://flowtv.org/?p=547 (accessed January 9, 2008).

Ginsburg, Faye, Lila Abu-Lughod, and Brian Larkin. "Introduction." In *Media Worlds: Anthropology on New Terrain.* Berkeley: University of California Press, 2002.

Hartley, John. "Television, Nation, and Indigenous Media." *Television and New Media* 5, no. 1 (2004): 7–25.

Hartley, John, and Alan McKee. *The Indigenous Public Sphere: The Reporting and Reception of Aboriginal Issues in the Australian Media.* Oxford: Oxford University Press, 2000.

Havemann, Paul, ed. *Indigenous People's Rights in Australia, Canada, and New Zealand.* Oxford: Oxford University Press, 1999.

Hourez, Sarah, ed. *Indigenous Voices: Celebrating the Journeys of Australian Film, Television, and Radio School Graduates.* Sydney: Australian Film, Television, and Radio School, 2003.

Kymlicka, Will. *Multicultural Citizenship: A Liberal Theory of Minority Rights.* Oxford: Clarendon Press, 1995.

Langton, Marcia. *"Well, I Heard It on the Radio and I Saw It on the Television."* Sydney: Australian Film Commission, 1993.

Marshall, T. H. *Citizenship and Social Class.* London: Pluto Press, 1987. Originally published in 1950 by Cambridge University Press.

McPherson, Shirley, and Michael Pope. *Promoting Indigenous Involvement in the Film and Television Industry.* Sydney: Australian Film Commission, 1992.

Michaels, Eric. *Aboriginal Invention of Television in Central Australia, 1982–86.* Canberra: Australian Institute of Aboriginal Studies, 1987.

Molitorisz, Sacha. "The Story of Black Australia." *The Age.* October 9, 2008, at www.theage.com.au/articles/2008/10/08/1223145363254.html (accessed May 2, 2009).

Myers, Fred. *Painting Culture: The Making of an Aboriginal High Art.* Durham, NC: Duke University Press, 2002.

O'Regan, Tom. *Australian National Cinema.* London: Routledge, 1996.

Peterson, Nicholas, and Will Sanders, eds. *Citizenship and Indigenous Australians: Changing Conceptions and Possibilities.* Melbourne: Cambridge University Press, 1998.

Povinelli, Elizabeth. *The Cunning of Recognition: Indigenous Alterities and the Making of Australian Multiculturalism.* Durham, NC: Duke University Press, 2002.

Riley, Sally. "Revolutions: The AFC Indigenous Branch." In *Dreaming in Motion: Celebrating Australia's Indigenous Filmmakers,* edited by Keith Gallasch, 1–6. Sidney: Australian Film Commission, 2007.

Young, Iris. *Justice and the Politics of Difference.* Princeton, NJ: Princeton University Press, 1990.

Emerging from Underground and the Periphery

Chinese Independent Cinema at the Turn of the Twenty-First Century

The concept of cinema at the periphery seems to designate film practices remotely located from the centers of power. For instance, we can talk about the situation of small national cinemas such as Scottish cinema and Danish cinema in such a framework. These are small nations relative to their immediate neighbors (England, Germany), or the huge European Union, or the biggest of it all, USA/Hollywood. The small-nation paradigm works perfectly well in analyzing such cinematic traditions at the periphery of major powers.

But the cinematic tradition I write about is China, the most populous nation in the world. Obviously, China does not fit in the boundaries of small national cinemas. However, the question of a cinema at the periphery is still a valid and important issue in the Chinese case. In fact, I argue that there does exist a cinema at the periphery, or there exist multiple cinemas at the periphery in Mainland China. The center of power is officially sanctioned mainstream cinema. Due to the mechanism of domestic censorship, Chinese cinema at the periphery is what has been known as independent film and underground film. Moreover, due to a peculiar turn of logic, marginal Chinese film under the guise of art film transforms into mainstream cinema in the circuits of international film festivals.

Setting the Terms: Underground, Independent, Peripheral

For a long time, the category of independent or underground cinema has been a convenient and conventional way of labeling films from the People's Republic of China, an (ex-)communist state. Defiant, independently financed films are banned by the censors of the regime but circulate and are applauded at international film festivals. These films may be suppressed in the national market, yet they are supported by benign transnational networks of film culture.

Recently, many formerly underground film directors have emerged to the surface, and their films are openly screened in public theaters across China, with uneven box-office sales. Independent films and their filmmakers are no longer at the periphery but move to the public domain, if not outright to the mainstream. The films of such celebrated underground figures as Jia Zhangke (*Shijie/The World,* 2004; *Sanxia haoren/Still Life,* 2006) and Wang Xiaoshuai (*Qinghong/Shanghai Dreams,* 2005) are available not just in bootlegged DVD copies sold at the street corner, but they also meet the eye in a legitimate theater.

The new film policies and film practices in China in the early twenty-first century call for a reexamination of old dichotomies in film studies and geo-aesthetics: periphery and center, marginal and mainstream, independent and studio, national and transnational, opposition and co-optation. While attempting to chart emergent patterns of production and exhibition of independent film in contemporary China, this chapter will focus on the films of a specific independent filmmaker, Jia Zhangke, whose *Still Life* received the Golden Lion Award at the Venice Film Festival in 2006. I will examine the specific style and textuality that mark such films as distinct from mainstream Chinese cinema.

Peripheral cinema, independent cinema, or underground cinema in the Chinese case can be defined at several levels: subject matter and theme, source of funding, networks of production and distribution, venue of screening, and film aesthetics. Paul Pickowicz offers to clarify the ambiguities in using the two terms *underground* (*dixia*) and *independent* (*duli*). He writes:

In general, "underground" is a term preferred by overseas media and embodies expectations of the subversive function of this alternative film culture in contemporary China. A majority of young filmmakers themselves, however, favor "independent," a term that has gained more currency in Chinese media and scholarship, not necessarily due to censorship pressures. More often than not, "independent" means a cinematic project's independence from the state system of production, distribution, and exhibition, rather than to its sources of financial support, for filmmakers increasingly depend on the private (*minying*) sector and foreign investment, thereby revealing their status of "in dependence" as joint or coproducers, or even contracted media workers.[1]

While agreeing with Pickowicz's broad description, I emphasize the fact that to obtain independence from the state system of production the filmmakers must seek funding from sources external to the state. Collaboration with sources from outside China, namely transnational coproduction, has been a major way of making films for independently minded directors. Independent filmmaking has been to a large extent part and parcel of the development of transnational Chinese cinema since the early 1990s.[2] More recently, as Pickowicz points out, funding from the private sector inside China has begun to play an increasingly important role in getting film projects off the ground.

As mentioned, a basic characteristic in the formation and evolution of Chinese independent cinema is its marginal status within China and its high profile in global film festival culture. This has a great deal to do with the perceived position of China as one of the last strongholds of communist states. Like the Chinese nation-state itself, its cinema is also politicized in international media. The fate of being "banned in China" often warrants entry to major Western film festivals, such as the Big Three in Europe (Cannes, Venice, Berlin) and many others around the world. Here we are dealing with old binary oppositions that had been established throughout the Cold War years—East versus West, communism versus capitalism, political oppression versus freedom.

We owe the rise of the New Chinese Cinema in a large measure to the groundbreaking works of the so-called Fifth Generation directors such as Chen Kaige, Zhang Yimou, and Tian Zhuangzhuang. Zhang Yimou is arguably the best-known director hailing from Mainland China. His martial arts features *Yingxiong/Hero* (2002), *Shimian maifu/House of Flying Daggers* (2004) and *Mancheng jindai huangjin jia/Curse of the Golden Flower* (2006) are global blockbusters. These recent films tend to be politically conformist with high entertainment values. People inside China jokingly call him the "official director" (*guanfang*) of China. Indeed, he was hand picked by Chinese officials to direct and choreograph a section of the closing ceremony of the Athens Olympic Games in 2004 and the entire opening ceremony of the Beijing Olympic Games in 2008. Zhang Yimou's complicity with the state notwithstanding, many of his early films are prime examples of what we call independent cinema at the periphery inside China and art house spectacles outside China. His films *Ju Dou* (1990), *Dahong denglong gaogao gua/Raise the Red Lantern* (1991) and *Huozhe/To Live* (1994) were banned in China but were award winners at major international film festivals such as Cannes. Hence, Zhang's career over the last twenty years is a good example of the transformation of independent cinema to mainstream cinema as embodied in the works of one single director.

It is the generation of filmmakers after the Fifth Generation, namely the so-called Sixth Generation that has been most closely associated with the phenomenon of independent and underground cinema. They graduated from the Beijing Film Academy in the late 1980s and early 1990s. This new generation could not compete with their elder classmates—the giants of the Fifth Generation—in obtaining funding. They usually started their career with low-budget films. Their style often departs from the glossy spectacles and the melodramatic mode associated with the Fifth Generation filmmakers, conveying a gritty, rough, documentary quality.[3] Their subject matter and interests are contemporary China—especially the urban China they see, witness, and live in. The unglamorous underbelly of China in the era of Deng Xiaoping's "reform and openness" (*gaige kaifang*) becomes the focus of their lens: marginal social groups, gay sexuality (which was not tolerated in socialist China for a long time), migrant workers, petty thieves, prostitutes, drug addicts, criminals, underground rock culture, and so forth. Due to the predilection for representing urban malaise in terms of subject matter and the directors' lack of rural experience in their personal upbringing, the Sixth Generation is also labeled the "urban generation."[4] There are several prominent elements that "characterize the world of vision of independent film practice: the portrait of the artist-self in film, the non-allegorical depiction of sexuality, and the construction of the coming-of-age narrative."[5] The leading directors of the Sixth Generation include figures such as Zhang Yuan, Lu Xuechang, Ning Ying, Lou Ye, Zhang Ming, Wang Xiaoshuai, and Jia Zhangke.

This new generation attempts to differentiate itself from the older generation in another important way. In the words of Gary Xu, "there arises a double bind for these directors: on the one hand, they consciously resist the tendency of self-Orientalization in Fifth Generation filmmaking, which focuses on 'traditional' and 'premodern' China; on the other hand, their realist representation of contemporary China's social issues continues to reinforce impressions of China's differences, of China being the violator of human rights and the dark realm of communism."[6] In other words, the point of departure of this new generation is the present moment rather than some mythical past that is exoticized for the gaze of the international audience. The nitty-gritty and the here and now with all the undisguised horrors constitute the focal point of their lens. Nevertheless, the frank unflattering portrayal of the socialist present can equally lead to a politicized reading of the East in international reception.

Beginning in the early twenty-first century, censorship became more lenient toward the erstwhile underground filmmakers, perhaps due to the inauguration of a new generation of Party leadership in the era of Hu Jintao. Their films begin to openly circulate in legitimate markets and are even screened in public theaters. The Chinese censors seem to have finally come to their senses: there is no need to regulate the film market in an old-style, heavy-handed manner, since audiences for these art films are small anyway. The big box-office draws are the commercial blockbusters from Hollywood, Feng Xiaogang's comedic "new-year-pictures" (*hesui pian*), and the films by the self-censored, self-reformed Zhang Yimou.

Many formerly underground directors have experienced a change of heart and are no longer so obstinate about the cherished themes and aesthetics of art cinema. They move with the times. For instance, Wang Xiaoshuai's early films *Dongchun de rizi/The Days* (1994) and *Jidu hanleng/Frozen* (1999) are quintessential experimental underground films in terms of subject matter (estranged marginal avant-garde artists) and style (low-budget features lacking in dramatic flourishes). But his later productions, *Shiqisui de danche/Beijing Bicycle* (2001) and *Qinghong/Shanghai Dreams* (2005), have been screened in theaters, becoming available to Chinese viewers not just as pirated DVDs but also in legitimate venues. He seems to have found a combination or compromise between art house aspirations and economic necessity.

It is a noteworthy development that an Annual Chinese Independent Film Festival (*Zhongguo duli yingxiang niandu zhan*) has been running in the city of Nanjing since 2003.[7] Although independent cinema has not been institutionalized to the extent of losing its edge and meaning, this phenomenon indicates that Chinese independent cinema is emerging from the underground into the public arena.

Jia Zhangke's Film Aesthetics in Still Life *(2006)*

The filmmaker who has persistently stood by the tenets of an austere independent art cinema is Jia Zhangke, the Wunderkind of the Sixth Generation. He has not bent to the allure of commercial cinema so far, and continues the pursuit of a rarefied aesthetics of art cinema. Jia's early career was a typical case of independent filmmaking. His first films were not permitted to be openly screened in legitimate venues due to their satirical social commentary, political subversiveness, and failure to get cleared by the proper channels of censorship. These films are *Xiaoshan huijia/Xiao Shan Going Home* (1995), *Xiaowu/Xiao Wu,* a.k.a. *Pickpocket* (1997), *Zhantai/Platform* (2000), and

*Ren xiaoyao/Unknown Pleasure*s (2002). Such works, funded by international sources, have been released abroad to high acclaim. Inside China, they only circulate via pirated DVD copies available in the black market. However, beginning with *The World* his films have started to emerge from the underground and are screened in Chinese theaters, with relatively low audience attendance.

Jia was officially banned from filmmaking by the Chinese Film Bureau in January 1999 for alleged violations of the regulations concerning filmmaking in China. The ban was not lifted until January 2004. In a casual yet troubling story that he wrote in a privately published newsletter, Jia revealed how he was banned by the government. He was summoned to the Film Bureau of the State Administration of Radio, Film and Television in January 1999. Upon arrival at the Film Bureau, he saw a revered master of the Fifth Generation schmoozing with officials. He had a more shocking discovery at the place. It was the screenwriter of that master of the Fifth Generation who reported on him to the authorities for spoiling "normal foreign cultural exchange" with his film *Xiao Wu*. Jia felt devastated by being betrayed by fellow film artists. He did not give the names of the "master" of the Fifth Generation and his screenwriter, but many people speculated that this has to be Zhang Yimou and his screenwriter Wang Bin. Wang Bin has denied this speculation, and Jia has not said any more words on the matter.[8]

The feud between Jia and art house director-turned-commercial-director Zhang Yimou flares up now and then. Zhang Weiping, the powerful producer of Zhang Yimou's films such as *Curse of the Golden Flower,* has criticized Jia and the Italian producers of *Still Life* for buying off the jury to win the Golden Lion Award at the 2006 Venice Film Festival. Jia has also lampooned Zhang Yimou for abandoning art cinema in favor of shallow but profitable commercial cinema. In the eyes of many observers and film viewers, Zhang Yimou, the once respected leader of Chinese art cinema, has lost his principles and has caved in to the pressure and allure of the regime and the market. Jia has thus emerged as the champion of serious art film in China. Moreover, he has also spoken out for Chinese national cinema at large. In May 2007, Hollywood blockbuster *Spider-Man 3* (Sam Raimi, USA 2007) was the rage in Chinese cinemas across the country. Cinema managers rushed to screen *Spider-Man 3* time and again in prime time slots. This foreign film out-performs local Chinese films in box-office sales and screening time. Jia offers his take on this trend of globalization as Hollywoodization:

Cinema managers always say the market and audience decide what they show, but it is not true. . . . The truth is cinema managers speculate on which films might be profitable and which are not. They make feature lists based on their assumptions and let audiences follow, which results in domestic small-budget films always being shown at the worst times.[9]

He calls for the establishment of a mechanism that would guarantee the screening of Chinese films in cinemas for a certain number of days during a year, as has been done in some other countries such as South Korea. The invasion and conquest of the Chinese film market by foreign films is the direct result of China's accession to the World Trade Organization. To be a member of the WTO, China has signed an agreement with the United States to allow a growing number of Hollywood blockbusters to be shown in China annually. Needless to say, globalization comes at a price for the native.

Jia is an auteur director in the old sense. His idiosyncratic film style stands out: very few close-ups; frequent use of medium shots, long shots, and long takes; slow pace; and minimal use of professional actors. Dramatic scenes of tension (fighting, intimacy, death) are not directly staged onscreen but indirectly suggested. Most extraordinary of all, there is not one single shot-reverse-shot pattern in all of his films. When two people are in conversation, a static camera is placed at ninety degrees to the characters or at a slightly oblique angle. Very often the viewer cannot see the face of the character due to the absence of a frontal shot. The effect that Jia is aiming at is a sense of objective distance, as if the camera (or the viewer) were a detached observer of a real-life situation. Moreover, Jia's characters often speak a dialect of Shanxi Province, his home province. Even native Chinese-language speakers must put in some effort in understanding the characters' speech, hopefully with the help of Chinese subtitles. Characters speaking a "quaint" provincial dialect further convey the marginal status of Jia's characters.[10] This is a film world populated by migrant workers from the countryside, petty thieves, delinquent adolescents, and misfits at the periphery of Chinese society. For all these qualities, Jia's persistently uncompromising style is not the usual dish for the taste of most domestic viewers who want to relax and have a good time with friends or loved ones in cinemas. Fast-paced, star-studded, and spectacle-ridden films from Hollywood prove more popular for the average Chinese spectator. Likewise, the handsome faces of superstars from Hong Kong and Taiwan, such as Andy Lau, Takeshi Kaneshiro (Jin Chengwu), or Chow Yun-fat; or the sexy appeal of Zhang Ziyi and busty middle-aged Gong Li, along with the scantily dressed palace maids in Tang-Dynasty China in Zhang Yimou's martial arts features *House of Flying Daggers* and *Curse of the Golden Flower,* are more palatable and enjoyable for mass audiences than the slow-paced social realism that starkly confronts the viewer with ugliness rather than beauty.

All the above factors make Jia Zhangke a darling of prestigious international film festivals. His award-winning feature *Still Life* repeats and exemplifies all the stylistic characteristics of his previous films. A new element is the more extensive use of horizontal pans because of the scenery at hand—the sprawling Three Gorges (*sanxia*) along the mighty Yangtze River. The story of the film unfolds against the background of the nearly completed controversial Three Gorges Dam project. The dam boasts of being the largest hydraulic project in the world. But this great achievement is not without disastrous side effects. Countless residents along the Yangtze River are dislocated, numerous towns and villages are flooded, archaeological sites are irretrievably buried under water, and ecological equilibrium is destroyed forever.

Still Life focuses on the human dimension of this impersonal national megaproject. Two Shanxi natives come to the city of Fengjie near Three Gorges to look for their loved ones. Coal miner Han Sanming wants to find his former wife, and nurse Shen Hong hopes for a reunion with her husband Guo Bin. The viewer then follows their steps and actions in Fengjie as they are entangled in an unfamiliar territory searching for their wife and husband. The viewer and the two main characters together embark on an ethnographic and social tour of the area. This is a place that is already partially flooded to the extent that Han Sanming cannot find the old address of his wife, which is under water now. Buildings are in the process of being demolished as the risk of total flooding increases by the day. People are told to leave their homes. Gangsters and thugs freely conduct their business in the area, where there is a very thin line between legitimate business and illegal transaction. The viewer sees the anger, discontent, frustration, and resignation of many local residents who must face up to dislocation. The two-thousand-year-old town, Fengjie, will be completely inundated soon.

While Han Sanming is stranded in the city and must wait for the arrival of his wife, he finds a temporary job as a demolition worker. The viewer is then presented with a double vision of the landscape. The pre-Deluge original scenery at Three Gorges unfolds like a beautiful Chinese landscape painting. Indeed, the very Chinese characters stand for landscape—*shanshui* means literally "mountains and water." The mountains and water along the Yangtze River, especially Three Gorges, have come to signify the essence of landscape in the Chinese tradition. The camera slowly pans horizontally to reveal the wonder and magnitude of the natural surrounding. At the same time, the demolition team goes on with its usual business. They must completely tear down all remaining buildings in the area. This is an ugly sight of ruins, rubble, and filth. Through mise-en-scène and camerawork, Jia drives home a feeling of horror in the jarring juxtaposition of man-made destruction on the one hand, and the serenity of nature on the other.

The sense of ruin and destruction is pervasive in Jia's oeuvre. In his first three films, a lonely young man (performed by amateur actor Wang Hongwei) experiences and lives through the spiritual emptiness and physical decay of post-Mao China. In his discussion of the first three films by Jia Zhangke, Xiaoping Lin perceptively points out that "this one man's journey starts from the capital city Beijing in *Xiao Shan Going Home,* continues in a small town called Fenyang in *Xiao Wu,* and finishes in an unknown, barren land in *Platform.*"[11] While continuing to depict human beings' alienation from society in contemporary China, *Still Life* carries a deeper and broader meaning of alienation in that this is humanity's alienation from nature itself. Ruins are portrayed in the most literal and graphic ways in *Still Life* as viewers' senses are pounded with the sight and sound of demolition. The vast expanse of nature (Three Gorges), as well as the colossal man-made destruction cum construction (the dam), reveals a catastrophe of a staggering magnitude.

A rather interesting character in the film is a young small-time gangster, nicknamed "Mark," in homage to the character Mark in the Hong Kong film *Yingxiong bense/A Better Tomorrow* (John Woo, 1986) starring Chow Yun-fat. Mark attempts to exhort money from the outsider Han Sanming in the early part of the film, but later on they become friends. Mark's is a dangerous, deadly profession. In one scene, he is seen sitting alone at the riverbank with his face covered in blood. He is eventually killed as the story unravels.

There is an intriguing scene of Mark and Han Sanming drinking and eating together. The entire scene is rendered in one continuous long take with a stationary medium shot, without any cuts or shot-reverse-shot. There is no close-up as the two characters speak to each other. The viewer cannot see their faces clearly. In this scene, coal miner Han Sanming gives a full account of his reason for coming to Fengjie to this stranger-turned-friend, and to the film audience in large:

MARK: You bought a wife from around here?

HAN SANMING: You are smart.

MARK: Nothing special. More women than men around here. Lots of women were sold off. How much did she cost you?

HAN SANMING: Back then, I paid 3,000 yuan.

Mark: Three thousand? You paid that much and still let her go?

Han Sanming: The police stepped in. . . . She kept crying and really wanted to go. She took our kid as well.

Mark: Well, it's a tough one. Can't really help.

Han Sanming: I asked her to leave an address when she left.

(Han Sanming shows Mark his wife's address in Fengjie, written on a piece of paper torn from a cigarette box.)

Mark: Okay, show me. "Mango?" What cigarettes are these?

Han Sanming: They were the best brand sixteen years ago.

Mark: You are nostalgic!

Han Sanming: We remember our own pasts.

Mark: You know what? Present-day society doesn't suit us because we're too nostalgic.

Han Sanming: Who taught you that?

Mark: Chow Yun-fat! Brother Fat! Brother Fat!

Han Sanming: If something comes up, please help me.

Mark: No problem. Tell you what, I will give you my mobile number. Call me if you need me. We're buddies. I will be there for you.

Han Sanming: Call my mobile.

(Mark dials Han's cell phone number. Han's phone rings, with the ringtone of a song.)

Mark: What's that song?

Han Sanming: "Bless Good-Hearted People."

Mark: Fuck, "Good-Hearted People"! None of those in Fengjie these days. Okay, call my mobile. Listen to mine.

(Han dials Mark's cell phone number. The phone rings, with the ringtone of a pop song about distraught immigrants leaving their home.)

The film cuts to televisual images of sorrowful immigrants on a boat leaving the area. There is a close-up of the face of a crying tearful old woman. A huge board on a mountain reads: THIRD PHASE WATER LEVEL: 156.3 METERS. A man in the mountain waves to the departing boat.

The conversation between two "old-timers" captures the mood and subject of much of Jia Zhangke's film world. "Criminals," gangsters, thieves are the heroes or antiheroes of his films, such as *Xiao Shan Going Home, Xiao Wu,* and *Unknown Pleasures.* The line between good guys and bad boys is blurred. In fact, legitimate and illegitimate are indistinguishable. "Mark" in *Still Life* worships the original "Mark" and the characters performed by charismatic Chow Yun-fat in John Woo's heroic gangster classics *A Better Tomorrow* and *Diexue shuangxiong/The Killer* (Hong Kong 1989). He mimics Chow's hand gesture as he repeats Chow's line, "present-day society doesn't suit us because we're too nostalgic." As the immobile camera is positioned sideways to his body and face, his silhouette does resemble Chow's body and posture. Characters at the periphery of Chinese society thus become the focal point of the film.

The original Chinese title of the film is plain and yet provocative. A literal translation of *Sanxia haoren* should be "Good People of Three Gorges," which is reminiscent of Bertolt Brecht's play *The Good Person of Setzuan* (*Der Gute Mensch von Setzuan*). Brecht reveals the untenable position of abstract morality and hollow idealism in the context of Chinese society in the early twenty-first century or in any society at any time. Both good and bad are faces of the same individual. Brecht's materialist critique calls for more attention to the concrete conditions of life rather than the imposition of unrealistic moral demands on people. Likewise, Jia's *Still Life,* or better still, *Good People of Three Gorges,* provokes the viewer to make an effort in understanding the real material conditions of life in the Three Gorges area. "There exist no more good people these days," as Mark exclaims. Yet, in this big batch of shady gray area that is China, ordinary people, whether from the underworld or out in the open, bond and help one another.

Later in the film, Mark goes on to a job with several youngsters to "get even" (*baiping*) with somebody in another city. They are all hired and paid by "Brother Bin," who is none other than the man that Shen Hong comes to look for as husband. Guo Bin has become a head of a large legitimate business in the area. Eventually he and Shen Hong decide to settle for a divorce, and she returns to Shanxi. One day Han Sanming is looking for his friend Mark, and dials his cell phone number. The song/ringtone of Mark's cell phone rings from under a pile of rubble. Mark's dead body is discovered under the pile. Characters such as Mark the thug, or the coal miner Han Sanming who illegally bought a wife sixteen years back make up the spectrum of good people in Jia's film. This is a properly independent cinema about characters at the periphery of Chinese society. It is noteworthy that *Still Life* passed the censors and has been screened in public theaters in China.

Conclusion: The End of Independent/Underground Film? Not Yet

Despite the overall relaxing of film censorship in China, there are still forbidden zones. Examples abound: for instance, Li Yang's film *Mangjing/Blind Shaft* (2003) startled the international film community with its unsparing depiction of the tragic condition and the darkness of human nature in Chinese coal mines. For that precise reason, the film was not allowed to be released in Chinese public theaters. When Sixth Generation director Lou Ye touched on the still politically sensitive subject of the events of June 4, 1989 in Tian'anmen Square, he crossed the line and invited himself into troubled water. His feature *Yiheyuan/Summer Palace* (2006) falls perfectly into the perceived image of underground/independent cinema from unsmiling communist China. In his review for *Variety,* Derek Elley notes:

Two star-kissed lovers meet, part, and finally are reunited against a backdrop of 14 years of contemporary Chinese history in *Summer Palace,* an occasionally involving but way over-stretched tapestry that plays like a French art movie in oriental dress. . . . Chinese-French co-prod played in competition at Cannes without prior official approval from China's Film Bureau, which could cause short-term hassles in Lou's local career. As well as being the first Mainland feature to show events around Tiananmen in the summer of 1989, *Summer Palace* is also the first to feature (in one shot only) full frontal nudity by its male and female leads. However, there's an unmistakable feeling throughout *Summer Palace* that Lou is deliberately pressing hot buttons to cater to Western auds. If the pic does end up banned in China, that will only add to its prestige in some Western critical circles—despite the fact that the pic is at least half an hour too long and poorly organized on a dramatic level.[12]

Elley's sarcastic yet perceptive remarks describe the precise geopolitics of a Chinese independent film. We see the repetition of a familiar scenario in East-West cultural relations. Due to the inclusion of sex (display of offensive, immodest frontal nudity) and politics (specifically, one of the remaining untouchables of China: the Tian'anmen incident in June 1989) the film was banned in communist China. Moreover, the director also violated the domestic politics of film regulation, since he did not obtain prior approval from the authorities to submit this film for competition at the Cannes Film Festival in 2006. As Elley observed, Lou pushed all the "hot buttons" for a film from communist China to succeed in a Western film festival. However, despite the fact that a fellow Chinese director from Hong Kong, none other than the legendary Wong Kai-wai, sat on the jury of that year's Cannes festival, Lou Ye did not bag any award to take home. And trouble was waiting for him at home nevertheless. He was censured, blacklisted, and banned from making film in China for the next five years.

The Chinese authorities took action to discipline a maverick domestic filmmaker because he transgressed the political bottom line. But they can be also oversensitive to imports from Hollywood. In summer 2006, as *The Da Vinci Code* (Ron Howard, USA, 2006) was screened in Chinese theaters across the nation and created impressive box-office figures, the film was suddenly pulled out of the market on the order of the authorities. This is a knee-jerk reaction to complaints of Chinese Catholics about the film's alleged negative portrayal of the Vatican. Some Catholics warned that "the film threatened social stability."[13] Another interesting turn of events is likewise indicative of the nature of China's level of tolerance. When Ang Lee's film *Brokeback Mountain* (USA, 2005) received major prizes at the Academy Awards, the official Chinese media equally basked in a moment of glory and pride. It praised the outstanding achievement of a diasporic Chinese. However, *Brokeback Mountain* was not released in China due to its patent gay theme. In China's slow march to a civil society, such paranoid reactions to public opinion are typical of the Chinese bureaucracy that is guarded and afraid of assuming responsibility. In a severely limited public sphere, China's film censors appear immature and do not know how to handle problems and complaints. Of course, the easiest and rudest way is to shut something down as soon as someone whispers something against it. Caution against foreign imports as well as discipline against unruly indigenous productions on the part of Chinese censors are likely to stay. It seems that we cannot completely detach ourselves from political considerations in the Chinese case. And for this reason alone, the category of the peripheral, independent, or underground will stay for a long time when film observers turn their gaze to the East.

Notes

1. Pickowicz and Zhang, "Preface," in *From Underground to Independent: Alternative Film Culture in Contemporary China*, viii–ix.

2. I first elaborated on the emergence and development of transnational Chinese cinema in the introduction to the anthology *Transnational Chinese Cinemas: Identity, Nationhood, Gender,* 1–31.

3. On the question of melodrama in Chinese cinema, especially in reference to Fifth Generation classics such as *Huang tu di/Yellow Earth* (Chen Kaige, 1984), see

Berry and Farquhar, "Realist Modes: Melodrama, Modernity and Home," in *China on Screen: Cinema and Nation,* 75–107. For a delineation of the distinctive features of the Sixth Generation in contrast to previous generations, see Zhang, "Introduction: Bearing Witness: Chinese Urban Cinema in the Era of 'Transformation,'" in *The Urban Generation: Chinese Cinema and Society at the Turn of the Twenty-First Century,* 1–45.

    4. See the anthology *The Urban Generation,* ed. Zhang.

    5. Cui, "Working from the Margins: Urban Cinema and Independent Directors in Contemporary China," in *Chinese-Language Film: Historiography, Poetics, Politics,* ed. Lu and Yueh-yu Yeh, 100.

    6. Xu, *Sinascape: Contemporary Chinese Cinema,* 48.

    7. See www.chinaiff.org.

    8. Zhangke, "A Record of Confusion."

    9. "China's Film Industry Rankles as Spiderman's Web Snares Cinemas," English. Eastday.com.

    10. I outline the politics of dialect in Jia Zhangke's film and contemporary Greater Chinese cinema in general in my essay "Dialect and Modernity in 21st-Century Sinophone Cinema," *Jump Cut* 49 (Spring 2007), www.ejumpcut.org.

    11. Lin, "Jia Zhangke's Cinematic Trilogy: A Journey across the Ruins of Post-Mao China," in *Chinese-Language Film,* ed. Lu and Yueh-yu Yeh, 187.

    12. Elley, review of *Summer Palace* (*Yiheyuan*).

    13. Kahn, "How China Banished 'Da Vinci,'" A15.

Bibliography

Annual Chinese Independent Film Festival website, www.chinaiff.org.

Berry, Chris, and Mary Farquhar, *China on Screen: Cinema and Nation.* New York: Columbia University Press, 2006.

"China's Film Industry Rankles as Spiderman's Web Snares Cinemas" (May 17, 2007). Available at http://english.eastday.com/eastday/englishedition/features/userobject1ai2837715.html (accessed June 15, 2007).

Cui, Shuqin. "Working from the Margins: Urban Cinema and Independent Directors in Contemporary China." In *Chinese-Language Film: Historiography, Poetics, Politics,* edited by Sheldon H. Lu and Emilie Yueh-Yu Yeh, 96–119. Honolulu: University of Hawai'i Press, 2005.

Elley, Derek. Review of *Summer Palace* (*Yiheyuan*). *Variety,* May 18, 2006. At www.variety.com/review/VE1117930547.html?categoryid=31&cs=1&query=derek+elley+summer+palace+lou+ye (accessed May 15, 2007).

Kahn, Joseph. "How China Banished 'Da Vinci.'" *Sacramento Bee,* June 10, 2006, A15.

Lin, Xiaoping. "Jia Zhangke's Cinematic Trilogy: Journey across the Ruins of Post-Mao China." In *Chinese-Language Film: Historiography, Poetics, Politics,* edited by Sheldon H. Lu and Emilie Yueh-Yu Yeh, 187–209. Honolulu: University of Hawai'i Press, 2005.

Lu, Sheldon H. "Dialect and Modernity in 21st-Century Sinophone Cinema." *Jump Cut* 49 (Spring 2007). At www.ejumpcut.org.

Lu, Sheldon H., ed. *Transnational Chinese Cinemas: Identity, Nationhood, Gender.* Honolulu: University of Hawai'i Press, 1997.

Lu, Sheldon H., and Emilie Yueh-yu Yeh, eds. *Chinese-Language Film: Historiography, Poetics, Politics.* Honolulu: University of Hawai'i Press, 2005.

Pickowicz, Paul G., and Yingjin Zhang, eds. *From Underground to Independent: Alternative Film Culture in Contemporary China.* Lanham, MD: Rowman and Littlefield, 2006.

Xu, Gary G. *Sinascape: Contemporary Chinese Cinema.* Lanham, MD: Rowman and Littlefield, 2007.

Zhang, Zhen, ed. The *Urban Generation: Chinese Cinema and Society at the Turn of the Twenty-First Century.* Durham, NC: Duke University Press, 2007.

Zhangke, Jia. "A Record of Confusion." *Danwei,* June 1, 2007. At www.danwei.org/film/jia_zhangke_vs_zhang_yimou.php (accessed June 14, 2007).

New Spaces of Empire

Quebec Cinema's Centers and Peripheries

In Denys Arcand's *Le Déclin de l'empire américain/ The Decline of the American Empire* (Canada, 1986), a group of Québécois academics and their partners spend a weekend at a country house. Amid the sexual chat and intrigue, they discuss the arguments of one of their number, Dominique Saint-Arnaud (Dominique Michel), concerning the inevitable decline of empires faced with the disintegration of collective purpose and the pursuit of individual gratification. Dominique notes: "Here we are lucky to live on the margins of the empire, the shocks are much less violent." On a nighttime walk by the lake, the friends speculate about being able to see the missiles during an American-Soviet nuclear exchange, concluding that they would no doubt witness the fireball if the U.S. base at Plattsburgh, in upper New York State near the Canadian border, were to be attacked.

These scenes, and indeed the film itself, are eloquent about the multiple implications of the term *periphery* when discussing cultural identities in Quebec, as well as its film industry. The analysis that follows seeks to explore the mobile and multifarious meanings of the term *periphery* in the Quebec context, in relation to an overwhelmingly Anglophone North America; to a French-speaking or French Atlantic world dominated demographically, culturally, and politically by metropolitan France; and to its marginal place in the global film industry. That mobility of meaning is also played out in the context of Quebec itself, where national cultural identities are located in a play of centers and peripheries, for the *periphery* in one viewpoint can become the *center* for another, and vice versa. The case of Quebec is thus a fruitful one for thinking through this relationship, challenging its binaries, and probing alternative mappings.

119

The Quebec Context

Quebec is the only Canadian province that is majority French-speaking (82 percent of its 7.5 million inhabitants), a figure that represents less than a quarter of the total population of Canada and 0.2 percent of that of North America. It is the site of an unresolved national question following two failed sovereignty referenda in 1980 and 1995, even if political nationalism there is currently in abeyance. The French Canadians are, historically, the other conquered and colonized people in North America, along with the native peoples (they share with the Afrikaners the distinction of being the only significantly numerous white settler group to be conquered by another empire). A play of majorities and minorities, and a widespread self-consciousness about boundaries and frontiers, colors much of Quebec's dominant self-image, and its cultural production. And yet, that peripheralization or marginalization must be qualified; its reality is paradoxical and multilayered. In *Le Déclin,* for example, Arcand the master ironist and student of history satirizes not only Quebec social realities by confronting them with the *longue durée,* but also that metahistorical discourse itself; his protagonists, caught insectlike in his gaze, are seen to be constructing alibis for their social and political inaction even as they write themselves into a grand narrative, be it of decline, and as they enjoy the fruits of their class privilege and cultural capital.

We shall return to the content of Arcand's analysis, for his *Les Invasions barbares/ The Barbarian Invasions* (Canada/France, 2003) takes up the same characters seventeen years later. But *Le Déclin* is also significant for industrial and economic reasons. Until *Les Invasions barbares,* it held the record for far and away the most successful Quebec film ever distributed in France, at 1.2 million tickets sold. The Quebec film industry that emerged from the (secularizing, modernizing) Quiet Revolution of the 1960s had developed with state aid at both federal and provincial levels, from organisms such as the National Film Board of Canada (which moved to Montreal from Ottawa in 1956), and, by the 1980s, as federal state-funding agency, Telefilm Canada.

It is thus extremely rare for a Quebec film to turn a profit over and above the subsidies it receives. *Le Déclin* and *Les Invasions,* aside from their intrinsic qualities, had going for them lots of (talk about) sex, and dialogue largely uttered in international French comprehensible to French audiences notoriously resistant to language variation. This resistance is a consequence of linguistic centralization dating from the foundation of the Académie française in the seventeenth century, and continuing through the revolution and the ensuing republican tradition, contaminating colonial policy from the nineteenth century onward. A center-periphery relationship most certainly exists in the Francophone world, as France remains by far the largest concentration of French speakers, unlike the former colonial powers Britain, Portugal, and Spain in relation to their respective national tongues. Hence the notorious difficulty of creating a French Atlantic film space, with Hollywood dominating cinemas in Quebec in similar numbers to the rest of Canada, which is regarded as an extension of the U.S. domestic market. In turn, as we shall see, Quebec films have to compete for distribution in France with all those other cinemas that are neither French national nor American, that is, less than 10 percent of the market. In 2003, *Les Invasions barbares* (a coproduction between Quebec and France's Canal Plus), with its 1.3 million spectators, ranked 29th at the French box office, with the only other non-French and non-American film achieving over a million that year, *Goodbye Lenin* (Wolfgang Becker, Germany, 2003), ranking 26th. In an interview with the French film magazine *Positif,* Arcand has fun with the confusing indeterminacy of Quebec for French audiences, relishing, despite his protestations, the "in-betweenness," the productive anomaly that Quebec represents. "The fact I make my films in French sometimes raises problems. It would be easier if my films were American. I think that they would then be better received in France. Whereas now it's like French, it refers to French culture, but it's something quite different. I'm the American Indian, the Danube peasant!"[1]

Nonetheless, Quebec cinema is currently on a roll. In 2005, domestic box-office share for Quebec films reached a peak of 18.2 percent, up from 13.6 percent the previous year. Even the figure of 8.8 percent in 2002 represented a then summit, far above the average 3.8 percent that was obtained during the 1990s. When numbers of tickets sold per projection are taken into account, films made in Quebec surpass those from Hollywood by 38.4 to 31.0. On average, Quebec has produced between ten and twenty-five feature films per year for theatrical release during the first decade of the century. The domestic box-office share for Quebec films now exceeds that for the national cinemas of Australia and, on average, the United Kingdom, but falls short, it is true, of comparable spaces such as Denmark (25 percent) and Sweden (20 percent), as well as the incomparable France (45 percent; these are 2006 figures). The Quebec figures for 2006 were in fact in decline, at 11.7 percent, and were heavily reliant on the phenomenon of *Bon Cop Bad Cop* (Erik Canuel, Canada, 2006), a bilingual police genre movie set, significantly, on the Quebec-Ontario border and that came in number one in the overall box office for that year, seeing off *Pirates of the Caribbean: Dead Man's Chest* (Gore Verbinski, USA, 2006) and *The Da Vinci Code* (Ron Howard, USA, 2006). In 2007, the absence of a similar big Quebec film event meant that audience share fell to between 10 percent and 11 percent.

Domestic Film Consumption:
Exportability and Inexportability

Despite high-profile auteurs such as Arcand, Quebec cinema is fundamentally inexportable. Its dominant audience remains located at the periphery of the French Atlantic world, in Quebec itself. Popular Quebec cinema means the costume or heritage film, or else comedy. The second biggest triumph at the domestic box office was *Séraphin—Un Homme et son péché/Séraphin—A Heart of Stone* (Charles Binamé, Canada, 2001), set in rural Quebec, more precisely in an area north of Montreal that is being settled for agriculture for the first time by French Canadians, at the turn of the nineteenth and twentieth centuries. Séraphin is the mayor of this community, manipulating the other characters through usury. He obliges a local shopkeeper to hand over his teenage daughter in marriage, which finishes off her affair with the local hunk (played by Roy Dupuis, best known internationally for his role in the TV series *Nikita* based on the Luc Besson film), and the whole business ends tragically. The story has a long pedigree in Quebec culture, first as a novel and then as two feature films, in 1949–50, which form part of a brief period of French-Canadian as opposed to Quebec filmmaking, when, at the height of cinema-going before the advent of television, fictional features were produced that are mostly to be characterized as Catholic melodramas. (*Aurore,* a melodrama about child abuse directed by Luc Dionne, is also a remake of perhaps the most famous film of this period, *La Petite Aurore l'enfant martyre/Little Aurore's Tragedy* [Jean-Yves Bigras, Canada, 1951], and it beat the blockbusters *The Fantastic Four* [Tim Story, USA/Germany, 2005] and *War of the Worlds* [Steven Spielberg, USA, 2005] on their opening weekend in July 2005.) The meanings these films provide for post–Quiet Revolution audiences are complex: the national "we" as origin, but also as difference, across the chasm of educational and social transformation that has since intervened. Descriptions of *Séraphin* as "Quebec's *Titanic*" suggest not only the box office but also a reference to a heterosexual romance that is prevented by the non-(post)modernity of the past, the difference being that the mobile, international space of the transatlantic liner is here replaced by a mythical national past largely incomprehensible to non-Québécois audiences. These big-budget heritage films also have their place in Quebec film historiography. Arguably inaugurated by lush 1970s art house productions such as Claude Jutra's *Kamouraska* (Canada, 1971) and Jean Beaudin's *J. A. Martin photographe/J. A. Martin Photographer* (Canada, 1975), they were further impelled by expensive coproductions directed by Gilles Carle in the early 1980s based on famous literary source material and/or radio and television programs from the 1950s and 1960s: *Les Plouffe/The Plouffe Family* (Canada, 1981) and *Maria Chapdelaine* (Canada/France, 1983). Then in the 1990s Radio Canada (SRC), the Francophone branch of the Canadian Broadcasting Corporation, developed a successful and sustained formula of big-budget, prime-time serial fictions, or *téléromans*. For while Quebec cinema has only recently managed to attain consistently high audience figures, Quebec television has since its inception been highly popular. Much more at ease with televisual culture than the French, the Québécois watch domestically produced fiction in massive numbers, single programs sometimes attaining half the audience (3.7 million for *Les Filles de Caleb* on January 31, 1991), unlike their English Canadian counterparts, who for 98 percent of their fiction viewing tend to watch the American networks.

This osmosis between film and television in Quebec is to some extent the trump card, as it has developed a mass, "national" audiovisual sensibility with its concomitant modes of recognition of places, faces, voices, storylines. One of 2005's top comedy successes was a satire of *Pop Idol/Star Academy* reality TV, *Idole instantanée* (Yves Desgagnés, Canada, 2005). It starred the comedienne Claudine Mercier, her talents honed on Quebec's extensive comedy circuit, including Montreal's annual Just for Laughs festival, playing the role of four different contestants. The most successful Quebec film of the first half of the 1990s, *Louis 19 le roi des ondes/King of the Airwaves* (Michel Poulette, Canada/France, 1994), was also a satire of reality TV, and, in a rare example of Quebec cinema voyaging to the center of the world film industry, albeit transformed, was remade in Hollywood by Ron Howard as *EdTV* (USA, 1999). Another major popular success of recent years, with implications for the metropolitan French center, as we shall see, has been the series of films based on *Les Boys* (directed by Louis Saïa), the first of which was made in 1997 and came second only to James Cameron's *Titanic* (USA, 1997) at the box office. These are comedies about an amateur ice hockey team, whose manager is played by Rémy Girard, who starred in *Les Invasions barbares*. The films emphasize the struggles and conflicts faced by a homosocial group, ending in euphoria as narratives of a hockey match and life end happily, a diegetic audience underlining the modes of participation central to popular culture. Some social differences are eradicated through team unanimity (the gay lawyer character scores the winning goal in the first film), performance and winning are what count, and women tend to be marginalized. The films trace the consequences for an older culture of the "new" (individualism, postindustrialism, gender instability), with the world outside left behind in favor of a utopian scene of success read in communal terms, with a masculinity under siege reasserted via the most minor of adjustments: an upward trajectory for masculinity and its changed contexts, to be contrasted with the downward trajectory of a film like *The Full Monty* (Peter Cattaneo, UK, 1997).

Les Boys II (Canada, 1998) took the team to France. Despite the fact that much Quebec comedy is based on mocking the French, the film was given a wide release there, with predictably negative results. One solution to the transatlantic Francophone divide has been the coproduced heritage film spoken in international French by an international cast. *Nouvelle France/ Battle of the Brave* (Jean Beaudin, Canada/France/UK, 2004), a big-budget (C$30 million,[2] enormous for Quebec) melodrama and love story set before and after the British Conquest of 1759, with Gérard Depardieu in the cast, was released on ninety-two screens in France in July 2005, but met with universal indifference there, averaging five spectators per projection in its first week. However, the film at number seven in the Quebec box-office rankings for 2001–3, *La Grande Séduction/Seducing Dr. Lewis* (Jean-François Pouliot, Canada, 2003), proved to be eminently exportable, and a comedy at that. Set in a remote coastal community on the north shore of the St. Lawrence, it recounts the efforts by the villagers to ensure the installation of a plastics factory in the vicinity, for which they need to have a doctor in residence. They thus set about wooing a doctor from Montreal, attempting to make him feel at home in a clash of rural and urban manners. What seems to be a rather conservative film, locking into a strand of Quebec culture that emphasizes the (ever so slightly "English") evils of the city, has in fact found audiences in surprising places—its first export market was South Korea—with an appreciation for the relation between local and global culture the film articulates.

The most successful film of 2005 both critically and commercially was *C.R.A.Z.Y* (Jean-Marc Vallée, Canada, 2005). Combining social comedy and family saga, it traces the itinerary of Zac, a young man born into a working-class Montreal family in the crucial year 1960. As he traverses the next twenty-five years (with a brief coda set in his forties), the film becomes a kind of primer for understanding post–Quiet Revolution Quebec, not in relation to public events (Expo '67 and the PQ election victory of 1976 are briefly glimpsed on the TV screen) but in terms of familial, affective, and sexual relations and the secularization of society (what Anthony Giddens calls "the transformation of intimacy").[3] Zac's slow awakening to homosexuality, a topic frequently used in Quebec culture as a touchstone for modernization and the distance traveled since the 1950s, is played out no less typically in the relation with his father (played by Michel Côté, one of Quebec's best-known actors), and, more inventively, through popular music; the film's title refers (as well as to the names of the five brothers) to the father's affection for Patsy Cline, and Zac's life and sense of self are negotiated via David Bowie and others (in his bedroom he performs a memorable rendition, like a prayer, of "Space Oddity").

Interrogating Center and Periphery through Minorization

So far, this overview of the current state of Quebec cinema has shown that it may certainly be described as "peripheralized" in terms of its access to world markets, and even to the main French-speaking market. However, Quebec's "peripheralization" in terms of meaning must be historicized, and in the main its unique geographical and historical situation generates inter-rogations rather than reaffirmations of the center-periphery nexus. A domi-nant feature of left-nationalist discourse in the 1960s was to align Quebec with the global anticolonial struggle. The famous title of a book written by a militant in the Front de libération du Québec (FLQ), Pierre Vallières's *Nègres blancs d'Amérique/White Niggers of America* (1968), encapsulated this homology. Quebec films of the Quiet Revolution period also explore this analysis, most notably Gilles Groulx's *Le Chat dans le sac/Cat in the Sack* (Canada, 1964), which combines techniques from direct cinema established in the previous six years by Groulx, Michel Brault, Jean Rouch, and others (synchronous sound, "interviews" to camera, hand-held mobile shots fol-lowing characters in the street) to portray the relationship between Claude (Claude Godbout), a twenty-three-year-old Francophone Québécois and aspiring journalist, and Barbara (Barbara Ulrich), a twenty-year-old Anglo-phone Jewish actress. The film opens with Claude holding up to the camera books on the black American revolt, the Cuban revolution, Jean Vigo, and copies of the works of Frantz Fanon, all coexisting with his rather Cartesian (or aspiring to be Cartesian) "I am French Canadian and therefore trying to find myself." But like most films of what I have termed Quebec's "cinema of modernization," the intellectual parameters and outcome of the film are very uncertain and inchoate. Claude rejects both the technocracy of the new Quebec state and the violence of the FLQ, and is dismayed by consumer cul-ture and its inauthenticities, impasses all bound up for him with the status of Quebec, colonized by American culture and peripheral to a Parisian center. His alienation prevents him from acting, but, arguably, his search for reas-suring fixity and wholeness to fill the lack in national (and, by implication, gender) identities prevents him from understanding Barbara, who is more at ease with the performativity and provisionality of identities, and more able to entertain fictions and allegorize her life.[4]

An alternative approach to Quebec's peripheral, marginal, and even in-between status can also be discerned in its 1960s cinema, one that avoids the straightforwardly oppositional stance evident in texts influenced by anticolonialism. In *Cinema 2: The Time-Image,* Gilles Deleuze famously analyzed the work of one Quebec documentary filmmaker working in the 1960s, Pierre Perrault. As with the (other) third world filmmakers he examines, such as Ousmane Sembene and Glauber Rocha, Deleuze sees Perrault's *Pour la suite du monde/For Those Who Will Follow* (Pierre Perrault, Canada, 1963) as an example of "minor" cinema in which "the people" are perceived as "lacking" rather than offering a full identity or presence:

What cinema must grasp is not the identity of a character, whether real *or* fictional, through his objective and subjective aspects. It is the becoming of the real character when he himself starts to "make fiction," when he enters into "the flagrant offence of making up legends" and so contributes to the invention of his people. The character is inseparable from a before and an after, but he reunites these in the passage from one state to the other. He himself becomes another, when he begins to tell stories without ever being fictional. And the film-maker for his part becomes another when there are "interposed," in this way, real characters who wholly replace his own fictions by his own story-telling.[5]

In Perrault's *Pour la suite du monde,* for example, the filmmakers encourage the reenactment of a traditional method of hunting beluga whale on an island in the St. Lawrence and overcome some of the dilemmas of ethnographic cinema and its subject-object relations. The peoples of the island are intercessors because they are real but engaged in creating fictions and legends, and a reciprocal communication and transformation characterize their relationship with the filmmakers. Time is the force that here puts truth in crisis. Through fabulation, Perrault and his cameraman Michel Brault are freed from a model of truth, and what Deleuze, drawing on Nietzsche, calls the "power of the false" breaks the repetition of the past and provokes, not a recalling, but a calling forth. However, the potential for Deleuzian thought to address the situation of Quebec does not end here in the pages of *Cinema 2: The Time-Image.* Explicitly in the "Postulates on Linguistics" section of *A Thousand Plateaus,* and implicitly in their work on Kafka and even the anti-Oedipal positions elaborated elsewhere in their collaboration, Deleuze and Guattari begin to suggest what a "minor" Frenchness might be.

In their ontology of becoming rather than being, of movement, process, and multiplicity rather than fixity and identity, and in their sidestepping of the binaries of self/other and subject/object, Deleuze and Guattari emphasize the fact that the "proper name" ("the instantaneous apprehension of a multiplicity"),[6] as in "Québécois," is always already pluralized, its bits, components, particles, molecules, arranged and organized according to bigger, molar, structures, but at the same time potentially taking off in new directions: "Signs are not signs of a thing; they are signs of deterritorialization and reterritorialization, they mark a certain threshold crossed in the course of these movements."[7] The Quebec national project is riven with the tension between territorialization and deterritorialization because of the competing discourses of "Québécité" and "Américanité," continental and Atlantic identities, the migrant flows of globalized capital into which it is unevenly inserted, the different relationships lived with Canada, and above all the shifting categories of majority and minority. Deleuze and Guattari conceive the "minor" not in terms of numbers but in terms of the relationship between becoming and the territorialization/deterritorialization process. The writings of Kafka, or of African Americans, or of the Irish, all possess an ambiguous relationship to the "major" language in which they write, which they affect with "a high coefficient of deterritorialization."[8] Kafka, for example, wrote German as a Jew excluded from the German-speaking minority in a peripheral city of an empire in which German was a commercial lingua franca but was not "at home." Quebec artists of the 1960s, to take another example, were conscious that their language was "minor" in relation not only to the vast North American and Canadian Anglophone majority, but was peripheral and relatively deterritorialized faced with the "major" language that is standard metropolitan French. This implies, as when Fredric Jameson, drawing on Deleuze and Guattari's work, writes of national allegory, that any individual utterance is always already in this context magnified to embrace politically the whole collectivity.[9] (Indeed, for Deleuze and Guattari, "There is no individual enunciation," since enunciation always implies "collective assemblages" and we all speak in indirect discourse.[10]) The point is not to talk about Quebec French as a particular dialect, but to realize that minor and major attitudes can be adopted toward this language and culture. One attitude is either to fall back on to a new territorialization: "the Canadian singer can also bring about the most reactionary, the most Oedipal of reterritorializations, oh mama, oh my native land, my cabin, olé, olé."[11] Or the other is to follow the logic of the minor status, its capacity for proliferation and innovation (becoming), its antithesis therefore to the rank of master, and its undermining of the major culture's pretensions to the natural, normal, and universal: "It is a question not of reterritorializing oneself on a dialect or patois but of deterritorializing the major language."[12] Minorities have their own territorialities but must also be considered as "seeds, crystals of becoming whose value is to trigger uncontrollable movements and deterritorializations of the mean or majority."[13] The minor languages and cultures that emerge may be completely innovative. In this context, the "national allegory" is best described as a "national-allegorical tension" between these centripetal and centrifugal forces.

Deleuze's canon of films in his cinema books is open to some question; for example, he tended to select one film director from a third world country, usually the one taken up by *Cahiers du cinéma,* hence his choice of Perrault. He might instead have alighted upon *A tout prendre/Take It All* (Claude Jutra, Canada, 1964) a little-known gem of world cinema, shot in 1961–63 and released in 1964, which revels in "the minor," but, paradoxically, a minor mode constructed from within the urban bourgeoisie (and whose main protagonist speaks impeccable metropolitan French). This quasi-autobiographical piece, produced in the private sector, portrays the affair between filmmaker Claude (the director Claude Jutra), and a black model, Johanne (Johanne Harel), who is still living with her (estranged and unseen) husband. The vicissitudes of the relationship—first encounter, obsession, other dalliances, Johanne's pregnancy, subsequent rejection by Claude, and miscarriage—are less important than the way the film combines the formal experimentation of its *cinematic* language with a sustained problematization of identity. *A tout prendre* joyously undercuts the self on which the film would seem narcissistically to center. From the opening scene in which Claude gets ready for the party, the spectator is confronted with the fragility of the self. The realism of body details in the shower (such as washing feet) combines with a montage of shots of Claude in various guises in front of the mirror, ending with him firing a gun so that it shatters and fragments. The self-proclaimed "quest" of the film is to "get rid of my youth and of the characters [*personnages*] inside me." The film proceeds to address this longing, but ultimately Claude discovers that there is no unified identity for him to step into. Claude and Johanne circle each other in the photography scene not in some closed repetition but in a relationship of mutual dependency and attraction; they consist of bits, fragments, atoms, rather than complete and finished persons or identities (although Johanne ultimately turns out to be trapped within the desire for wholeness predicated on heterosexual romance). In fact, "Je est un autre," "I is another" (the quotation from Rimbaud's *Lettre du voyant* of 1871 that Deleuze uses to describe the nonidentical in time and the nonidentity of image and concept, and which he sees manifesting itself in Jean Rouch's practice in *Moi, un noir*). The way forward is through fabulation. Crucially, a gay element in *A tout prendre* (Johanne asks Claude if he "likes boys," Claude, it is implied, has an affair with a male actor) also contributes to the film's "minorization" of Quebec by side-stepping Oedipal categories associated with lack and heterosexual masculinity to be found in, for example, *Le Chat dans le sac.*

New Spaces of Empire

If we return to the contemporary period and Denys Arcand's *Les Invasions barbares,* we may say that while his making explicit of the buffetings of identity has thus always existed in Quebec cinema, it is played out, even accelerated, here in the new context of Quebec postmodernity, in relation both to time (the lost past of religious and political certainty) and space (the realities of globalization). Rémy (Rémy Girard), the most philandering of the academics from *Le Déclin,* is dying of cancer, and Sébastien (Stéphane Rousseau), his wealthy futures-trading son from London, organizes for him a refurbished private room in a dilapidated state-run Montreal hospital, procures heroin for him via Nathalie (Marie-Josée Croze, winner of the Best Actress award at Cannes), the addicted daughter of another of the characters from the earlier film, and assists his suicide at a lakeside chalet where Rémy is surrounded by friends and family. In a slight shift of emphasis from *Le Déclin,* Quebec, or at least Montreal, is here to be seen as firmly within, if not quite at the center of, "empire" (if we are now to read the latter not in the strict spatial and territorial terms of "the American empire" but in the Hardt and Negri analysis of the capitalist global order).[14] The "barbarians" are not at the gates but are with us: the 9/11 hijackers (footage of the attacks on the twin towers is followed by an analysis by the now no doubt tenured graduate student from 1986, mouthing Dominique's thesis), but more notably the corrosive gratification of drug culture, and Sébastien himself, or at least the triumphant capitalism he represents.

The difficulty of the film lies in Arcand's slippery irony, satirical of but also nostalgic for the past, scathing about public health provision but leaving open a very liberal-economic reading from that criticism. That ambiguity is there in the border crossings made by Rémy and Sébastien in an ambulance for treatment in Burlington, Vermont. On the one hand, the United States, at least for those in the income bracket of the protagonists, seems to offer a present that works. On the other hand, the United States is a foil, to Rémy's continuing socialist or progressive views, and to both Canadian and Quebec national identity constructions. At the border, the two men are greeted by a smiling female immigration official. In a two-shot edit, to her "welcome to America" they reply "Hallelujah" and "Praise the Lord." The brief scene is significant, for the two Québécois humorously undercut American euphoria, and any identification with it, by an invocation of the religious fundamentalism that marks a widely perceived *difference* between Canada/Quebec and the United States. But they do so in of all places Vermont, the state of Howard Dean and free health care for children, and of Bernie Sanders, the only self-proclaimed socialist in the U.S. Senate. The scene serves as a reminder of Slavoj Žižek's fundamental argument that borders, margins, and peripheries are in fact an inherent part of what we take identity to be. Identities are always about nonidentity, a split between what for example a nation is, and what it purports or ought to be, that totalization or plenitude that can never by definition be achieved or grasped. The *boundaries* of national identification have to be understood as being reflected in the nation's internal *limits,* the impossibility of being fully, purely and unproblematically Canadian, Québécois, American: "every boundary proves itself a limit: apropos of every identity, we are sooner or later bound to experience how its condition of possibility . . . is simultaneously its condition of impossibility."[15]

These observations open out the possibility of "minorizing" Quebec cultural identities, as we have seen, but Arcand is often unwilling to follow this path, as if it would make too many concessions to the present and to contemporary culture. The reason Montreal seems much nearer the center of the empire in 2003 is that since the 1980s it has reinserted itself within international capital flows, including within the multimedia industry (but also biotechnology and aircraft engineering). This is due partly to technical and industrial factors (the branch plant phenomenon, the animation tradition), and partly to cultural hybridity (Montreal as linguistically rich and as located between European and North American culture). For instance, Daniel Langlois, founder of Softimage, which had provided animation software for *Jurassic Park* (Spielberg, USA, 1993) and *Toy Story* (Lasseter, USA, 1995), has invested in the Festival of New Cinema and New Media, and sponsored the new C\$16 million cinema complex on the Boulevard Saint-Laurent devoted to experimental and auteur cinema.[16] One consequence of Montreal's economic relaunch since the mid-1990s has been a certain reconfiguring of space within Quebec itself, within which it is possible to talk of new centers and new peripheries. Such is the fate of the provincial and historic capital, Quebec City, which struggles gamely to compete with Montreal. The other eminently exportable Quebec auteur of the contemporary period, Robert Lepage, was born there in 1957, and is somewhat more at ease than Arcand with the consequences of globalization and the possibilities for cultural hybridity it brings. By 1995 and his first feature film, he was already a well-established theater director with an international career, making extensive use of multimedia, video screens, and translation in his productions. *Le Confes-*

sionnal/The Confessional (Robert Lepage, Canada/UK/France, 1995) travels back and forth between 1952 (when Alfred Hitchcock came to Quebec City to shoot *I Confess* and when Quebec was still languoring in pre-1960 clericalism) and 1989, unraveling a family mystery and tragedy in ways that establish tiny circuits of contrast, confidently juxtapose the local (Quebec City, a much smaller and less cosmopolitan urban space than Montreal) and the global (Japan and a whole world of difference), as well as past and present. These minimal circuits include: womb and cinema screen (and beyond it Hollywood and the world), as the mother attends the premiere of *I Confess,* an event narrated in voice-over by her adult son; and the astonishing cut as a little girl, Renée Hudon, auditions for Hitchcock, is handed the script and begins reading news of 1989's Tian'anmen Square demonstrations, wherein we see the television image of the adult Renée Hudon reading the news on Quebec City's CBC/SRC channel (a cross-reference only fully understood by a local TV audience). In Lepage's follow-up film, *Le Polygraphe/Polygraph* (Robert Lepage, Canada/France/Germany, 1996), a juxtaposition of the city walls (enclosure, the weight of the past, but also a reference to the Berlin origin of one of the protagonists) and a night sky empty save for whirling particles—snowflakes—continues this rhythm of contraction and dilation. *Le Confessionnal* thus leapfrogs over the metropole of Montreal, disrupting center-periphery binaries.

A periphery of Quebec City is also evoked in this film, namely the suburb of Charny, with its motel and strip bar. Here a native Canadian character participates in an erotic dance, perpetuating the cliché of nonthreatening sexuality (unlike that of African American men), and serving as a go-between for the white characters, transmitting not only a leather jacket and hairstyle but also a nomadic and polymorphous notion of identity.[17] This evocation of the Amerindian is also eloquent in relation to the complexity of power configurations in the Quebec context, and the shifting senses of majority and minority as well as center and periphery. In Quebec cinema, the representation of native peoples has often been a displacement of white Franco-Québécois anxieties: the relationship with the (Catholic) past (*Le Festin des morts/Mission of Fear* [Fernand Dansereau, Canada, 1965]) or sexual anxieties (*Red* [Gilles Carle, Canada, 1969]; *Visage pâle/Pale Face* [Claude Gagnon, Canada/Japan, 1985]; *L'Automne sauvage* [Gabriel Pelletier, Canada, 1992]). Native issues have been most fully explored in documentary, notably by Arthur Lamothe (*Mémoire battante,* 1983). Although no director of native origin has yet made a fictional feature in Quebec, Alanis Obomsawin, born in 1932 to an Abenaki community, is a leading documentary filmmaker (*Kanesatake: 270 Years of Resistance,* 1993). In parallel fashion, Quebec's "visible minorities" (in fact Montreal's, for 92 percent of Quebec's population of recent immigrant origin lives in the city's greater area) have for long been relatively invisible in Quebec film production, although this is gradually changing given the emphasis on diversity and *transculture* in the public sphere in the periods following the two referenda. While some directors of immigrant origin have made features, such as the Italian Paul Tana (*La Sarrasine* [Canada, 1992]; *La Déroute/Mr. Aiello* [Canada, 1998]) and the North African Michka Saäl (*La Position de l'escargot* [France, 1998]), sustained reflection or representation has to be sought in modest television films (*Manuel le fils emprunté* [François Labonté, 1989]) or in documentary, such as the work of Tahani Rached, born in Cairo in 1947 (*Les Voleurs de job,* 1980; *Haïti-Québec,* 1985). An exception is *Clandestins* (Denis Chouinard and Nicolas Wadimoff, Switzerland/Canada/France/Belgium, 1997). This international coproduction, directed by a Québécois and a Swiss and with French dialogue, tells the story of six stowaways—Arab, Gypsy, and East European—bound for Canada. Set almost entirely in the claustrophobic container of a cargo ship, the film communicates the physical hardships and psychological pressure with the kind of documentary realism associated with Canadian cinema (the directors-writers based their account on testimonies). But the film also denounces both the desperation that provokes such migrations and the injustices of the immigration system; because Canada fines ships C$5,000 per illegal immigrant, on discovering them the captain puts them off the ship into an open boat (although the gypsy teenager remains at liberty with the little girl, offering at least some promise of renewal). Chouinard's follow-up feature, *L'Ange de goudron/Tar Angel* (Canada, 2001), narrates a father-son relationship in an Algerian immigrant context as the son is tempted by terrorism.

It will be interesting to see whether the current euphoria in film circles in Canada and Quebec is sustained over the next few years, dependent as it is on one or two films per year really taking off in the domestic and international markets. Recent successes to an extent ratchet up the pressure on filmmakers to deliver a significant return, if not profit, on the majority public investment that is made. Filmmaking costs in Montreal remain high, partly as a result of the city's success in the Hollywood North phenomenon of attracting American filmmaking; some of the infrastructure and personnel is beyond the financial reach of local filmmakers. The average budget for a Quebec feature is less than C$2 million, clearly a fraction of Hollywood budgets for both production and the crucial activity of promotion. Interesting directors such as Manon Briand (*La Turbulence des fluides/Chaos and Desire* [Canada/France, 2002]), Chouinard, André Turpin (*Un Crabe dans la tête/Soft Shell Man* [Canada, 2001]), Denis Villeneuve (*Maelström/Maelstrom* [Canada, 2000]), and even Léa Pool (whose last two films have been made in English) struggle to get films made. In many countries the undeveloped or marginal fraction of the market for nondomestic and non-Hollywood films is overcrowded and difficult to penetrate (this is nowhere more true than for the place of Quebec films in France). Thus, the national, central, or peripheral—and therefore contradictory—status of Quebec cinema is implicated in the meanings of its film texts, the shifting interface between the exportable and the inexportable, and the vagaries of its production and place within the global film industry.

Notes

1. Ciment and Rouyer, "Entretien: Denys Arcand. Comme le sourire d'une nuit d'été," 8–12, at 12.

2. All monetary sums in this chapter are in Canadian dollars, which, at time of writing, is practically equal to the U.S. dollar.

3. Anthony Giddens, *The Transformation of Intimacy: Sexuality, Love, and Eroticism in Modern Societies* (Cambridge: Polity Press, 1992).

4. For a more lengthy analysis of *Le Chat dans le sac,* see Marshall, *Quebec National Cinema,* 55–59.

5. Deleuze, *Cinema 2: The Time Image,* 150.

6. Deleuze and Guattari, *A Thousand Plateaus: Capitalism and Schizophrenia,* 37.

7. Ibid., 67.

8. Deleuze and Guattari, *Kafka: Toward a Minor Literature,* 16.

9. Jameson, "Third-World Literature in the Era of Multinational Capitalism," 65–88.

10. Deleuze and Guattari, *A Thousand Plateaus,* 79–80.

11. Ibid., 24.

12. Ibid., 104.

13. Ibid., 134.

14. Michael Hardt and Antonio Negri, *Empire* (Cambridge, MA: Harvard University Press, 2000).

15. Žižek, *For They Know Not What They Do: Enjoyment as a Political Factor,* 110.

16. For more on this general topic, see Bellemare Brière, "Montréal capitale multimédia," 54.

17. See Cornellier, "Absence et présence de l'Indien: Identité, nationalité et indianité dans *Le Confessionnal* (1995)."

Bibliography

Bellemare Brière, Véronique. "Montréal capitale multimédia." *Séquences* 197 (July–August 1998): 54.

Ciment, Michel, and Philippe Rouyer. "Entretien: Denys Arcand. Comme le sourire d'une nuit d'été." *Positif* 512 (October 2003): 8–12.

Cornellier, Bruno. "Absence et présence de l'Indien: Identité, nationalité et indianité dans *Le Confessionnal* (1995)." Master's diss., Concordia University, 2006.

Deleuze, Gilles. *Cinema 2: The Time-Image*. Translated by Hugh Tomlinson and Robert Galeta. London: Athlone Press, 1989.

Deleuze, Gilles, and Félix Guattari. *Kafka: Toward a Minor Literature*. Translated by D. Polan. Minneapolis: University of Minnesota Press, 1986.

———. *A Thousand Plateaus: Capitalism and Schizophrenia*. Translated by Brian Massumi. London: Athlone Press, 1988.

Jameson, Frederic. "Third-World Literature in the Era of Multinational Capitalism." *Social Text* 15 (1986): 65–88.

Marshall, Bill. *Quebec National Cinema*. Montreal: McGill-Queen's University Press, 2001.

Žižek, Slavoj. *For They Know Not What They Do: Enjoyment as a Political Factor*. London: Verso, 2001.

Part 2

PERIPHERAL VISIONS

(Re-)conceiving Identities and Histories

The Palestinian Road (Block) Movie
Everyday Geographies of Second Intifada Cinema

> We travel like other people, but we return to nowhere. As if travelling
> is the way of the clouds. We have buried our loved ones in the
> darkness of the clouds, between the roots of the trees.
> And we said to our wives: go on giving birth to people like us
> for hundreds of years so we can complete this journey
> To the hour of a country, to a metre of the impossible.
>
> —Mahmoud Darwish, "We Travel Like Other People"

It is a cliché to begin writing about modern Palestine by quoting Mahmoud
Darwish,[1] one of the country's most renowned poets. Yet it is also a cliché
for any of us to drift from literal to metaphorical allusions to the road, and
a cliché like "the Palestinian on the road" perforce grabs us by way of its
familiarity, stretching outward both to reach us and to incorporate the specific: "We travel like other people, *but* . . ." The "but" here is not only the
relentless inconstancy of diaspora life but also its ruptured relationship with
another Palestinian reality: one of curfew, checkpoint, and forbidden access
to territories supposedly, although not in practice, protected by international
law. How might these two very different accesses to mobility, to "the road"
work dialectically? Neither condition stands still, much as it might long to
pause for rest. Neither, thankfully for a necessary sense of identification and
solidarity, is uniquely Palestinian.

Given these conditions, roads have understandably haunted the film
culture of this tiny and potentially easily traversed country, particularly since

the inception of the Second Intifada in 2000, while roadblocks, curfews, and checkpoints render cinematic production and dissemination uniquely difficult. A national identity dominated by territorial war and the collective dispossession of Palestine's seven million plus refugees,[2] displaced both internally and within the diaspora, prompts director Rashid Masharawi to claim, "I am trying to make films that look like us: roads, maps. This colours our cultural behaviour . . . I like road movies and I make them without planning to."[3] There are long productions about roads and there are short ones, fictional narratives, documentaries, and many more in between. Palestine's two most prominent feature films wind around road systems. *Divine Intervention* (Elia Suleiman, Palestine,[4] 2002) maps out a love affair at a checkpoint and peppers its storyline with arguments about driveway expansions and car license plates. *Paradise Now* (Hany Abu-Assad, 2005) commences on a road to a checkpoint and ends with a potential suicide bomber on a bus. In between, there are all manner of aborted and successful road journeys for the two lead characters (Kais Nashif and Ali Suliman) who mend cars for a living. The epic Israel-Palestine documentary *Route 181* (Michel Khleifi and Eyal Sivan, 2003) is structured by a drive along the original and now largely invalidated 1947 border. The dramatic highpoint of *Be Quiet* (Sameh Zoabi, 2005) unfolds during a roadside toilet stop; *Like Twenty Impossibles* (Annemarie Jacir, 2003) depicts a film shoot that is dangerously interrupted by a "flying" (temporary) checkpoint; the quasi-fictional *Ford Transit* follows the travails and escapades of a minibus (also known as transit or *servees*) driver; *Crossing Qalandia* (Sobhi al-Zobaidi, 2002) documents the difficulties of doing just that by car; *25 Kilometers* (Nahed Awwad, 2004) chronicles the lengthy, arduous, and hazardous task of trying to reach Bethlehem from Ramallah, once possible along a road whose length the title reveals and which is, since the film's completion, a journey now entirely blocked by the Wall; the titular subject of *Rana's Wedding* (Hany Abu-Assad, 2002) takes place at a checkpoint; *Going for a Ride?* (Nahed Awwad, 2003) explores car culture in Ramallah via an art installation that positioned vehicles destroyed by Israeli tanks along a "road to nowhere"; *A Few Crumbs for the Birds* (Nassim Amaouche and Annemarie Jacir, 2005) is set within a gas filling station and a brothel employing Palestinian refugees on the road to the Iraqi border. *Hopefully for the Best* (Raed al Helou, 2004) and *Palestine Blues* (Nida Sinnokrot, 2006) are distinguished by lengthy shots of the road captured from onboard vehicles; *Trafic* [sic] (Mohanad Yaqubi, 2006) satirizes the stagnancy and disruption of the Palestinian situation with a road-based metaphor of crossing signals flashing between the red and the green man. Finally, even when roads do not physically feature, such as in *The Fourth Room* (Nahed Awwad, 2004), there is prolonged and nostalgic mention of trips, usually ones that are currently off limits. Many of these films contain raw and covertly captured footage of brutal checkpoint encounters, or the dramatization of them. *Road Map* (Multiplicity,[5] 2003), more an art installation than a movie, is split between two screens in order to juxtapose the separate Israeli and Palestinian experiences of traveling between roughly the same points, but along very different, segregated roads. The majority of these movies use the West Bank as their primary mise-en-scène, although not their greater imaginary, so, for the sake of brevity, I will concentrate my more sociohistorical attentions "there" too.

How different these works are from the traditional road movie of whose values Palestinian directors can only dream. "Imagine, you're just traveling on the highway for hours, nobody stops you,"[6] ruminates filmmaker Nahed Awwad. "The road becomes a hero in Palestinians' lives . . . it's freedom. . . . Wow, we never drive for one hour and a half. . . . From Ramallah to Nablus: stop, start, stop, start, it's psychologically there in the back of the mind at all times,"[7] stresses director Enas Muthaffar. If a road movie frequently champions rebellion against staid social structures, the right to roam and be free, then its aims are upheld, yet cruelly ironized by circumstances in Palestine and the movies that are its offspring. Most road movies resist the notion of "home," while Palestinians are still fighting for the right to a home(land). While more typical incarnations of this genre might trace their lineage to the frontier ethos of nation-building and the conquest of space, where then does Palestine, if it is allowed to, stand?[8]

Amid the fantasies and impositions of state (multiple states') expansions, the road has become an actual participant and a driving metaphor, and its navigation is unremittingly challenging, not just for motorists but also for researchers. There can be no correct or authentic departure point to the geography of such a study, no overarching theories from "there" or "elsewhere" to wield upon Palestine's roads and cinema. If at all possible, one should surely avoid creating a separate and fainter track of the ideas in these movies by merely describing them. Instead, shouldn't we aspire to join them in a road-building process of sorts, one that is hopefully a communications network rather than another unwanted imposition on the landscape? It may well be, let us hope, that the policing of scholarship is less restrictive than the policing of actual roads in this instance. As will become apparent, the strategists of the current intifada are adept at unanticipated detours and, by weaving together cultural production, the imperialist history of road building in the West Bank and the international comprehensibility of cinematic genres in this chapter, I am hoping to draw strength from these tactics of unexpected selection and combination.

I do not dwell lightly on the borderline between the real and the improbable. With, for example, USAID proudly declaring its stake in the current regeneration of the West Bank road from the southern border to Ramallah, while America simultaneously funds Israeli armament, with the territory illegally crisscrossed by Israeli-only thoroughfares, the near-surrealism of the current situation in Palestine provokes a disordering of fiction's opposition to fact ("can this possibly be happening?"), a breakdown that is also common to so many Palestinian movies. Seemingly impossible political narratives are created at the international level, and we all assume roles in their realization. Could we divert ourselves from more injurious endeavors by tinkering with the myths of "the road," by casting Palestine and "Palestine" in a newly interconnected understanding of what cinema and travel can mean and can identify to us all?

These are the complexities that consume this chapter. As allegories and as a geopolitical tarmac, dust, and grit reality, how do these roads sit within a violently disputed topography? If there is little more ordinary in life than a road, how is the road's very everyday-ness to be conceptualized, reordered, even subverted through the practices of occupation, intifada, and cinema alike? What can it mean that a road is a communication system with international(ist) potential and might the road movie genre work in these ways too, not as a group of goods transported from A to B, but as the thoroughfare itself?

The Landscape and Its Vanishing Points

Browse any library catalogue for texts on the Israel-Palestine conflict and you will find a significant number containing the word "road" in their title. One of the more recent proposals for a two-state solution bore the moniker the "Road Map to Peace"[9] and, when the RAND Corporation think tank launched an initiative to imagine a postconflict regeneration of Palestine, a land-based communications network was its key principle for the ignition of national pride and a national economy.[10] Transport networks are crucial to the flows of both trade and troops (not to mention, in Palestine, pilgrims). They also allow for an often-desirable schism between public and private life, as the commuter incentives for Jerusalem employees to move out to now well-connected West Bank settlements attest.

Historically less popular than the easily navigable coastal and the commercially advantageous internationally bound roads, the core artery road of the West Bank (now known as route 60) has been overdetermined, since the Israeli occupation of Canaan in the Iron Age, by colonial design. Traversing difficult terrain, its role was primarily to hold ground, rather than to interlock with a regional trade infrastructure. "Clear the way of the Lord in the Wilderness," incites Isaiah 40:3, revealing the historical extent of the correlation among roads, a modernizing and civilizing agenda, and, one could argue, religious imperialism. Think here, as I have just pointed out, of how the road from the border into the West Bank is regularly damaged by the actions of the Israeli military, as well as wear and tear advanced by the prevention of network expansion, and then repaired through the munificence of USAID.

Leaving the sullied connotations of "development" to one side for a moment, Eyal Weizman argues that roads are simply one dimension of a supra- and subterranean complex of imperialism, a central and unique example within it nonetheless.[11] Of the 5,146.9 km of roads in the West Bank, for instance, 764.4 km were built without permission by Israeli authorities beyond its designated borders to exclusively serve Israeli users and largely to facilitate movement that bypasses Palestinian towns and villages.[12] Most Palestinians are forbidden from traveling by these routes, even if they are the purported owners of the land being crossed, and this schema effectively prohibits Palestinians from visiting the breadth of their own country. Although justified as military requirements, the primary function of these thoroughfares is to connect the isolated and resource-dependent illegal settlements in the West Bank with Israel proper.[13] Furthermore, the institution of what is increasingly dubbed an "apartheid road system"[14] has no firm foundation in Israeli law, making the implementation of this infrastructure extremely opportunistic, arbitrary, and unregulated.[15]

At the same time, Israeli forces mete out a form of collective punishment by rendering the roads that remain for Palestinian passage inefficient, unpredictable, and often dangerous through a series of closures, roadblocks (manned or otherwise), and permanent and flying checkpoints: a system that is hard to quantify, but which, at one point in 2003, amounted in the West Bank to 734 such obstacles.[16] Furthermore, the Wall (which, at times, hits long-established roads at a perpendicular and now invalidating angle) more obdurately bars Palestinians access to their land and its resources, ultimately disallowing anyone without specific Israeli-issued identification from, say, moving between the north and the south of the West Bank. Access into and out of Gaza, even via the border with Egypt, has now been almost completely halted, creating what many are now calling "the largest prison in the world."[17] It is not hard to piece together how these measures contributed to the fact that 85 percent of West Bank villagers did (or could) not leave their villages between 2000 and 2003,[18] and that the country's per capita GDP slumped by 30 percent between the start of this intifada and 2005,[19] leaving it in an even worse situation now that Hamas has come into power.

At this point we run into the cruel contradiction that certain Palestinians are hostages in their villages, even homes, while others travel incessantly. Furthermore, until Palestine is granted total statehood, all of them unsettle global notions of "the nation." As Hamid Dabashi argues, these conundrums provoke a serious ontological debate for film culture: "The very proposition of a Palestinian cinema points to the traumatic disposition of its origin and originality. The world of cinema does not know quite how to deal with Palestinian cinema precisely because it is emerging as a stateless cinema of the most serious national consequences."[20] Thus Palestinian cinema refracts, multiplies, and complicates stable concepts at one and the same time. Even "the land" is painfully, if not also usefully chimerical. Rashid Masharawi claims of his own film *Waiting* (Rashid Masharawi, 2005), shot in Jordan, Syria, and Lebanon because his refugee crew was denied access to their homeland: "There are two maps of Palestine, the geographical and the humanitarian. *Waiting* is a road movie through a humanitarian map."[21] Palestinian cinema, then, radically reorganizes social and political space; his crew, he declares, become family, in lieu of the real one from whom he has been separated through exile. It would be irresponsible to claim that these forms of fractured and partial access to a "home culture" should be celebrated without a sense of the pain they also affect,[22] yet the tenacity with which these situations are dealt and the communicative gestures they afford are crucial to the creative and egalitarian road-building process to which so many filmmakers and critics aspire.

Cases like Masharawi's assert that we cannot purely conceive of Palestine as a localized site, nor can we untangle it from greater transnational flows. Palestine's roads (all roads, in fact) also intersect with larger arrangements of geopolitics and, ultimately, oil distribution. Palestine's part in all this features obliquely in *A Few Crumbs for the Birds,* a film tracking petrol smugglers, oil tanker drivers, and the Palestinian prostitutes in a roadside brothel. While Palestine may seem like a geographically specific crisis zone on one level, issues of expansionism, freedom, democracy, and privatization resonate outward from within its borders (and vice versa) through current global policies impinging upon oil-producing nations and the supposed liberties of "the open road" that are exhorted by road movie mythologies. It is no accident that *Palestine Blues* compares the Israeli West Bank settlements to Californian suburbs, and thus to a mode of petrol-dependent privilege. Remarking upon the resemblance seriously interrogates the peripherality of Palestine to the rest of the world, while eliding the typical semantics of suburban aspirations with the more unsavory features upon which its foundations rest.

The paradoxical and shifting interchange among Palestine, its cinema, and peripherality not only opens up avenues for critiques like this one but also makes space for a certain limberness of thought that is well worth examining. The conflict's dominance of audio-visual current affairs coverage (despite a lower death toll than other disputes) belies an absence of concern in the form of state support, film education, or funding unless, as is often the case, stipulations enforcing a partnership with an Israeli cinema body are adhered to, something most Palestinians boycott.[23] On the one hand, there is arrested movement within and into the territory itself (the denial of the legal right of return for Palestinian refugees); on the other, we witness the rootlessness of the refugee population. Furthermore, Palestine exists largely beyond the traditional economic sense of the periphery—an out-of-sight servant class—in that it is now largely disenfranchised from global production and is certainly losing this role it once had in relation to the state of Israel. Not that any of this exempts the country from market exploitation. All of these characteristics add nuance to the never-so-simple semantics of the periphery. Few people would wish for the lack of a state to call their own, but could this ever work to revolutionary or at least artistic advantage? There is little officialdom to hold court either economically or ideologically over Palestinian cinema, prompting director Rashid Masharawi to claim, "We have the best international cinema in the Arab world because we don't have an industry."[24]

In all of these senses, peripherality is a mobile concept, epistemologically and spatially. Palestine can, at times, expertly negotiate the tension between resolute, nationalistic permanence and tactical or enforced transience. A balance of this sort is held most acutely and consciously within Palestinian refugee camps, but also by several mobile cinema projects that have traveled throughout the whole of historic Palestine and, more specifically, within the very aesthetics of Palestinian cinema. I have already noted these movies' refusal to reinscribe the car on the open road as a neoliberal personal space; instead, the films more typically work like the *servees* mode of shared transportation creating a public sphere (destroyed by the day by the Occupation, although unwittingly reestablished through the commonality of checkpoint queues) in surprising and engaging new ways.

Everyday Detours and Traveling (through) Shots

Director (Hany Abu-Assad): You often use detours?
Transit Driver (Rajai Khatib): They saved us. We use them
    more often than asphalt.

—*Ford Transit*

"We thought they [the *servees* drivers] were the best Palestinian artists because they were all the time finding new roads,
finding new ways, being very creative."[25]

—Sandi Hilal, part of the Multiplicity Project, makers of *Road Map*

Throughout the Second Intifada, the drivers of *serveeses* (privately owned minibus taxis) ascended to a heroic, iconic, though never static position, not least within films such as *25 Kilometers, Road Map,* and, in particular, *Ford Transit. Servees* drivers have been distinguished by their indefatigable opposition to occupation, their quick-fire transmission of information about obstacles to one another, their deliberate violation of routes prohibited by Israeli forces, their creation of politicized and often educational community spaces, and their subversion of the original meanings of their vehicles (these Ford Transits were once Israeli police vans given to collaborators as gifts and herald from a company—Ford—that is the bastion of historical U.S. economic domination). "If they find out one [trick], we'll invent a hundred more," boasts Rajai in *Ford Transit.* Within the current shared project of communication networks, there are valuable lessons to be learned from these drivers. I want less to describe these skills than to transport them to another place (as it were) where their adhesive propensities are also much needed.

With Palestinian state structures fragile or nonexistent, the revolutionary inscription of everyday life becomes more urgent than ever, and it is crucial to understand how roads, their travelers, and the art that interacts and amalgamates with them work accordingly. As ever, the insistence is upon "we travel like other people, *but* . . ."; the supportive and inquisitive observation of road users who are, in many ways, "like us" (in simply trying to arrive as promised) and, in others, utterly unique. Here contemporary Palestinian cinema entices us to reconsider not only, as I have argued, the power dynamics of the center-periphery divide but also the stamina required for quotidian (versus "spectacularized") existence under occupation.

In seeking out atypical typicality, many strands of Palestinian cinema simultaneously challenge the hegemonic preconditions of sadly more customary images of the country (of "suicide bombers," of "terrorists"), insisting that we not cordon off Palestine exclusively within these terms. This is not just a matter of policing stereotypes. As Alessandro Petti, one of the artists behind *Road Map,* maintains, "'real' violence . . . is easy to represent, everybody knows it,"[26] it is the ongoing structure, the *temporality* of the Occupation's maneuverings and how all this concurrently underpins the moments of danger and high (newsworthy) drama that this group project aims to convey. Ultimately, he continues, "99 percent of your time is under Occupation because of this [restriction on] movement,"[27] something subtler, more pervaded by the wait than the (inevitable) event, than the cruder conceptions of violence that consume the media.

Thus everyday life, infused as it is with this lurking brutality, becomes central to the rhythms of Palestinian cinema—itself, however, a fairly extraordinary achievement during these times and within these spaces. *Divine Intervention,* like all of Elia Suleiman's work, toys with seemingly boring actions like arguments between neighbors; the movie relays, through a dark and wry ludicrousness, how habitually invested a Palestinian can become in the minutiae of a shrunken daily repertoire. *Hopefully for the Best* likewise revolves around everyday folk in everyday jobs such as food preparation. Markedly, though, the movie is punctuated, as is all (Palestinian) life, with road encounters. On one plane, there lies the film's documentation of checkpoints, the weariness of unpredictable waits for ID verification exacted by unsympathetic soldiers on a daily basis. Tedium for the occupier should be noted here too, and Hannah Arendt's conception of "the banality of evil" does not go amiss on any Palestinian who has read her work.

Also, there are lengthy sequences, including the one that opens the film, that are shot through a car windscreen (this one is nearly two minutes in total, unedited). We become party to another side of Occupation here, where conflict is not manifestly present in terms of an occupier in our sight lines. The car's aimless cruising in one sense hooks into practices undertaken the car-owning world over; in another sense, it carries the specific resonances of people trapped within very small boundaries. As we move from nights to days and the seasons change, the journey remains the same, later rendered in fast motion, as if to fulfill an impossible wish to zoom past this tired backdrop.

The interplay between the shared (the global everyday) and the exceptional (the specific contraventions of Palestinian human rights) is also embodied within *Road Map.* A split-screen depiction of two differently experienced journeys (one impossible to a Palestinian, the other the only viable route for one) is deliberately wearisome—as is the stultified journey itself. As we are dragged through the distinctly more frustrating Palestinian experience, in a fractional fashion we face the injustices imposed according to nationality in this region, as well as a comradeship that is lacking in the sealed, silent, and uninterrupted drive along the more uniform Israeli-only route.

Road Map is composed of jerky, point-of-view cinematography that not only draws in its viewers through a replication of the motion sickness–inducing ride but also speaks of a particular Palestinian sensibility. The technique has become a stalwart of the Second Intifada aesthetic repertoire: *25 Kilometers, Palestine Blues,* and *Route 181,* to name but a few, all feature abundant traveling shots from within vehicles that are featured within the frame. Necessarily, in a conflict over territory, it is crucial that a resistant cinema document the land, but why so through the frame of a vehicle, especially given the centrality of fuel to the viciously skewed negotiations of rights and democracy in the Middle East?

One reason is purely pragmatic and exposes the guerrilla nature of Palestinian cinema. The answer erupts when a *servees* passenger in *25 Kilometers* expresses concern that Awwad's filming will endanger the entire group of them; they might be shot for shooting. Yet the automobile is the safest place from which to film when traditional, static establishing shots leave one more vulnerable than exiting the protective vehicular space or provoking suspicion by parking. Is this not a rewriting of the promotional logics of capitalistic automotive production, with the raw materiality of the commodity splayed before us, faith held within it, but not unrealistically? How secure, then, is the liberal individualist ideal of the car owner, materially or ideologically, within such a scenario? This privatized space offers simple, risible pleasures in *Divine Intervention* where a car allows a character to politely wave at his community while spewing an unheard torrent of obscenities at them. On all levels, the easily understood benefits of these enclosed spaces are presented but then complicated by the dynamics of warfare.

The same could also be said of the camera. Filmmakers such as Sandi Hilal and Alessandro Petti[28] point out how risky it can be to carry a camera, while Nahed Awwad states, "At the beginning the camera was a kind of protection; I was hiding behind the camera in a way, or maybe I was trying to deal with things through the camera to forget my real emotions."[29] In *Ford Transit,* a factual-fictional crossover of sorts, an Israeli soldier asks, "Are you mocking me because of the camera?" before punching Rajai. The security of technology—the camera and the car alike—is called into question by all these instances.

The restlessness of both the driving car and the mobile framing not only betrays the fidgetiness of endangering activity, not only brings us back to the trope of ceaseless wandering that insinuates the refugee experience, but also works dialectically with the precious few static shots in recent Palestinian cinema. *Around* (Mohanad Yaqubi, 2006) is a film that deliberately presents relaxed, motionless shots of the beauty one faces when one finally *arrives* after the monotony of the checkpoints that it also depicts. The land, the territory—what is left of it—is celebrated, recaptured, as it were, in this road trip documentary, a deliberate defiance to one depicted Israeli soldier who seems aghast, through a lifetime's evasive spatio-political education, that there is anything to actually visit in Palestine.

A similar incentive to use cinematography as reclamation is also evident in *Going for a Ride?* which depicts double-exposed phantom images of cars that partially bring back to life what the conflict has destroyed. Like vehicles, film is not just a mode of transportation, it can also usefully warp time and space. As Third Cinema activist Tomás Gutierrez Alea once averred, "Cinema can create genuine ghosts, images of lights and shadows which can't be captured. It's like a shared dream."[30] And this sense of (national history as) diffused, collective ownership is something to which I shall return presently. The wish-fulfillment tendency looms large in Palestinian cinema more generally, for instance in the scene in *Divine Intervention* when E. S. (played by Suleiman himself) hurls a peach pit from his car window and it blows up an Israeli tank. Such inclinations are also noticeable in the willful refusal to dichotomize fact from fiction noticeable in the quasi-documentary, quasi-fantastical proclivities of, say, Hani Abu-Assad and Annemarie Jacir's work. Enas Muthaffar puts it another way: "I'm talking about inventing a new genre . . . Occupation Fiction, like Science Fiction: something surreal because it's fiction, but at the same time related to a certain frame."[31] Within these aesthetic decisions is embedded both the politically vital need to convey the particularities of the everyday, as well as the specific, often unbelievable strangeness of Palestinian life, something, it would appear, that is also a fundamental spark to its filmmakers' creativity and methods.

Primarily, this is a style marked by, as well as discussing, unpredictability, an eagerness to work with, rather than against the Palestinian situation. "There's no use fixing down the script because reality will interfere,"[32] notes Rashid Masharawi of his feature film, conspicuously about a taxi driver, which is currently in preproduction and would, originally, have been shot in now-out-of-bounds Gaza. "It's part of the process, it adds to the film,"[33] claims Nahed Awwad. And so the movies are deliberately random and freewheeling in their structure; improvisation (as with the *servees* drivers) abounds and "acting" and "being" run into each other. In a country without a firm internal system of authority and with multitudinous stateless compatriots, governance—including how a film production is ordered and controlled—must be handled differently.

This strange, proxy freedom is grasped for what it is: simultaneously an intensely marshaled nonfreedom. For those of us watching from spaces of supposedly greater liberties, however, an imbalance of vitality and capacity for new thought becomes surprisingly evident through our own deficiencies. There is little sense that Palestinian movies will change anything—what films ever do in these earth-shattering terms—but the situation is constantly and creatively picked over. For certain directors, making these rather anarchic films is a product of freedom of expression, a living out of the quotidian that insists upon social autonomy within Palestine, rather than something that aims primarily to "convert" an "outside" audience.[34] The movies are also conceived of as an archive of resistance for present as well as future use, concretizing its benefits in a location where change is rapid and destructive.[35]

Via an engagement with these use-values, we confront a refusal for cinema to act solely as a service provider, particularly one that easily assuages guilt about conflict by allowing a compartmentalized, harrowing vision that is almost as easily abandoned upon exiting the screening space. Yes, we run into a lexicon of heroic or tragic figures within these films, but they are too mercurial to ever remain just that. Rashid Masharawi angrily recounts attending a Q&A in Cairo where audience members cried before his film had even begun. "They damage Palestinian cinema," he remarks. Pity of this order is not a preferred endpoint.

Instead there is frequently a difficulty in extracting exact meaning from these films as a method of, on one level, calling for freedom through the very mechanisms and choices of interpretation, and, on another, by disavowing the justice that has rarely been forthcoming through clear, ethical statements about the "truth" of the situation. Representations of the conflict are in constant, blurring motion, never allowed (within these spaces at least) to ossify or to become reified (in a capitalistic-fetishistic sense) so that an audience member might take away something supposedly valuable that is, in essence, already dead. This imperative drives my desired orientation of what lies above: that what I have written might be taken up not as a poor replication of something so vital but as an active intersectional node in a transportation matrix, like cinema, constructing rather than conveying, making rather than carrying.

The Road to "Elsewhere"

Edward Said, that most famous of Palestinian exilic thinkers writing in English, coined a term that has multiple significances for how these road movies activate—he called it *traveling theory*. Through Said's concept, we might begin to engage (with the films) in ways that do justice to and learn from the topic in (and out of) hand. Said argues:

It is never enough for a critic taking the idea of criticism seriously simply to say that interpretation is misinterpretation or that borrowings inevitably involve misreadings. Quite the contrary: it seems to me perfectly possible to judge misreadings (as they occur) as part of a historical transfer of ideas and theories from one setting to another. . . . I see no need here to resort to the theory of limitless intertextuality as an Archimedean point outside the two situations. The particular voyage . . . with all that entails, seems compelling enough, adequate enough for critical scrutiny, unless we want to give up critical consciousness for critical hermeticism.[36]

And so I wish to briefly embark, with Said, on this type of voyage by thinking of cinematic experience and its academic coverage not as description of what supposedly exists (road cartography, as it were), but as shared *constructions* of thoroughfares, as an international endeavor that draws upon certain, often different, skills and knowledges to link together tactical points. One such action is the pooling of a variety of seemingly suitable resources. Within the context of this argument, I would like to draw upon a perception of "the road movie" that does not deny a Westernized knowledge or placement and that acts, at one and the same time, as small-scale subversion and as a direct invitation to audiences to identify (just as they may have done with the references to everyday life). More of this in a moment. Another necessary endeavor is to sincerely learn from the intermediary role that is so often assumed by artists inside and outside of what formal structures exist in a "place" like Palestine. Add to this the negotiating skills of refugees who straddle at least two (often competing) cultural communities, regularly dismantling what blocks obstruct the movement of similarities between the two.

Let us take the case of Annemarie Jacir, a Palestinian with three passports, none of them Palestinian, and a director whose films almost always feature roads. She describes her fascination with them as follows: "it's that never having a base, a home, a place that has been permanent. [It] affects my work and the way I see the world. The only constant place I have ever known is Palestine—it's the only place I have known all my life—and yet I am not allowed to legally live there, to feel secure there. . . . I am not allowed to have residency, to get an ID. . . . It is a place that can be taken from me at any moment."[37] Yet this mobility, so evident in the very structures and themes of these films, prompts a migration of thought too. If we switch metaphors for a moment, mindful of how communication systems require multiple forms of communication, then aren't dislocated peoples often endowed with heightened skills of comparison (which is vital to social change)[38] as well as a multilingual fluency that, despite its frequent imperial legacy, can transmit and translate liberationist struggle with enormous effectiveness? We cannot be naively optimistic about the transferability of all expression, let alone the appositeness of certain specific emancipation gestures in every given environment, but surely there is scope here.

This is where the road movie, as an international genre, comes in. Certainly only a handful of directors would explicitly call their films road movies unprompted, but, then again, it is also the critic's job to forge such links, not in any sense to propose a sort of degraded mimesis, but to hint at the potential for both collectivity and insurrection against the unthinking and politically dubious resonances of established genres. The idea of "the road movie" is not "foreign" to Palestine because Palestine's borders are, as has been demonstrated, not ever themselves closed or secure (whether or not its people wish them to be so). The insinuation of a Palestinian participation in the traditional preoccupations of the road movie—rebellion and freedom[39]—not only democratizes these aspirations, not only exposes how Western ideals (as embodied in the car and road mythologies) are often founded, as we have seen, on extreme exploitation, but also speaks to us from and about that very topography that is consequently reinscribed and colonized. In so doing, Palestinian road movies might work to confuse the hierarchies of expression and create a space for identification that undercuts the more negative, abject implications of the periphery.

Such internationalism permeates Palestinian cinema, as ever, on the stylistic level too. *Divine Intervention* is equally at home with references to Hollywood musicals and Hong Kong martial arts flicks as it is with in-jokes about national politics. *Ford Transit*'s soundtrack draws on Dr. Dre's "Big Ego" and scores from westerns precisely to imply a continuation of various territorial and economic inequities so manifest in this music, to link up various resistance movements and share modes of dignified survival, to point out how porous our world (of ideas) actually is. As Nida Sinnokrot asserts at the beginning of his movie, quite naturally, as an exilic Palestinian, "When I'm in New York, I listen to Palestinian hip-hop. But when I'm in Palestine, I listen to the blues."

Working in unison with the references to everyday life, with the point-of-view shots, these contributions to the international road movie genre insist that "otherness" is ultimately an illusion, but, at the same time, an enforced and very much experienced condition. This too is why I have awkwardly positioned myself as a participant within this road building and road travel.

The overlaps *and* the vehement separations that distinguish my journeys into Palestine and its cinema from those of others insist, through their similarities, a commonality and, through their variations, an urgency to liberate access to all the ways through. This act of comparison happens, and must repeatedly happen, on unstable ground as the Occupation mutates so rapidly and dramatically.

Within the seismography of all such conflicts, opportunities are afforded at the same time as others are ripped away, and one of the road-building skills that has been constantly maintained—ironically, through Palestine and its diaspora's spatial instability—is a concentration upon dialogical dexterity. Certainly there are forces at work attempting, often successfully, to block Palestinian voices, but there may be other, partial modes of arrival, including film production. As director Raed El Helou[40] points out, "I don't speak English well; I speak no other language except Arabic and that is one of my weak points. But I speak cinema."[41] From here, it makes sense to now return to the end of Mahmoud Darwish's poem because it deals with the paradoxical and concomitant fragility and power of expression, the sharing of the territories of metaphor and everyday life:

> We have a country of words. Speak speak so I can put my road on the stone of a stone.
> We have a country of words. Speak speak so we may know the end of This travel.[42]

Notes

I am enormously grateful to the following filmmakers for their help with this project: Nahed Awwad, Sandi Hilal, Annemarie Jacir, Rashid Masharawi, Enas Muthaffar, Alessandro Petti, Nida Sinnokrot, and Mohanad Yaqubi. Thanks also to Nick Denes for doing most of the driving and for creating a new Palestinian subgenre: the segway movie. As ever, I am deeply indebted to Reem Fadda for being a wonderful host, for discussing these ideas with me, for introducing me to some of the most exciting artists in Palestine, and for putting up with my inexpert handling of forbidden roads of all kinds.

1. Darwish, "We Travel Like Other People," 31.

2. It is difficult to accurately gauge how many Palestinian refugees there are globally, but the current estimate is 7.2 million (Al-Awda: The Palestinian Right to Return Coalition, "FAQs on Refugees," www.al-awda.org/faq-refugees.html). Of these, according to 2005 figures, 4,283,892 were officially registered by the United Nations Relief and Works Agency (UNRWA) as holding refugee status in either Jordan,

Syria, Lebanon, or Palestine (United Nations Relief and Works Agency, "Number of Registered Refugees," at www.un.org/unrwa/refugees/pdf/reg-ref.pdf).

3. Rashid Masharawi, interview with author, September 10, 2007.

4. To avoid repetition, I would like to point out here that all the movies mentioned in this chapter should be considered Palestinian. However, "Palestine," as I argue throughout, is a fragile and amorphous concept. In order to honor these filmmakers' aspirations toward national liberation and self-determination, even films partially shot outside Palestine or financed by funding bodies from other countries (including Israel) are best thought of as primarily Palestinian.

5. Multiplicity is a group of visual and spatial culture activists comprised of, at this point, Stefano Boeri, Maddalena Bregani, Marco Gentile, Maki Gherzi, Matteo Ghidoni, Sandi Hilal, Isabella Inti, Francesco Jodice, Anniina Koivu, John Palmesino, Alessandro Petti, Cecilia Pirovano, Salvatore Porcaro, Francesca Recchia, Eduardo Staszowski, and Kasia Teodorczuk.

6. Nahed Awwad, interview with author, September 4, 2007.

7. Enas Muthaffar, interview with author, September 5, 2007.

8. For further explorations of this idea, see Cohan and Hark, "Introduction," in *The Road Movie Book*, 1.

9. See Office of the Spokesman, *A Performance-Based Roadmap to a Permanent Two-State Solution*.

10. See Suisman et al., *The Arc: A Formal Structure for a Palestinian State*.

11. This is a topic imaginatively and persuasively discussed throughout Weizman, *Hollow Land: Israel's Architecture of Occupation*.

12. Palestinian Central Bureau of Statistics, "PCBS: Released the Results of the Annual Report on Transportation and Communication Statistics in the Palestinian Territory, 2006." A B'Tselem (Israeli Information Center for Human Rights in the Occupied Territories) report of 2004, working with the total 732 km of Israeli-claimed of two years previous, breaks down the usage into totally forbidden roads (124 km) and roads that require a permit (608), which de facto prohibits most of the Palestinian population. B'Tselem, *Forbidden Roads: Israel's Discriminatory Road Regime in the West Bank*, 14, 16, 18.

13. So claims B'Tselem, *Forbidden Roads*, 5.

14. Ibid., 3, likens the state of play in Palestine to the former South African regime, and this phrase is in common parlance among a good number of pro-Palestinian activists (although many others think the conflation of the two very different political and historical situations should be avoided).

15. Ibid.

16. According to the UN Office for the Coordination of Humanitarian Affairs (OCHA) Report, December 2003, cited in "Fact Sheets—Health."

17. I heard this phrase repeatedly during a trip to Palestine in 2007, as well as from pro-Palestine activists in the United Kingdom.

18. Figures derived from Weizman, *Hollow Land*, 147, where he cites statistics from the Union of Palestinian Medical Relief Committees.

19. An uncited reference to the OCHA report, cited in Hass, "Israeli Restrictions Create Isolated Enclaves in West Bank."

20. Dabashi, "Introduction," in *Dreams of a Nation: On Palestinian Cinema,* 7.

21. Rashid Masharawi, interview with author, September 10, 2007.

22. For a full account of this debate, see Stam, "Beyond Third Cinema: The Aesthetics of Hybridity," in *Rethinking Third Cinema,* 33.

23. For the rationale behind this boycott, see Palestinian Campaign for the Academic and Cultural Boycott of Israel, "Palestinian Filmmakers, Artists and Cultural Workers Call for a Cultural Boycott of Israel."

24. Rashid Masharawi, interview with author, September 10, 2007.

25. Sandi Hilal, interview with author, September 5, 2007.

26. Alessandro Petti, interview with author, September 5, 2007.

27. Ibid.

28. Sandi Hilal and Alessandro Petti, interview with author, September 5, 2007.

29. Nahed Awwad, interview with author, September 4, 2007.

30. Gutiérrez Alea, "The Viewer's Dialectic."

31. Enas Muthaffar, interview with author, September 5, 2007.

32. Rashid Masharawi, interview with author, September 10, 2007.

33. Nahed Awwad, interview with author, September 4, 2007.

34. Some of these sentiments were expressed by Rashid Mashrawi, interview with author, September 10, 2007.

35. Sandi Hilal, in particular, points to this as one of her motives (interview with author, September 5, 2007.).

36. Said, *The World, The Text, and the Critic,* 236–37.

37. Annemarie Jacir, e-mail correspondence, August 10, 2007.

38. See, for example, this comment by Nahed Awwad: "I'm considered luckier than other Palestinians because I have the chance to travel outside and when you travel outside you can see the difference. You can see normal life and then you can compare and then you can start to say, 'No, it should not be like this.' People who have only lived within Palestine, especially over the last fifteen to twenty years and haven't left either for economic reasons, or because they've not been permitted to leave . . . begin to believe that things are normal and this is the way it should be. This becomes a way for them to protect themselves. It's adjustment, I don't think it's the healthy way to do it, but it's protection." Later on she continues, "Even when I travel outside, I become more attached to Palestine, it's something inside me." Nahed Awwad, interview with author, September 4, 2007.

39. For a more detailed account of these generic characteristics, see Laderman, *Driving Visions: Exploring the Road Movie,* 19–23.

40. Also known as Raed Al Helou (see above) and Raed Helou. These inconsistencies are fairly typical when a language with a different alphabet, such as Arabic, is transliterated into Roman lettering.

41. Raed El Helou interviewed in Habreich-Euvrard, *Israéliens, Palestiniens que peut le cinema? Carnet de route,* 95. Interestingly, this book is published in French and I have had to retranslate a quotation that was almost certainly originally delivered in English.

42. Darwish, "We Travel Like Other People," 31.

Bibliography

Al-Awda: The Palestinian Right to Return Coalition. "FAQs on Refugees." At www. al-awda.org/faq-refugees.html (accessed October 10, 2007).

Abu-Rabi', Ibrahim. *Contemporary Arab Thought: Studies in Post-1967 Arab Intellectual History.* London: Pluto Press, 2007.

B'Tselem. *Forbidden Roads: Israel's Discriminatory Road Regime in the West Bank.* Jerusalem: B'Tselem, 2004.

Cohan, Steven, and Ina Rae Hark, eds. *The Road Movie Book.* London: Routledge, 1997.

Dabashi, Hamid, ed. *Dreams of a Nation: On Palestinian Cinema.* London: Verso, 2006.

Darwish, Mahmoud. "We Travel Like Other People." In Victims of a Map. Translated by Abdullah al-Udhari. London: Al-Saqi Books, 1984.

Dorsey, David A. *The Roads and Highways of Ancient Israel.* Baltimore: Johns Hopkins University Press, 1991.

"Fact Sheets—Health." *Palestine Monitor.* At www.palestinemonitor.org/spip/health. html (accessed August 22, 2007).

Fischer, Moshe, Benjamin Isaac, and Israel Roll. *Roman Roads in Judaea II: The Jaffa-Jerusalem Roads.* Oxford: Tempus Reparatum, 1996.

Gutiérrez Alea, Tomás. Translated by Julia Lesage. "The Viewer's Dialectic." *Jump Cut* 29 (February 1984): 18–21. Available at www.ejumpcut.org/archive/onlinessays/JC29folder/ViewersDialec1.html (accessed September 8, 2007).

Halbreich-Euvrard, Janine. *Israéliens, Palestiniens que peut le cinema? Carnet de route.* Paris: Éditions Michalon, 2005.

Hass, Amira. "Israeli Restrictions Create Isolated Enclaves in West Bank." *Occupation Magazine—Life under Occupation.* At www.kibush.co.il/show_file. asp?num=12852 (accessed September 4, 2007).

Isaac, Benjamin, and Israel Roll. *Roman Roads in Judaea I: The Legio-Scythopolis Road.* Oxford: B.A.R. International Series, 1982.

Laderman, David. *Driving Visions: Exploring the Road Movie.* Austin: University of Texas Press, 2002.

Office of the Spokesman. *A Performance-Based Roadmap to a Permanent Two-State Solution.* Washington, DC: U.S. Government, 2003.

Palestinian Campaign for the Academic and Cultural Boycott of Israel. "Palestinian Filmmakers, Artists and Cultural Workers Call for a Cultural Boycott of Israel." At www.pacbi.org/boycott_news_more.php?id=315_0_1_0_C (accessed August 25, 2007).

Palestinian Central Bureau of Statistics. "PCBS: Released the Results of the Annual Report on Transportation and Communication Statistics in the Palestinian Territory, 2006." At www.pcbs.gov.ps/DesktopDefault.aspx?tabID=3355&lang=en (accessed September 13, 2007).

Said, Edward. *The World, the Text, and the Critic.* London: Vintage, 1991.

Stam, Robert. "Beyond Third Cinema: The Aesthetics of Hybridity." In *Rethinking Third Cinema,* edited by Anthony R. Guneratne and Wimal Dissanayake,

31–48. London: Routledge, 2003.

Suisman, Doug, Steven N. Simon, Glenn E. Robinson, C. Ross Anthony, and Michael Schoenbaum. *The Arc: A Formal Structure for a Palestinian State.* 2005; Santa Monica, CA: RAND Corporation, 2007.

United Nations Relief and Works Agency. "Number of Registered Refugees." At www.un.org/unrwa/refugees/pdf/reg-ref.pdf (accessed October 10, 2007).

Weizman, Eyal. *Hollow Land: Israel's Architecture of Occupation.* London: Verso, 2007.

Islands at the Edge of History

Landscape and the Past in Recent Scottish-Gaelic Films

This chapter examines the Scottish-Gaelic-language films *An Iobairt/ The Sacrifice* (Gerda Stevenson, UK, 1996), and *Seachd: The Inaccessible Pinnacle* (Simon Miller, UK, 2007). Produced on the periphery of Scotland, Gaelic films have been all but ignored in academic debates until now. Yet the engagement of the Gaelic oral storytelling tradition with cinema in certain of these films is on a par with that often celebrated in African cinema. Gaelic films in Scotland emerged along with a Gaelic Renaissance that has flourished since the 1980s. Accordingly, certain Gaelic films deploy epic, mythical, or otherwise allegorical narratives to reconsider stereotypical conceptions of Scotland's remoter edges as somehow "lost" in the past. Instead, situating themselves within the storytelling tradition, and through a dynamic use of landscape, they examine how the periphery's past remains active in the Gàidhealtachd (Gaeldom). In this way, in contrast to many previous films set in the Gàidhealtachd, these Gaelic films actively explore the potential that film offers for assisting the survival, if not the rejuvenation, of Gaelic culture.

Scotland's Cinematic Islands

The Gàidhealtachd includes certain remote parts of the Highlands and Islands of Scotland, in particular the Western Isles where the Gaelic language is still spoken by over 60 percent of the population. Once the dominant language in Scotland, Gaelic is now in decline, with less than 60,000 Gaelic speakers in Scotland (1.2 percent of the population). Even so, the Gàidhealtachd retains a distinctive linguistic and cultural identity that is evident in recent Gaelic films.

There is a long tradition of films set on Scotland's remoter islands, including, but not limited to, those in the Gàidhealtachd. As Duncan Petrie points out in *Screening Scotland* (2000), the island is a "literal and metaphorical figure" frequently used to represent Scotland, "a space in which remoteness or isolation is enhanced by virtue of its detachment from the mainland."[1] There is simply not space here for an exhaustive list of these films, which ranges from the ethnographic *St. Kilda: Britain's Loneliest Isle* (Paul Robello et al., UK, 1928) through Ealing comedies like *Whisky Galore!* (Alexander Mackendrick, UK, 1949) and cult classics like *Madame Sin* (David Greene, UK, 1972) to recent mainstream dramas like *The Rocket Post* (Stephen Whittaker, UK, 2004). With the possible exception of certain recent art films like *Play Me Something* (Timothy Neat, UK, 1989), in the majority of such films it is the supposedly dangerous, romantic, or fantastic attributes of the peripheral wilderness, those characteristics that have come to epitomize Scotland's existence at the extreme edge of the world, that are evoked by a Scottish island location or setting. This stereotypical view of Scotland as a primitive wilderness was first defined during the eighteenth and nineteenth centuries, in particular during the visit of King George IV to Scotland in 1822, when Sir Walter Scott was responsible for solidifying tartanry as the overarching symbol of Scotland and Scottish identity.[2] The deployment of tartanry in cinema has received extensive coverage since Colin McArthur's groundbreaking anthology, *Scotch Reels* (1982), which was influenced by Malcolm Chapman's book, *The Gaelic Vision in Scottish Culture* (1978). In the types of film listed above, the islands continue to resonate with mythical conceptions of Scotland as a savage wilderness, or a romantic, untamed land bypassed by the advances of civilization. The major difference in the Gaelic films *An Iobairt* and *Seachd* (both shot and set on Skye) is that they are based on native characters, rather than visitors to the islands, and attempt to tap into and recover a rejuvenative, local past from within the local landscape. This search within history both preserves tradition and ensures future progression of the Gàidhealtachd. It is this difference that ensures that these indigenous Gaelic films stand out from the other island-based films that are—with the notable exception of *Play Me Something,* which has some Gaelic dialogue and singing—their English-language counterparts. Before I analyze these Gaelic films, however, they need to be placed in a more localized context.

Gaelic Renaissance, Gaelic Films

In *Reimagining Culture: Histories, Identities, and the Gaelic Renaissance* (1997) Sharon Macdonald describes the Gaelic Renaissance that has taken place in the Highlands and Islands of Scotland since the 1980s. For Macdonald this renaissance, although admittedly the forefront of a much longer process that began in the late eighteenth century, marks a significant "reimagining of Gaelic culture."[3] Not surprisingly, this revival focused on the rejuvenation of the Gaelic language, a process that first received significant state support in the 1960s.[4] A number of other measures followed over the coming decades, including recognition—in the Education (Scotland) Act of 1980—of the need for Gaelic to be taught in schools in Gaelic-speaking areas, and the subsequent Grants for Gaelic Language Education (Scotland) Regulations of 1986.[5] A Minister for Gaelic was first appointed by the Scottish Executive in 1997, the European Charter for Regional or Minority Languages was signed by the Labour Party in 2000, in 2003 the Scottish Executive published a draft of a Gaelic Language Bill,[6] and the Gaelic Language Act (given Royal Assent in 2005) established the Bòrd na Gàidhlig (with the responsibility of preserving Gaelic as an official language in Scotland), in 2006.[7]

In this context, Gaelic media emerged due to the Broadcasting Acts of 1990 and 1996, which established state support for Gaelic broadcasting in Scotland.[8] In 1990 the Broadcasting Act established the Gaelic Television Fund with an annual sum of £9.5 million (around U.S. $15.5 million). In 1993 Comataidh Telebhisein Gàidhlig (Gaelic Television Committee) (CTG), began broadcasting Gaelic television. The Broadcasting Act of 1996 introduced Gaelic radio to the remit of the fund, although without any additional funding, and in 1998 the budget was slightly reduced. In 1997 the committee changed its name to Comataidh Craolaidh Gàidhlig (The Gaelic Broadcasting Committee) (CCG). In 2003 the Communications Act replaced CCG with the Serbheis Nam Meadhanan Gàidhlig (Gaelic Media Service) (GMS), with the aim of establishing a "dedicated Gaelic television channel."[9] In 2007 the Scottish Executive backed this venture by adding an additional annual £3 million (around U.S. $4.8 million) to the GMS budget,[10] which renamed itself again, to MG ALBA (Meadhanan Gàidhlig ALBA, Gaelic Media Scotland). The channel, BBC ALBA, was launched in September 2008.

Practically all Gaelic-language films have been part-funded by CTG, CCG, or GMS. As such, although *Seachd* is a feature film designed for cinema release, prior to its release the majority of Gaelic-language films were made initially for television. *An Iobairt* (1996) was part of the Geur Ghèarr

158

scheme, which ran from 1996 to 1998 and was part-funded by CTG/CCG, the Scottish Film Production Fund, and BBC Scotland.[11] *An Iobairt* is a twenty-four-minute color short, shot on 35 mm, directed by the actress Gerda Stevenson (who previously starred in *Blue Black Permanent* [Margaret Tait, UK, 1992]), and produced by Lucy Conan on a budget of around £50,000 (around U.S. $80,500) mostly supplied by CTG, BBC Scotland, and the SFPF, with an additional £5,000 (around U.S. $8,050) coming from Skye and Lochalsh Enterprise. It was scripted by Skye native Aonghas MacNeacail. Several other short films were made under the Geur Ghèarr scheme, *Roimh Ghaoth A'Gheamhraidh/Before Winter Winds* (Bill MacLeod, UK, 1996), *Ag Iasgach/Fishing* (Roddy Cunningham, UK, 1997), *A'Bhean Eudach/The Jealous Sister* (Domhnall Ruadh, UK, 1997), *Dathan/Colours* (Iain F. MacLeod, UK, 1998), *Keino* (Iseabil Maciver, UK, 1998), and *Mac* (Alasdair Maclean, UK, 1998). Two feature films were also made, *As An Eilean/From the Island* (Mike Alexander, UK, 1995) and *Seachd: The Inaccessible Pinnacle* (2007). These features follow in the footsteps of what is arguably the first Gaelic feature, *Hero* (Barney Platts-Mills, UK, 1982), and the first short, *Sealladh/The Vision* (Douglas Mackinnon, UK, 1992). *Hero* was funded by Channel 4 (unaware it was to be in Gaelic), whose authentic Gaelic status is often questioned because of its cast of nonnative speakers. *Sealladh* is a fifteen-minute color short shot on 35 mm, partly funded by CTG and Channel 4, and starring Peter Mullan. *Sealladh* was directed by Douglas Mackinnon, a filmmaker born on Skye who—after many years in television—gained international esteem with *The Flying Scotsman* (UK, 2006). *As An Eilean* cost around £750,000 (around U.S. $1.2 million), £500,000 (U.S. $805,000) of which came from the CTG with the rest from Channel 4, Grampian TV, the Ross and Cromarty District Council, Highlands Regional Council, and Highlands and Islands Enterprise. Incredibly, a decade later, *Seachd* was shot on HD at a cost of £680,000 (around U.S. $1.1 million), again with approximately two-thirds of the funding from GMS and the rest from BBC Scotland and Scottish Screen. *Seachd* is a reworking of *Foighidinn: The Crimson Snowdrop/Patience* (Simon Miller, Scotland, 2003), a fifteen-minute color short, shot on 35 mm Anamorphic film stock taken from the remains of reels from *Wimbledon* (Richard Loncraine, UK/France, 2004) and *Bridget Jones: The Edge of Reason* (Beeban Kidron, UK/France/Germany/Ireland/USA, 2004), which director Simon Miller persuaded the production company Working Title to donate.[12] A Young Films production, *Foighidinn* cost £60,000 (around U.S. $97,000), half of which came from Scottish Screen with the other half from GMS and BBC Scotland. The original script for *Foighidinn* was reworked into Gaelic by Aonghas MacNeacail, who also worked on the script for *Seachd*.

Macdonald positions the Gaelic Renaissance within a national context, stating: "The Gaelic Renaissance is part of Scottish national identity and part of the wider movements of ethnonationalism within the established nation-states of Europe."[13] The revival of interest in Gaelic culture coincides with the drive for national independence that culminated in Scotland's devolution from the state of Britain in 1997. Indeed, Scotland's cultural outpourings of the 1980s and 1990s are often attributed to the discovery of North Sea oil, the growth of the Scottish National Party, and the failed referendum on devolution and the election of the Conservative Party, both in 1979. For instance, in *Contemporary Scottish Fictions* (2005), Duncan Petrie draws this conclusion, noting the upsurge in literary, televisual, and cinematic creativity that followed in the 1980s and 1990s. Following the direction of critics like Macdonald and Petrie, then, it is possible to see the emergence of Gaelic media as part of this cultural upsurge, as Scotland attempted to redefine itself culturally in ways that seemed impossible politically. Thus although the short-lived Geur Ghèarr initiative may in retrospect appear a blip in the history of Gaelic broadcasting, the precedent set by *Hero* and *Sealladh,* and the recent emergence of *Foighidinn* and *Seachd* (both produced by Chris Young on the Isle of Skye) suggest that Gaelic filmmaking remains a, albeit intermittent, facet of the Gaelic Renaissance.

Although the films under discussion are not representative of all Gaelic films, or television dramas generally, I have selected them for two reasons. Firstly, because of their shared concerns with storytelling, the history of the islands, and landscape. Secondly, in addition to their pertinence to the theme of this collection, their existence should be made known to a wider audience. Although there is a growing body of work on Scotland and cinema, with the exception of two postgraduate theses by students from Glasgow University languishing in the Scottish Screen archive, and a discussion of Gaelic television drama in a recent article by Mike Cormack,[14] there is practically nothing published addressing these Gaelic-language films. As a nonnative speaker and an outsider of the region I am not the ideal voice to begin a discussion of these films, yet I do so nonetheless in the hope that it will open up space for further debate.

The Storytelling Tradition and Gaelic Films

The oral tradition in the Gàidhealtachd is usually associated with the singing of Gaelic songs and verses by bards, whose practice acted as a living preserve of history since before the arrival of the Romans in the first century AD.[15] In *The Last of the Free: A History of the Highlands and Islands* (1999), James

Hunter discusses how the fourteenth- and fifteenth-century bardic family the MacMhuirichs "made it their business to be repositories of the Gaelic-speaking world's history, myth and lore,"[16] a practice that stemmed from the arrival of their ancestors from Ireland in the thirteenth century.[17] However, the power of the bards has diminished over the centuries since the forfeiture of the Lordship of the Isles in 1493, the most deliberate curtailment of their power arriving with pronouncements against the bards, and the Gaelic tongue in general, in the Statutes of Iona of 1609.[18] Yet Gaelic folklore was preserved orally in local communities, for instance in songs to accompany agrarian work and to suit various everyday occasions.[19] Despite the debilitating effect on the Gàidhealtachd of the aftermath of Culloden in 1746, the Protestant reformations of the sixteenth and seventeenth centuries, and the clearances, famine, and emigrations of the eighteenth and nineteenth, bàrd baile (township or village poets)—that Thomas McKean describes as "heirs of the professional bards"[20]—emerged in the nineteenth century, and continue to exist today.[21]

Existing discussions of an oral storytelling tradition in cinema often focus on African cinema. In *Black African Cinema* (1994), Nwachukwu Frank Ukadike discusses how the African oral tradition of "making a point with stories" was incorporated into African cinema,[22] emphasizing the deployment of "metaphor and proverbs, the mythic components and poetic resonances of the oral tradition,"[23] to confront ideology and engage with discussions of national significance.[24] Although this is not the place for a detailed examination of these ideas, suffice it to say that the same type of argument can be applied to certain Gaelic films.

The mythical story told in *Foighidinn* began life as an idea of English director Simon Miller, who wanted to capture on film the visceral excitement of being in the presence of a storyteller.[25] As the script developed, however, the narrative of *Foighidinn* was framed by a seanair/grandfather telling a story to a captive audience of young children, the story being dramatized for the benefit of the film's viewers. Significantly, in *Foighidinn* this seanair is played by the Gaelic bard and novelist Aonghas Padraig Caimbeul, who begins by telling the children—in response to their impertinent query, "Is this going to be *another* story?"—that

there is a whole world of difference . . . between a story and the truth. The history books tell you that Levingstoun—where I was born—was founded by Leving of Levingstoun in the reign of King Edgar. The history books will also tell you that Leving of Levingstoun had three sons. . . . What the history books do not tell you is that they lie!

After this framing scene valorizing the oral tradition over written versions of history, a story from the past is then enacted. The seanair narrates the events we see taking place. His voice is heard on the voiceover, effectively positioning the audience among the children as they/we learn of the Gaelic past. Thus, when the story cuts back to the present, and the children ask questions of the storyteller, there is a sense of engagement between audience and film in the act of storytelling. In this way, *Foighidinn*—and later *Seachd,* which includes a re-creation of this sequence—demonstrate the need to pass on Gaelic history to future generations through the oral storytelling tradition.

This recurring theme in Gaelic film can also be explained by the various roles played by writers with a background or interest in the oral storytelling tradition. For instance, the Gaelic bard Aonghas MacNeacail worked on many of these films. He was the Gaelic-language consultant on *Hero,* scripted *An Iobairt,* reworked Simon Miller's script for *Foighidinn* into Gaelic, and co-wrote *Seachd.* MacNeacail's poetry examines the ancient past of the Gàidhealtachd and its relationship to the landscape, as seen in poems such as *an catadh mór/the great snowbattle* (1984). The Gaelic playwright Iain F. MacLeod also worked on the script for *Seachd,* perhaps bringing to it something of his previous role as Callum—a young man interested in the oral tradition—in *As An Eilean.*

Thus, although Gaelic films do not yet demonstrate the often formally sophisticated representation of the griot of the African films of directors like Ousmane Sembene, their recurring emphasis on storytelling demonstrates the central positioning of the act of mythologizing Gaelic culture and folklore in these films. *An Iobairt* is set in the present day, but explores the informing presence of the past on modern-day Gaelic society, and *Foighidinn* and *Seachd* are both mythical stories of ancient kingly warrior heroes and sleeping maidens that obliquely reflect upon the future of Gaelic traditions in the contemporary world. Indeed, a number of the Geur Gheàrr shorts could be analyzed in this way. *Roimh Ghaoth A'Gheamhraidh* starkly contrasts nature and industry, past and present, and innocence and guilt in a modern-day setting that has very deliberate epic overtones; *A'Bhean Eudach* is a mythical examination of empowered and dangerous female sexuality in the style of Angela Carter; by pastiching film noir *Keino* also explores female sexuality as a motivating force for narrative and society; *Dathan* attempts to reinspire an uplifting love of life into religion through embracing art and the landscape; and *Mac* examines the role of fantasy in constructing Gaelic identity in an increasingly globalized culture. Finally, *Sealladh,* while set during the nineteenth-century potato famine, explores the debilitating effect of religious dogma and the equivalent vice of self-serving capitalism.

Recent Gaelic films, then, are part of both the Gaelic Renaissance and the more general, national flourishing of culture in Scotland, and they consider the past as a potentially active force for changing the future. Their evocation of the past also resonates with other cultural developments of the 1980s and 1990s in Scotland, such as literary explorations of the resonance of the past in the present in the works of writers like Iain Chrichton Smith and George Mackay Brown, the latter's *Beside the Ocean of Time* (1994) being a case in point. Douglas Gifford considers this development as typical of contemporary Scottish literature, where he notes a "rediscovered sense of the limitless imaginative possibilities of the idea of Scotland, or Scotlands, a matrix of myths, attitudes, possibilities, histories."[26] Similarly, discussing Scottish drama, Adrienne Scullion (1995) argues that "the role of mythology, legend and fable, the Gothic, the supernatural and the unconscious within the development of the Scottish imagination" illustrates "a sophisticated engagement with the fantastic that some cultures might celebrate as magic realism."[27] Alongside developments in these other artistic spheres, then, a return to mythology and the imagined possibility of different histories (or different "Scotlands") is clearly evident in certain Gaelic films. I will now examine the different ways the past is deployed in two Gaelic films that engage with the renaissance of Gaelic culture, *An Iobairt* and *Seachd*.

Landscapes of the Past

An Iobairt features two friends who go peat digging on Skye. The allegorical quality of the narrative is foregrounded by their names, Esan (Domhnall Ruadh) and Ise (Ceit Kearney), *he* and *she* in Gaelic. The husband of Ise, also the business partner of Esan, went missing on Halloween. He was a boat repairer who recently fell on hard times. There is a suspicion that his disappearance may have been suicide, or simply contrivance to ensure an insurance payment. As the couple disturb the peat they are interrupted by the ghostly specter of a figure clad in the black robes of a monk. In fact, the narrative is interrupted on several occasions by scenes from a pre-Christian past, when this druidic monk was a willing sacrifice, his ghost's reappearance being due to the two friends' disturbance of his grave in the peat. After his skeleton is uncovered, police and an archaeologist arrive. Elsewhere on the island, the car of the husband of Ise is recovered from a loch.

Throughout *An Iobairt,* scenes from the Gàidhealtachd's pre-Christian past interrupt the narrative without warning, as do shots of swirling red water that are only explained at the very end of the film when the door of the red car of the husband of Ise is pulled from a loch. Time is thus confused in the film, as past, present, and future crowd in on one another without warning. The flashbacks to the pre-Christian past are not motivated by character memory and belong instead to the landscape in which the monk is buried. Similarly, the meaning of the shots of red water cannot be known to Ise, even though they are signaled by eyeline matches as though premonitions on her part. In both instances, past and future are brought together in the present by place and mingle in the experiences of the characters in the landscape.

Initially the evocation of the Gàidhealtachd's past seems somewhat stereotypical. The willing sacrifice of the monk is depicted in a wooded glade, complete with mist and eerie musical accompaniment. A druidic past in which willing sacrifices were made to the land could evoke eighteenth-century constructions of the Gael as prehistoric druid, its depiction of a misty past of weird rites expressing precisely the mysticism that has surrounded the Gàidhealtachd ever since.[28] Instead, however, *An Iobairt* deliberately engages the past with the present to suggest its continued relevance in the process of Gaelic Renaissance.

Evoking Bergsonian or Deleuzian layers of the past like those Patricia Pisters uncovers in Tangier in this collection, the appearance of the monk's ghost in the present is depicted using a conventional shot-reverse-shot pattern that suggests the copresence of past and present. The first time it appears the shot frames Esan and Ise in the foreground, on either side of the monk, who is a centered but out-of-focus figure in the middle distance. The reverse shot shows their puzzled faces, and the return to the original position, an empty landscape. Again, when the two characters shelter from the rain in the van, and briefly kiss, the monk is seen through the misted windshield. When they leave the van, however, he is gone. A cyclical narrative that begins and ends with the two characters arriving and departing in the little gray van, *An Iobairt* suggests that rather than lost to time, the peripheral islands of the Gàidhealtachd contain a layered past that must be revived, or excavated, if its relevance to the present is to be uncovered. In this respect the film's conflation of the monk, a willing sacrifice in the past to ensure a good harvest, and the husband of Ise, a willing sacrifice in the present for insurance money, is most telling. Like the monk, the husband of Ise also returns from the submerged depths, as the door of his car is pulled from the loch. Past and present are also shown to match when the monk's ghost lays its hand over the hand of its own skeleton, and again when a graphic match is used to seamlessly link the ax stroke that beheaded the monk in the past with the spade digging into the peat in the present.

In these ways the missing husband comes to replace the monk, representing a new founding sacrifice for the land. The jumbling of time through the use of unmotivated flashbacks, and flash forward suggestive of second sight, formally demonstrate a belief in the interaction of different layers of the past in the Gàidhealtachd. The landscape is figured as a repository of time, a giant, shifting memory in which past, present, and future collide, and where the past has the ability to inform the present, to be recycled, or revived. Notably, the archaeologist who examines the skeleton and informs Ise and Esan (and the viewer) of the fate of the willing sacrifice in the past was played by Margaret Bennett the folklorist and Gaelic singer. In Bennett's presence there is a deliberate blending of reality with fiction. The Gaelic singer embodies a physical memory of the oral past, and accordingly it resides with her to inform us of events that took place in the past, which are now a part of the landscape.

An Iobairt is ambivalent as to the future, as the revival of the past has also brought with it another sacrifice. The husband of Ise, finding his traditional way of life no longer tenable, has willingly given his life for his wife. Yet what the consequences of this will be for the future of the island and its inhabitants simply cannot be seen. In this way, as part of a general context, in *An Iobairt* the Gaelic Renaissance seems to be considered potentially rejuvenative for the Gàidhealtachd, but with as yet entirely unclear consequences.

Made nearly a decade after the end of the Geur Gheàrr scheme, *Seachd* views the context of the Gaelic Renaissance in a far more positive manner. *Seachd* is a reworking and expansion of a previous short film, *Foighidinn,* made by the same director and producer team of Simon Miller and Chris Young. *Foighidinn* begins in the present day, on Christmas Eve, with three young children impatient to open their presents. Caught by their seanair/ grandfather (Aonghas Padraig Caimbeul), they listen attentively as he tells them a story about patience, an allegory for the need for phenomenal patience throughout history if the once-powerful Gaelic culture is to survive in the present day. The mythical story is set 800 years ago, and tells of a young medieval nobleman, Am Mac Bu Shine (literally, The Eldest Son) (Aonghas MacDhomhnaill), the son of Leving of Levingstoun. On the verge of marrying for his father's wishes, Am Mac Bu Shine falls in love with a sheep farmer's daughter Ailsa MacLeod (Kathleen NicDhomhnaill). Presenting his young love with a lip balm that he has manufactured, Am Mac Bu Shine unwittingly poisons her, sending her into a deep sleep. A local sea-witch (Gerda Stevenson, director of *An Iobairt*) tells him that the only remedy is a similar brew concocted with the flower of the crimson snowdrop, but that this flower is now extinct. For seven years Am Mac Bu Shine searches for the flower. Finally, he finds one on top of the mountain Sgurr Dearg (Inaccessible Pinnacle) of the Cuillin mountain range, on Skye. Returning to Ailsa, however, Am Mac Bu Shine arrives only to witness her sudden death. The curse he suffers as a consequence is that his heart beats once for every ten times that of a normal man. The story ends with Aonghas, one of the three young children, listening to the abnormally slow heartbeat of his seanair!

In *Foighidinn* the quest for the crimson snowdrop is clearly intended to illustrate the unlikely survival of Gaelic culture in the Gàidhealtachd. When Am Mac Bu Shine reaches the summit of the peak, his final chance to find the flower, he states: "Nothing could live up here, nothing." However, it is precisely there that he finds the crimson snowdrop, stressing the hardiness of Gaelic culture, its endurance and stoicism in isolation, its patience. The shot of the crimson snowdrop dissolves to a shot of the storyteller in the present, to emphasize that the mythical hero can and did live "up here" at the edge of the world for centuries. He survives into the present day despite the decline of Gaelic culture, as seen in the failure of Am Mac Bu Shine to reach Ailsa before she died, which led to a slowing down of time (the storyteller's slowed heartbeat is matched by repeated shots of the clock as it edges toward midnight on Christmas Eve), as Gaelic culture awaits its renaissance.

As the three children in the present mirror Am Mac Bu Shine's posture in the past, placing their hands on their hearts, the hands of the clock are shown standing at midnight. It is on this generation that *Foighidinn* places the responsibility of maintaining Gaelic culture into a new dawn. Accordingly, the final word the storyteller speaks to the sleepy Aonghas and his siblings is "foighidinn" (patience). In the context of the Gaelic Renaissance there is a similar sense of sacrifice involved here as there was in *An Iobairt*, with Gaelic culture shown to only survive at a dreadful cost. However, there is also a great deal of strength in Gaelic culture, as symbolized by the heart that only needs to beat once for every ten beats of a normal man, a heart strengthened by the crimson snowdrop, the flower that represents a history of suffering and isolation at the peripheral summit of the world. Significantly, the burden of renaissance is placed on the children, the target audience of the film.

Seachd keeps the major themes and preoccupations of *Foighidinn* intact, especially the focus on the storytelling tradition in certain Gaelic films. However, it greatly develops the previous film's examination of the landscape. The narrative of *Seachd* tells of three young children, suddenly orphaned when their mother and father fall to their deaths mountaineering on Sgurr Dearg. Brought up by their grandparents, they are told a number of stories by their grandfather Aonghas (Aonghas Padraig Caimbeul), including the story of the Crimson Snowdrop, which is represented by footage from *Foighidinn* cut into the feature film. The youngest of the three, Aonghas, aged nine (Pàdruig

Moireasdan), is embittered by his parents' death and rejects the role of story-telling in his upbringing. However, the film begins with the adult Aonghas (Colla Dòmhnallach) visiting his grandfather's deathbed, and concludes with their visit to Sgurr Dearg. There, the magically young again Aonghas climbs the mountain and releases into the wind the remaining petals of the crimson snowdrop. On his return to the bottom of the mountain, his grandfather has died, and Aonghas (now magically adult again) has become reconciled to his position—as inheritor of his grandfather's oral history—within Gaelic history and tradition.

As in *Foighidinn,* in *Seachd* the duty to keep alive the oral tradition of the Gàidhealtachd is passed on to the younger generation, in this case Aonghas, who—he tells us at the start of the film—shares his name with his grandfather, and his great-great-grandfather before him. The adult Aonghas's visit to his dying grandfather in the hospital prompts the flashbacks to his childhood. At two points during the flashbacks the young Aonghas rejects his Gaelic heritage, on both occasions due to the deaths of members of his family. Firstly, following his parents' death on Sgurr Dearg, Aonghas—shouting his bitterness in English—decries Gaelic. In reply, his grandfather informs him of his duty to the Aonghas's who went before him, and proceeds to tell a magical story set during the clearances of the nineteenth century, clearly indicating the need to remember the sufferings of the past in Gàidhealtachd. The second occasion occurs when his grandmother dies while grandfather Aonghas is telling a mythical story of a young girl, his grandmother's death

Aonghas releases the remaining petals of the crimson snowdrop. *Seachd: The Inaccessible Pinnacle* (Simon Miller, UK, 2007). Courtesy of Simon Miller and Christopher Young.

coinciding with the death of the girl in the story. In his grief Aonghas throws his grandfather's storybook at him, rejecting the storytelling tradition for what he sees as the damage it causes by distracting people from "reality."

Yet the film ultimately takes an extremely positive stance on storytelling, positing an oral tradition as the most effective way of keeping the past alive. As with all historical records, stories can never express an objective truth, so they remain only stories. Even so, they maintain the distinctive identity of the Gàidhealtachd, as, through its depiction of the landscape (especially the mountainous landscape of Skye), *Seachd* conflates the storytelling tradition with the physical context of the Gàidhealtachd. At the opening, when Aonghas drives toward his grandfather in the hospital, he says: "When my parents died on the mountain, it wasn't a story—it was the truth. But thanks to my grandfather my life was full of stories, and sometimes it was hard to tell the stories from reality. My name is Aonghas—like my grandfather, and his grandfather before him." This voiceover is heard over a static shot of Sgurr Dearg, ensuring that the landscape of Skye is initially positioned as integral to the passing on of oral history down the generations, "like my grandfather, and his grandfather before him."

In fact, from the very opening shot of the film, the landscape, and in particular Sgurr Dearg, is integral to the narrative. This is just as it was in *Foighidinn,* the most striking shot of which occurs when Am Mac Bu Shine begins to climb Sgurr Dearg. He is hooded, and his faceless figure blends entirely into the rocky landscape. The angular shape and gray-brown tone of his hooded cape, along with the overcast surroundings of the close, misty, gray sky, ensure that climber and mountain become indistinguishable, as though the climber's crouching figure were just another boulder on the mountainside. Director Simon Miller notes that the entire costume of Am Mac Bu Shine was briefed to create this effect.[29] Thus *Foighidinn* blends the mythical hero into the mountainous landscape to illustrate that in the Gàidhealtachd the past still exists in the present and is to be found in the surroundings, much as it was in the peat bog in *An Iobairt.* Tradition, myth, and place have become indistinguishable in the landscape.

For its part, *Seachd* begins with a white screen, which only gains definition and perspective as a snowbound mountainside when two figures appear in the center of the screen. These figures soon become lost when mist descends, transforming them into silhouettes that merge with the rock formations. When the children's parents fall to their deaths, they become literally lost in the landscape. From the opening shot, then, *Seachd* establishes the importance of the landscape in the lives of its characters. In *An Iobairt* the editing shows how the landscape brings together past, present, and future,

Am Mac Bu Shine begins to climb Sgurr Dearg. *Foighidinn: The Crimson Snow-drop/Patience* (Simon Miller, Scotland, 2003). Courtesy of Simon Miller and Christopher Young.

shifting layers of time and bringing them into contact through the shot-re-verse-shot pattern that reveals the coexistence of peat diggers in the present and the monk in the past. In *Foighidinn* and *Seachd* the cinematography shows how the landscape captures characters from the mythical past, blending them into the wildest edges of the world to patiently maintain them for the future. In this respect, the most telling moment in the film occurs when Aonghas leaves his grandfather's deathbed, rejecting the storytelling tradition, and determined to return to his "normal" life in Glasgow.

Driving away from the hospital, Aonghas looks out of the car window and sees several characters dotting the changing landscape. They are all fictional figures from the stories his grandfather told him as a child, characters who represent history in a fantastical form, and whose lives are kept alive by the link between the Gàidhealtachd and the oral storytelling tradition. As the stories come to life for Aonghas in the landscape, his grandfather appears in the back seat of the car, and together they return to the house where Aonghas grew up. Awaking the next morning, adult Aonghas finds himself magically transformed into a little boy, illustrating both the magical quality of stories for transforming reality, and indeed, the imperceptible slippages between layers of history that are made possible by the oral history of the Gàidhealtachd. This ensures that in the film's conclusion, myth and reality blur, once again on the most significant feature of the landscape of Skye, Sgurr Dearg.

Like the character in his grandfather's story, and like his parents before him, the young boy Aonghas climbs Sgurr Dearg on his grandfather's request. As he does so, he becomes lost among the boulders, just as his ancestor Aonghas did 800 years ago. Dwarfed by the astonishing mountains of the Cuillin range, at times young Aonghas almost disappears, or becomes a silhouette barely distinguishable from the outline of the mountainside. On the pinnacle he releases the last petal of the crimson snowdrop, releasing his grandfather from his place in the storytelling tradition, as a mythical character who has lived for over 800 years, passing on an oral history of the Gàidhealtachd in stories. Thus the young Aonghas becomes a character in a mythical story that takes place on the island, becomes literally a part of the landscape.

When he returns from the summit his grandfather passes him his storybook. The young boy Aonghas opens it, only to find it blank. The close-up on the blank pages cuts back to the present, where the adult Aonghas finds that his grandfather has died. Here Aonghas realizes his inheritance, his grandfather's oral history of stories, having become a living embodiment of local history, a character in a story about Sgurr Dearg like his grandfather before him. Thus, in *Seachd,* the passing on of history in the Gàidhealtachd is a matter of actions within a setting, a landscape marked by history, and the telling of stories that records these deeds as history.

Conclusion: Gaelic Films in the World

It is tempting to view the depiction of the landscape in *Seachd* as serving an additional purpose, as has recently been the case with so many Scottish films, of promoting the countryside as a tourist destination.[30] The numerous shots of the stunningly beautiful scenery of Skye that take up so much screen time are an undoubted draw to any potential tourist watching the film. Skye's biggest tourist pull, the Inaccessible Pinnacle, is even mentioned in the title. Thus, *Seachd* can be seen to aim to promote and regenerate Gaelic culture, and perhaps even the economy on Skye. However, while there is an element of truth in such an interpretation, things are not as clear-cut as they seem. Most importantly, the way the landscape is depicted as integral to the preservation of the oral history of the region ensures that its function within the diegesis does not simply serve as a picture postcard backdrop to the action. Moreover, despite the best efforts of Chris Young, local film agencies like the Highlands and Islands Film Commission did not support the project financially, as they were more focused on servicing the location shoots of major Hollywood films in the region. Instead, it was the local Gaelic College

Aonghas climbs Sgurr Dearg on his grandfather's request. *Seachd: The Inaccessible Pinnacle* (Simon Miller, UK, 2007). Courtesy of Simon Miller and Christopher Young.

on Skye, Sabhal Mòr Ostaig (the island's major employer) that provided the production base that enabled the film to be made.[31]

Seachd played at festivals in, among other places, Cannes, Edinburgh, and Rome, and gained a multiplex and art house distribution deal for the United Kingdom and Ireland with Soda Pictures as a result. It then secured a deal with Altadena Films (part of Hollywood Classics) to market the film internationally, under the title: *Seachd: The Crimson Snowdrop.* However, *Seachd* also found itself at the center of controversy when the British Academy of Film and Television Arts (BAFTA) decided not to nominate it for a foreign language Oscar. In an unexplained move, BAFTA did not nominate any film from Britain, despite considering both *Seachd* and the Welsh-language film, *Calon Gaeth/Small Country* (2006).[32] This move prompted producer Chris Young to quit BAFTA, and it provoked criticism from the Academy of Motion Picture Arts and Sciences (AMPAS).[33] It would seem, then, that (GM ALBA funding notwithstanding) Gaelic films cannot necessarily rely upon either the Scottish nation or the British state to support it internationally. At the time of writing, then, it remains to be seen whether the interest of outsider directors like Miller in the Gàidhealtachd, or the presence of Young Films on Skye (which has produced a number of other Scottish films, none of them in Gaelic) will be enough stimulate the continued growth of Gaelic filmmaking, or whether it will remain a sporadic manifestation of a peripheral culture on the edge of a nation without a state (Scotland) whose own "national" cinema is struggling to maintain momentum from its Lowlands base in and around Glasgow.

Notes

My thanks to Simon Miller and Chris Young for generously spending hours of their time talking to me about *Foighidinn, Seachd,* and Gaelic cinema. Heartfelt thanks to Gerda Stevenson and Aonghas MacNeacail for answering all my lengthy e-mails, and Lucy Conan for extremely helpful information on *An Iobairt.* I am also grateful to Fidelma Farley and Mike Cormack for productive discussions during the research and preparation of this piece. Thank you to the staff at the Scottish Screen archives, in particular Allan MacKay, and the various people who found out information for me: Belle Doyle at Scottish Screen; Douglas Ansdell, head of the Scottish Executive's Gaelic Unit; Margaret Cameron at GMS; and Jenny Yeomans and Trish Shorthouse at the Scottish Highlands and Islands Film Commission.

1. Petrie, *Screening Scotland,* 35.

2. Devine, *The Scottish Nation, 1700–2000,* 46–47; Devine, *Scotland's Empire, 1600–1815,* 354–55.

3. Macdonald, *Reimagining Culture: Histories, Identities, and the Gaelic Renaissance,* xv.

4. Ibid., 57.

5. Scottish Executive, "Gaelic in Scotland Factsheet."

6. Cormack, "Gaelic in the Media," 23–43, at 23.

7. The Bòrd na Gàidhlig website is www.bord-na-gaidhlig.org.uk/welcome.html (accessed March 29, 2007).

8. Scottish Executive, "Gaelic in Scotland Factsheet."

9. The Serbheis Nam Meadhanan Gàidhlig/Gaelic Media Service website is www.gms.org.uk (accessed March 29, 2007).

10. The Serbheis Nam Meadhanan Gàidhlig/Gaelic Media Service website:// www.gms.org.uk/news/07/PatriciaFergusonvisit.php (accessed April 2, 2007). The relative merits and outcomes of these initiatives have been discussed at length in Cormack, "Problems of Minority Broadcasting: Gaelic in Scotland," 101–17; Cormack, "Programming for Cultural Defence: The Expansion of Gaelic Television," 114–31; and Cormack, "Gaelic in the Media," 23–43.

11. Cormack, "Gaelic in the Media," 30.

12. Interview with director Simon Miller, April 19, 2007.

13. Macdonald, *Reimagining Culture,* xvi.

14. The Scottish Screen archives in Glasgow contain two unpublished MLitt (postgraduate) theses written in the 1990s by students from the University of Glasgow's Department of Film and Television Studies: Myers, "At the Edge of Europe: The Emergence of a Gaelic Language Media in Scotland and the Potential and Cultural Necessity for a Gaelic Cinema" (1994) and Kirkwood, "Inviting the Outsider In" (1998). See also Cormack, "Gaelic in the Media," 29–30.

15. Hunter, *The Last of the Free: A History of the Highlands and Islands*, 176.

16. Ibid., 129.

17. Thomson, *An Introduction to Gaelic Poetry*, 12.

18. McKean, "Celtic Music and the Growth of the Féis Movement in the Scottish Highlands," 245–59, at 246; and Hunter, *The Last of the Free*, 176.

19. Thomson, *An Introduction to Gaelic Poetry*, 57–98.

20. McKean, "Celtic Music and the Growth of the Féis Movement," 247.

21. Neat and Macinnes, *The Voice of the Bard*.

22. Nwachukwu Frank Ukadike, *Black African Cinema*, 201.

23. Ibid., 202.

24. Ibid., 25.

25. Interview with director Simon Miller, April 19, 2007.

26. Gifford, "The Return to Mythology in Scottish Fiction," in *Studies in Scottish Fiction: 1945 to the Present*, 17–50, at 32.

27. Scullion, "Feminine Pleasures and Masculine Indignities," in *Gendering the Nation*, 169–204, at 201.

28. Chapman, *The Gaelic Vision in Scottish Culture*, 37.

29. Interview with director Simon Miller, April 19, 2007.

30. For a much fuller discussion of this phenomenon, see Martin-Jones, "Kabhi India, Kabhie Scotland: Bollywood Productions in Post-Devolutionary Scotland," 49–60.

31. Interview with producer Chris Young, May 14, 2007.

32. Pendreigh, "And the Oscar Will Not Go To."

33. Pendreigh, "Producer Quits Bafta over Gaelic Film Snub."

Bibliography

Bòrd na Gàidhlig. At www.bord-na-gaidhlig.org.uk/welcome.html (accessed March 29, 2007).

Chapman, Malcolm. *The Gaelic Vision in Scottish Culture*. Montreal: McGill-Queen's University Press, 1978.

Cormack, Mike. "Gaelic in the Media." *Scottish Affairs* 46 (2004): 23–43.

———. "Problems of Minority Broadcasting: Gaelic in Scotland." *European Journal of Communication* 8, no. 1 (1993): 101–17.

———. "Programming for Cultural Defence: The Expansion of Gaelic Television." *Scottish Affairs* 6 (1994): 114–31.

Devine, T. M. *Scotland's Empire, 1600–1815*. London: Penguin, 2003.

———. *The Scottish Nation, 1700–2000*. London: Penguin, 1999.

Gifford, Douglas. "The Return to Mythology in Scottish Fiction." In *Studies in Scottish Fiction: 1945 to the Present*, edited by Susanne Hagemann, 17–50. Frankfurt: Peter Lang, 1996.

Hunter, James. *The Last of the Free: A History of the Highlands and Islands*. Edinburgh: Mainstream Publishing, 1999.

Kirkwood, Holly. "Inviting the Outsider In." MLitt diss., Glasgow University,

1998.

Macdonald, Sharon. *Reimagining Culture: Histories, Identities, and the Gaelic Renaissance.* Oxford: Berg, 1997.

MacLeod, Murdo, and Alastair Gray. "Speed Bonnie Boat Like a Bird on the Wing, Over the Sea to Eilean a' Cheò." *Scotland on Sunday,* April 29, 2007. At http://scotlandonsunday.scotsman.com/index.cfm?id=659562007 (accessed May 5, 2007).

Martin-Jones, David. "Kabhi India, Kabhie Scotland: Bollywood Productions in Post-Devolutionary Scotland." *Journal of South Asian Popular Culture* 4, no. 1 (2006): 49–60.

McKean, Thomas. "Celtic Music and the Growth of the Féis Movement in the Scottish Highlands." *Western Folklore* 57, no. 4 (1998): 245–59.

Myers, Kenneth. "At the Edge of Europe: The Emergence of a Gaelic Language Media in Scotland and the Potential and Cultural Necessity for a Gaelic Cinema." MLitt diss., Glasgow University, 1994.

Neat, Timothy, and John Macinnes. *The Voice of the Bard.* Edinburgh: Canongate, 1999.

Pendreigh, Brian. "And the Oscar Will Not Go To . . ." *Scotland on Sunday,* September 16, 2007. At http://news.scotsman.com/movies.cfm?id=1482232007 (accessed October 7, 2007).

———, "Producer Quits Bafta over Gaelic Film Snub." *Scotland on Sunday,* September 30, 2007. At http://news.scotsman.com/entertainment.cfm?id=1560962007 (accessed October 7, 2007).

Petrie, Duncan. *Screening Scotland.* London: British Film Institute, 2000.

Scottish Executive. "Gaelic in Scotland Factsheet." At www.scotland.gov.uk/library/documents6/eid_ach_gisf_1.htm (accessed March 29, 2007).

Scullion, Adrienne. "Feminine Pleasures and Masculine Indignities." In *Gendering the Nation,* edited by Christopher Whyte, 169–204. Edinburgh: Edinburgh University Press, 1995.

Serbheis Nam Meadhanan Gàidhlig/Gaelic Media Service. At www.gms.org.uk/ (accessed March 29, 2007).

———. At www.gms.org.uk/news/07/PatriciaFergusonvisit.php (accessed April 2, 2007).

Thomson, Derrick. *An Introduction to Gaelic Poetry.* London: Victor Gollancz, 1974.

Ukadike, Nwachukwu Frank. *Black African Cinema.* Berkeley: University of California Press, 1994.

Filming the Times of Tangier

Nostalgia, Postcolonial Agency, and Preposterous History

Tangier, peripheral city par excellence at the border between Europe and Africa, is nowadays mostly known for its illegal immigrants who want to cross the ocean to Spain. Leila Kilani's documentary *Tanger, le rêve des brûleurs/ Tangier, the Burner's Dream* (Leila Kilani, France, 2002) powerfully presents the sociopolitical dreams of people wanting to leave North Africa and "burn" their IDs. However, Tangier has also always attracted many Europeans and Americans to settle or seek adventure in the Maghreb. In André Téchiné's film *Les Temps qui changent/Changing Times* (France, 2004) the main character, Antoine (Gérard Depardieu), has just left Europe to arrive in Tangier with the very individual aim of regaining the heart of Cecile (Catherine Deneuve), of regaining a lost love in Tangier. Granted, Téchiné also acknowledges the burners. In one scene, Antoine and Cecile pass by a group of people waiting for an opportunity to leave and they briefly discuss their fate. But at first sight, these burners do not directly concern the main characters. Struck by these apparent oppositional types and directions of desire that traverse Tangier in these films, this chapter investigates the different attractions of this peripheral location.

Many film crews took their cameras to capture the whimsical magic of Tangier. Since the nineteenth century the city has occupied an important place in the imagination of the West and East as an extremely complex, chaotic, dangerous and at the same time alluring and open city. Locals, settlers, smugglers, secret agents, travelers, tourists, and migrants of all sorts have moved to and from the city, throughout history, in always changing dynamics. Because of these changing dynamics, and Tangier's status as both peripheral city and transnational meeting point, I want to propose the hypothesis that Tangier might offer a paradigmatic case for discussing the ways in which the dynamics between center and periphery have changed in the contemporary world. In order to develop this hypothesis I will focus on the concept of time (as history, memory, and temporality). Because Tangier is such a complex and even legendary city, in the first part I will sketch some of Tangier's history. I will do this by looking at several (of the many) films shot in Tangier and considering these as "sheets of the past" that make up the city as it is today.[1] In this section the films serve as bits and pieces of actual history, as traces of the past that can be partially reconstituted in the image. A brief tour of this cinematic landscape is necessary at this stage to sketch in the contours of the temporal map of Tangier. This mapping then provides a preliminary discussion of the image of the city that will be challenged in the second part, where I will move to contemporary postcolonial Tangier. Here I will address the concept of time as it has been developed in postcolonial theory, looking at the postcolonial condition and the question of agency, described by Homi Bhabha as a "temporality of Tangier." This temporality of Tangier, I will finally argue, is what we might need in order to understand the shifting dynamics between center and periphery.

"Sheets of the Past": Imagining Tangier's History

According to Henri Bergson the present, every present perception, is already in the past. Bergson argues that we live in the past that is preserved in recollection—images that are stored in a not necessarily chronological order. Each moment in the present invites us to jump to other layers of the past.[2] Gilles Deleuze has developed this model further in respect to cinema and cinematographic consciousness.[3] This conception of the past stored in images that we can address in a nonchronological order at a metalevel can be used as a very basic methodology to briefly sketch Tangier's history through several films. Of course, these films are not history itself but they are related to historical circumstances and events that I will address. Moreover, as imaginations in themselves they also have a role to play in our historical consciousness. All films include at least three layers of time that cause disjunctive perspectives: the time that the film's story addresses; the time in which the film was produced, which influences the film's form and content implicitly or explicitly; and the time in which we view the film, which can alter our perception of the events earlier presented. In this section I will mainly focus on the first time, the time of the film's story. This will reconstitute an account of the main historical developments of the city, which implies a chronological notion of time. This classical notion of time will be challenged by the "temporality of Tangier" that will be developed later on in this chapter.

The American film *The Wind and the Lion* (John Milius, USA, 1975) presents Tangier in 1904 as a location where several imperialistic powers try to gain a foothold in Morocco and to have access to Africa and the Arab world. From the nineteenth century onward Tangier was the place where France, Spain, Germany, England, and the United States sent most of their diplomatic and commercial missions. The film is set several years before Morocco would become a French and Spanish protectorate and one year before the German emperor Wilhelm II provoked a scandal by expressing his antipathy to the French machinations for influence. This led in 1906 to the Algeciras conference that declared Tangier as an open and independent zone, and eventually to the 1923 declaration of Tangier as an International Zone, governed by an international board that consisted of representatives of seven countries (England, France, Spain, Italy, Germany, United States, and Morocco, which had both Jewish and Arab representatives).

The plot of the film is loosely based on a real event known as the Perdicaris Affair, which involved the kidnapping of a supposedly American citizen, Ion Perdicaris (played in the film by a woman, Candice Bergen). The kidnapper is a tribal headsman from the Rif called Raisuli (Sean Connery in the film), who wanted to fight Western influence by putting pressure on the Moroccan sultan, whom he considered a marionette of the Europeans. An important role is also assigned to President Theodor Roosevelt (Brian Keith) who in 1904 sends warships to Tangier in order to put pressure on the Moroccan officials to release the American citizen. The fact that Perdicaris turned out to be a Greek citizen is not mentioned in the film, right in line with official historical accounts. The French and especially the Germans in the film are depicted as much less civilized and less powerful than the Americans and the nationalistic self-portrayal of America is quite interesting, even if it is not topical here. What I mainly want to emphasize is how Tangier is presented as an arena for the international struggle among several imperial powers, which eventually led to its status as an international zone.

During the Second World War, Tangier, because of its international status, became known as a spy's nest and a dangerous place to be. It was also the place from which resistance against Vichy France was organized. The French film *Mission à Tanger/Mission in Tangier* (Hunebelle, France, 1949) is one of several espionage films that refer to this reputation of Tangier. It is a classic thriller, complete with a Hitchcockian McGuffin, an undefined secret message that has to get across the sea.[4]

Mission in Tangier combines actual footage of the city, initially seen from the periscope of a submarine, with scenes shot in a studio in Paris. Besides Tangier's historical role in international resistance and espionage, here I want to mention the ways in which both the Spanish and (again) the Germans are represented in this film. The Spanish, who occupied Tangier during the war, are rendered foolish by the performance of a young Louis de Funes, the Germans by the depiction of German officials that kill and capture French spies and by the strategic use of historical footage of Hitler.

After the war Tangier regained its international status and was famous for its libertinous climate. Peter Goedel's 1996 documentary *Tanger, Legende einer Stadt/Tangier, Legend of a City* (Germany, 2000) is interesting in this respect. The film is about Tangier's "golden years," the 1940s and 1950s, when it built its legendary reputation as a playground for eccentric millionaires and famous artists, a continuing meeting place for secret agents and all kinds of crooks and gamblers. The film combines four sorts of images: found footage and historical documentary images of the city during the war and during the independence struggles; images of actor Armin-Mueller Stahl in the present who arrives in Tangier to recall his fictitious past in Tangier; dramatized flashback images of this past where Stahl spent happy days with his French fiancée, Marie, who was killed accidentally during the liberation riots in 1956; and interviews with Europeans and Americans (most famously Paul Bowles) who remember the good old days, when Europeans were throwing parties all over the city, when American and European writers (William Burroughs, Tennessee Williams, Samuel Becket, Jean Genet, to name but a few) went to the city to have a "white Christmas" ("white" of course not referring to snow as Paul Bowles jokes in the film), and when the city seemed to be a happy and magic meeting place for all nationalities, Western nationalities that is. The Europeans recall that on the Moroccan side only three influential aristocratic families could participate in the magic dream of the legendary city. Writer Mohamed Choukri is the only Moroccan in the film who talks from a nonprivileged Moroccan perspective and mentions the fact that the Europeans always considered the Moroccans as servants. In these same golden years, however, Tangier nevertheless also played a key role in the struggle for independence, which is also shown in this film. In 1947 the sultan Mohamed V proclaimed in his famous Tangier speech his full support to the Istiqlal—the Party for Independence. In 1952 riots in Tangier made the call for independence louder, which in 1956 became a reality. Tangier was no longer an international zone and became part of the Moroccan kingdom. *Tangier, Legend of a City* speaks of these historical moments by showing important archival footage. But all these images are centered on the individual tragedy of Mueler-Stahl's character who loses his fiancée at the moment of independence and who dies after he has "relived" all the important memories with his fiancée in Tangier in 1956.

Alexandre Arcady's *Dernier été à Tanger/Last Summer in Tangier* (France, 1987) is also set in 1956. The film pays homage to the classic film noir, with a private detective who tells the story in voice-over, a femme fatale, cigarettes, nightclubs, and of course a few dead bodies. The film on the one hand refers to Tangier's wild reputation, and on the other hand to the important political changes that took place in that year. But again these changes are not the central concern of the film. They form the background of the story and explain why many people, like the European main character, detective Richard Corrigan (Thierry Lhermitte) have to leave. In an interview on the DVD of the film, Alexandre Arcady admits that for him, filming in Tangier was a sort of replacement. As a *pied noir* (person of French origin born and raised in Algeria), at the time of making the film in the 1980s it was still not very easy for French people to revisit the country they had to leave about twenty-five years earlier during the War of Independence. Tangier therefore symbolizes European regrets for having to leave the Maghreb when colonialism ended. I will return to this point soon. To conclude this chronological overview of Tangier's history: After the death of Mohamed V in 1961, during the reign of Hassan II the city was largely neglected. Since 1999, the new King Mohamed VI has spent as much time as possible in his palace in Tangier and the city has undergone large construction works. Tangier has slowly regained its old attractive reputation. Nowadays many tourists from Spain cross the ocean on the speedy ferryboats from Tarifa and Algeciras. Moroccans who live in Europe visit the city to spend their holidays at the seaside. Its dangerous reputation too has regained importance. The harbor still attracts smugglers (*contrabandeurs*). Since Spain, following the Schengen Agreements in 1991, closed its borders and started to demand visas for entrance into Europe, the city has also become the place from which illegal immigrants from all over Africa and the Maghreb try to reach the European coast that is visible from everywhere in the city.

The Temporality of Tangier versus the Nostalgia of Casablanca

Having sketched some of Tangier's historical dimensions through its recollections-images, I will now move to Tangier as a postcolonial city as it emerges in recent films. Historically the postcolonial era of Tangier starts in 1956. Acknowledging the possible problematic aspects of the term *postcolo-*

nial, I take Homi Bhabha's definition in his article "The Postcolonial and the Postmodern" as a starting point. Here Bhabha states:

Postcolonial perspectives emerge from the colonial testimony of Third World countries and the discourses of "minorities" within the geopolitical division of East and West, North and South. They intervene in those ideological discourses of modernity that attempt to give a hegemonic "normality" to the uneven development and the differential, often disadvantaged histories of nations, races, communities, peoples.[5]

Now, what I have been doing so far, by and large, was giving exactly such a "hegemonic" account of the city's history, which is a problem at the heart of center-periphery discussions. As Bhabha argues, the testimony of third world countries and their emancipation require a radical revision of the social temporality in which emergent histories may be written, a rearticulation of the cultural text or the "sign" in which different identities may be inscribed. Bhabha calls this a "strategy of survival" that is both transnational and translational. It is transnational because contemporary discourses are rooted in specific histories of cultural displacements (and all films set in Tangier talk about displacements of various sorts). It is translational because such dynamic histories make the question of how culture signifies a rather complex issue involving translations between different languages and other cultural signs.

Bhabha refers to Roland Barthes' visits to Tangier. Interestingly, Tangier was very instructive for the white French semiotician, enabling him to learn how to open up language and cultural signs for transnational and translational revisions. Bhabha recalls how Barthes describes his Tangier experience: "Half-asleep on a banquette in a bar, of which Tangiers is the exemplary site, Barthes attempts to 'enumerate the stereophony of languages within earshot': music, conversations, chairs, glasses, Arabic, French," when suddenly he feels how the sentence is opened up with the carnality of the voice and the incomprehensibility of language.[6] "I was myself a public place, a souk; words, small syntagmas, bits of formulations, and no sentence could be formed."[7] This is what Barthes calls "the outside of the sentence" and what Homi Bhabha renames as the "temporality of Tangier," a temporality that is changing and open, full of ambiguities.

Bhabha contrasts this temporality with the temporality of Casablanca, for which he refers not so much to the city as, significantly, to the film *Casablanca* (Michael Curtiz, USA, 1942).

In *Casablanca,* the passage of time preserves the identity of language; the possibility of naming over time is fixed in the repetition:

> You must remember this
> A kiss is still a kiss
> A sigh is but a sigh
> The fundamental things apply
> As time goes by

"Play it again, Sam" which is perhaps the Western world's most celebrated demand for repetition, is still an invocation to similitude, a return to eternal verities.[8]

This tendency is evident in the opening scene of *Last Summer in Tangier,* in which a poster of *Casablanca* on the wall of Corrigan's office now becomes significant in that it refers to a specific temporality that is related to a desire for a repetition of fixed time, a signification of closure.[9] It explains the nostalgic dimension of the film. *Last Summer in Tangier* acknowledges the changes that have taken place but with regret: the hero has to leave. It is as if the only redemption that can be found is in repeating a classic genre, the return of the film noir. On top of this, at the end of the film, the beginning of the film is exactly repeated: the femme fatale offers the hero a light, this time not in a hotel in Tangier but on a boat to America. It is as if the temporality of Casablanca could be repeated by creating a repetitive "sheet of the past" and moving normative history to America. In a similar vein it can be argued that *Tangier, Legend of a City* gives a nostalgic account of the past, especially in its emphasis on the individual love story of the French lovers and repetition of their past, which means that "Casablanca" as a temporal sign can be very easily found in images of Tangier.

Yet, in contrast to this filmic representation, what actually happens in Tangier? I have to go back to Bhabha, who relates Tangier to a very different type of signification: "In Tangier, as time goes by, it produces an iterative temporality that erases the occidental spaces of language—inside/outside, past/present, those foundationalist epistemological positions of Western empiricism and historicism. Tangier opens up disjunctive, incommensurable relations of spacing and temporality *within* the sign."[10] This disjunctive character of Tangier for Barthes leads to a form of discourse he named "writing aloud": the disjunctive moment, the time-lag "between the event of the sign

(Tangier) and its discursive eventuality ('writing aloud') exemplifies a process where intentionality is negotiated retrospectively."[11] In this way, Bhabha argues, "the temporality of Tangier is a lesson in reading the agency of the social text as ambivalent and catachrestic."[12]

The next question is, is it possible to conceive of historical agency in that disjunctive, indeterminate, and contingent moment of discourse in the "temporality of Tangier"? What other narratives can be read in the ambivalence of cultural texts? Put in Bhabha's words: "How does the time-lag signify individuation as a position that is an effect of the intersubjective (negotiation)?"[13] This would imply that those elements of social consciousness imperative for agency can now be thought outside that (Western) epistemology that insists on the subject (individuality) as always prior to the social. Bhabha develops the idea of the intersubjective further with Mikhail Bakhtin's notions of heteroglossia and dialogism and especially Hannah Arendt's concept of the human interest:

It is this public sphere of language and action that must become at once the theater and the screen for the manifestation of the capacities of human agency. Tangier-like, the event and its eventuality are separated; the narrative time lag makes the who and the what contingent, splitting them, so that the agent remains the subject, in suspension, outside the sentence. The agent who "causes" the narrative becomes part of the interest, only because we cannot point unequivocally to that agent at the point of outcome. It is the contingency that constitutes individuation—in the return of the subject as agent—that protects the interest of the intersubjective realm. The contingency of closure socializes the agent as a collective "effect" through the distancing of the author. Between the cause and its intentionality falls the shadow. Can we unquestionably propose that a story has a unique meaning in the first place?[14]

The implication of this is that the contingency of the Tangier-sign enables revisions and negotiations that are not necessarily defined in antagonisms, polarities, and pure oppositions. "Polarities come to be replaced with truths that are only partial, limited and unstable."[15] Contrary to Arendt (who argues for a consensual community), Bhabha is most interested in human togetherness or human interest where subaltern, minority, or peripheral agency seeks revision and reinscription. Therefore, let me now return to some postcolonial images of Tangier and look at some of the revisions that have introduced subjects with postcolonial agency.

Postcolonial Agency and Revisionist Perspectives

First, it has to be acknowledged that there are certainly forms of "oppositional history" that are proposed as a kind of strategic counterperspective, to rewrite and re-present history from a postcolonial perspective. Mohamed Choukri (who appeared briefly in *Tangier, Legend of a City*) is the author of one of the best-known modern Moroccan novels. *El Khoubz el Hafi* (translated in English as *For Bread Alone*) is his autobiographical story that is also set in Tangier after the Second World War and around 1956. In 2004 the Algerian director Mohamed Rachid Benhadj filmed the book. *For Bread Alone* is a case in point in postcolonial revision and regaining postcolonial agency from an antagonist perspective. The film in itself does not speak of limited or partial truths, but seen on a metalevel in relation to the other images of Tangier described above, it certainly renders the historical truth more partial and limited and can therefore be seen to be revising the history of Tangier.

Like *Tangier, Legend of a City* this film also uses archival material combined with dramatization. However, the archival footage is now framed in a completely different story: that of a child (later young man) from the Rif whose family fled to the city in the hope of finding bread. At the beginning of the film the images (both archival and dramatized) emphasize the enormous difference between the wealth and decadence of the French and other Europeans and the incredible misery of the common Moroccan people. We see happily dancing Europeans in found footage and then in dramatized scenes the poverty of Choukri as a child who searches waste bins for food.

Second, other archival images are introduced that show people from the Rif Mountains fleeing from starvation by drought, which provides an explanation for the poverty and misery in the city, a perspective that is absent from the other films discussed so far. The Tangier riots are also dramatized. Choukri as a young man (played by Said Taghmaoui) gets arrested even though he is at the riots more by accident than by political conviction. In prison he learns how to write Arabic, which changes his life. This has a large symbolic and political meaning. Here postcolonial agency is literally acquired by accessing and mastering language and the ability to revise history. It is clear that this film proposes a new agent as a collective intersubjective effect, where the subject is not prior to the social as in the story of Mueller-Stahl and his Marie told in *Tangier, Legend of a City*. There is still individuation, but it is through the social and the contingencies of history that Choukri gains agency.

Another example of a revisionist film is Leila Kilani's *Tangier, the Burn-*

er's Dream, mentioned above. Here the revisionist project is not so much related to the revising of history but to changing our perception of the current image of illegal immigrants who do not get a voice in mainstream media (other than perhaps a sound bite). I have discussed this documentary elsewhere more elaborately, arguing that the main strategy of the film is to provide these characters with dignity and agency by showing them as people with a dream, a dream of conquering the frontier like cowboys.[16] Also the film makes their story seem like an adventure: after hearing about the dangers of hiding under trucks, the images in close-up of the trucks become very suspenseful. The film changes one's perception of "minority people" like illegal immigrants and turns the camera into an emancipatory tool of the periphery.

This affects the temporalities of the center as well. There are basically two strategies for the old center (the West as the source of history that puts others in the shadow/at the periphery) to deal with the temporality of Tangier. On the one hand, as demonstrated with contemporary films like *Last Summer in Tangier* and *Tangier, Legend of a City*, it remains difficult for the former colonizer to let go of the past, which is therefore revisited very often in a nostalgic fashion, projecting personal loss onto the collective loss, sticking to a "temporality of Casablanca." I am not arguing that this is not legitimate, or that it is always completely excluding of the other perspective. Both *Last Summer in Tangier* and *Tangier, Legend of a City* do acknowledge these perspectives, but always in the framework that puts Western individual mourning before the social.[17]

On the other hand, an increasing number of filmmakers from the West fully acknowledge that the center and periphery have shifted in whimsical and unpredictable ways, and that moving between different centers (or different peripheries) is a reality for everybody as we are in constant circulation. This implies that the white Western character is no longer always controlling signification, that positions can shift, or that self-criticism is allowed to be screened. It does not imply that power relations have become equal, but the massive migratory movements are changing these relations slowly but surely. The relation to the past in these films is not nostalgic but preposterous, referring to the necessity to put the present and future before the past (a reversal of the *normal* temporal order).[18] This implies a revision of the past in order to have a future. This is the strategy of survival of the temporality of Tangier.

The Temporalities of Téchiné

André Téchiné's film *Loin/Far* (France, 2001) presents such a preposterous approach to history. The film shows how we are all implicated in the constant circulation of people, ideas, and goods, which infuse discourse with a lot of the ambiguities that give agency to different people at different moments.[19] At the beginning of the film a clear statement is made about the transnationalism and translationalism of the postcolonial condition mentioned by Bhabha. It also shows how the "out of the sentence" of Barthes can create agency and empowerment. Serge (Stéphane Rideau), a French truck driver who travels regularly between Algeciras and Tangier, is tempted to practice *contrabande* and transport illegal merchandise to Europe. He is completely dependent upon his Moroccan contact who gives him his assignments. Serge is clearly not in control. He does not master the language nor does he know what is going to happen.

Stylistically the transnationalism and translationalism of the film can be sensed by the fact that everything is constantly in movement, everybody is constantly in circulation. The camera also moves constantly, and even fixed scenes have movement in them since the camera is handheld. Somewhere at the beginning of the film, Serge's friend Said (Mohamed Hamaidi) takes him to the house of an American ex-pat, James (Jack Taylor). Before entering the house we see the moving bodies of Africans and Moroccans in the narrow streets of the casbah, many of whom are probably burners. The house is full of movement: on the ground floor ballet lessons are taking place, people are moving up and down the stairs and the camera moves between the first and second floor. On the terrace Serge is welcomed by James who offers him tea. Several languages are spoken, people are dancing and making music, Said tells his "burner's story" to Nabil and François, a French film director (played by Téchiné's alter ego Gaël Morel). François and Serge discover they know each other from high school back in France.[20] When they tell James about this coincidence he is not surprised: "Time doesn't exist in Tangier," James says.

This remark could mean two things: James is clearly modeled on Paul Bowles. His homosexuality, his love for the city and its people but also his arrogance of knowing the city and its people better than themselves is striking and could refer to his desire for a time in which nothing changes and the past can remain fixed, a time of Casablanca, nostalgia. However, "time doesn't exist in Tangier" could perhaps also be read as "chronological time does not exist." If we can jump between layers of the past according to the needs of the present this also implies that the present can shed new light on the past, that revisions can take place. Indeed, the constant movement of the camera, the languages, sounds, and voices: "music, conversations, chairs, glasses, Arabic, French" and English.[21] It could have been the scene that Barthes inspired for his opening up to the temporality of Tangier, where not every sign is comprehensible, where the time-lag creates ambiguity and post-colonial agency can be acquired. When Said, for instance, starts telling his story, Nabil addresses him jokingly as Sheherazade who tells a well-known story. But Said replies that he is going to change the end of his story, thus claiming agency. And Serge again is clearly not in control. He smokes too much of a joint and leaves feeling nauseous, falling down the stairs. Yet, in the course of the film as a whole he is not completely without agency either. At the end it will appear that he is tested by his Moroccan contacts, something he only discovers when the police check his truck and, contrary to his own beliefs, do *not* find any illegal goods. Instead of illegal merchandise, he will take an "illegal body" with him, when he tells Said to jump in his truck and drives onto the ferry to Europe. The film ends abruptly, but the story of transnational circulation continues, implicating everybody in a truly "becoming-minoritarian."[22]

Changing Times

And this brings me back to my starting point. The opposition I noticed initially between *The Burner's Dream* and *Changing Times* is actually a false opposition. While Kilani's film moves the burners more to the center by presenting them as cowboys who will stop at nothing to achieve their dream of conquering the border, Téchiné's film moves his French stars more to the periphery. First by introducing (like in *Far*) many other characters next to Deneuve and Depardieu (Cecile's bisexual son Sami and his Moroccan wife Nadi; Nathan, the Jewish husband of Cecile who starts a friendship or perhaps even an affair with Nadi's sister). The characters are presented in a heterogeneous assemblage that relates them explicitly to the social.[23] Second, Téchiné moves all these characters out of the old center, Paris, and brings them to Tangier, which he does not present in a nostalgic fashion. Granted, the main focus of the story is still on the very individual love story between Antoine and Cecile. But, and this is my third point, the difference with nostalgia films is that the story of Cecile and Antoine is brought into connection with the fate of the immigrants. Or, at least there is an ambiguity in the way Téchiné presents this connection that allows for a double reading. At first instance, as I said at the beginning, the scene in which Cecile and Antoine pass by a group of burners can be considered as terribly bourgeois. They are only concerned with their own former passion, and their life has nothing to do with that of the illegal immigrants. There is no contact, they are just there as a fact of life that they discuss as though watching them on television.

But on second and third viewing, listening to the words of Antoine who speaks with respect, hope, and even admiration for the dream of the burners to fight for a future, and considering what happens to Antoine (he becomes very much like an illegal immigrant who has only one dream: for him the future is Cecile), things appear rather differently. Like many of the burners, Antoine almost drowns for his dream, albeit not out at sea but in the earth and soil of Tangier, which literally almost buries him alive when he is at the construction site of the media center he is building. This brings the possibility of an allegorical reading of the film.[24] Cecile is Antoine's Europe, and their fate is as uncertain as that of the burners, comparable to that of Serge and Said at the end of *Far.*

Finally, the references to the media in *Changing Times* are also significant. The images that will be produced and broadcasted from the media center should not bury the sheets of the past under the soil of Tangier, but neither should one constantly want to go back to the same past. The past needs to be revised, put into a different perspective according to the needs of the present and in order to have a future that is different from the past.

As time goes by, the choice between temporalities of Casablanca and Tangier will keep on presenting itself in the image. The temporality that Tangier inspires could be seen as an indication of how center and periphery keep on changing places in intersubjective encounters in which no one can claim absolute authority. The contingency of the time lag provides opportunities for agency and strategies for survival for both the (former) centers and peripheries. Times have changed indeed.

Notes

1. See Bergson, *Matter and Memory* and Deleuze, *Cinema 2: The Time-Image*. In "Passagen 2000: The City, Pace and Space," Bal and Vanderburgh refer to the layers of time that make up the city: "the city as we now inhabit or know bears bits and pieces of pasts." Bal and Vanderburgh, "Passagen 2000," 1–8, at 3.

2. Bergson, "Of the Survival of Images: Memory and Mind," in *Matter and Memory,* 133–77.

3. Deleuze, *Cinema 2,* third and fourth commentaries on Bergson, 44–126. See also Bogue, *Deleuze on Cinema;* Colebrook, *Gilles Deleuze;* Pisters, *The Matrix of Visual Culture: Working with Deleuze in Film Theory;* and Martin-Jones, *Deleuze, Cinema, and National Identity: Narrative Time in National Contexts.*

4. Spanish and Italian directors made similar films with titles like *Los misterios de*

Tanger/The Mysteries of Tangier (Carlos Fernandez Cuenca, Spain, 1942), *Agguato a Tangeri/ Trapped in Tangier* (Riccardo Freda, Italy, 1958), and *Requiem per un agente secreto/Requiem for a Secret Agent* (Sergio Sollima, Italy, 1967). In 1987 John Glen directed agent 007, James Bond, in Tangier the spy nest during the end of the cold war in *The Living Daylights.*

5. Bhabha, *The Location of Culture,* 246.

6. Ibid., 258.

7. Barthes, *Le plaisir du texte,* 79. My translation.

8. Bhabha, *Location of Culture,* 261.

9. In his article "Casablanca's Regime: The Shifting Aesthetics of Political Technologies (1907–1943)," Jorge Otero-Pailos demonstrated how the film *Casablanca* aimed at uniting the American nation: "Inside the dark theatres, the camera's lens became America's prosthetic eye, and where there once was an incomprehensible and chaotic world, now a clear image of right and wrong came sharply into focus." In Otero-Pailos "Casablanca's Regime, 18.

10. Bhabha, *Location of Culture,* 261.

11. Ibid., 263.

12. Ibid.

13. Ibid., 264.

14. Ibid., 272.

15. Ibid., 278.

16. See Pisters, "Arresting the Flux of Images and Sounds: Free Indirect Discourse and the Dialectics of Political Cinema," 175–94.

17. Many films that present memories of colonial times from the colonizer's perspective have this nostalgic desire for a lost past. For instance, Michael Radford's *White Mischief* (UK, 1987) presents the decadent lives of the British in Kenya during the Second World War.

18. Mieke Bal has developed this term in respect to art history, where works of art that appear chronologically first operate as an aftereffect caused by the images of subsequent artists. See Bal, *Quoting Caravaggio: Contemporary Art, Preposterous History.*

19. An example of another film that is influenced by the temporality of Tangier, albeit in a less explicit way, is *A costa dos murmurios/The Murmuring Coast* (Marida Costaderas, Portugal, 2004) about the Portuguese in Mozambique. Also films by Claire Denis would fit into this category.

20. This is an intertextual reference to Téchiné's earlier film *Les Rosaux sauvages/ The Wild Reeds* (1994), where the same actors play Serge and François in a small village in France during the Algerian Independence War.

21. Bhabha, *Location of Culture,* 258.

22. For an elaboration of the Deleuzian notion of "becoming-minoritarian" see Marrati, "Against the Doxa: Politics of Immanence and Becoming-Minoritarian," 205–20.

23. Significantly, most reviews of both *Far* and *Changing Times* reject these other characters for they distract from the "real story" of Sarah (Lubna Azabal, who plays Serge's Jewish ex-girlfriend), Said, and Serge in *Far* and from Cecile and Antoine in

Changing Times. Postcolonial sensibilities of different temporalities are not evident among these film critics. See Burg, "Drama ontbreekt in Tanger" (Drama is missing in Tangier).

24. Concerning the political significance of allegory, see Wayne, *Political Film: The Dialectics of Third Cinema,* 129–36.

Bibliography

Bal, Mieke. *Quoting Caravaggio: Contemporary Art, Preposterous History.* Chicago: University of Chicago Press, 2001.

———, and David Vanderburgh. "Passagen 2000: The City, Pace and Space." *Parallax* 5, no. 3 (1999): 1–8.

Barthes, Roland. *Le plaisir du texte.* Paris: Éditions du Seuil, 1973.

Bergson, Henri. *Matter and Memory.* Translated by N. M. Paul and W. S. Palmer. New York: Zone Books, 1991.

Bhabha, Homi. *The Location of Culture.* London: Routledge, 2004.

Bogue, Ronald. *Deleuze on Cinema.* New York: Routledge, 2003.

Buchanan, Ian, and Adrian Parr, eds. *Deleuze and the Contemporary World.* Edinburgh: Edinburgh University Press, 2006.

Burg, Jos van der. "Drama ontbreekt in Tanger" (Drama is missing in Tangier). *Parool.* At www.parool.nl (accessed December 15, 2007).

Colebrook, Claire. *Gilles Deleuze.* London: Routledge, 2002.

Deleuze, Gilles. *Cinema 2: The Time Image.* Translated by Hugh Tomlinson and Robert Galeta. London: Athlone Press, 1989.

Marrati, Paola. "Against the Doxa: Politics of Immanence and Becoming-Minoritarian." In *Micropolitics of Media Culture: Reading the Rhizomes of Deleuze and Guattari,* edited by Patricia Pisters, 205–20. Amsterdam: Amsterdam University Press, 2003.

Martin-Jones, David. *Deleuze, Cinema, and National Identity: Narrative Time in National Contexts.* Edinburgh: Edinburgh University Press, 2006.

McGavin, Patrick Z. "Away, So Close: Téchiné's Trip to Morocco." *IndieWireMovies.* At www.indiewire.com/movies.

Otero-Pailos, Jorge. "Casablanca's Regime: The Shifting Aesthetics of Political Technologies (1907–43)." *Postmodern Culture* 8, no. 2 (1998).

Pisters, Patricia. "Arresting the Flux of Images and Sounds: Free Indirect Discourse and the Dialectics of Political Cinema." In *Deleuze and the Contemporary World,* edited by Ian Buchanan and Adrian Parr, 175–94. Edinburgh: Edinburgh University Press, 2006.

———. *The Matrix of Visual Culture: Working with Deleuze in Film Theory.* Palo Alto, CA: Stanford University Press, 2003.

Wayne, Mike. *Political Film: The Dialectics of Third Cinema.* London: Pluto Press, 2001.

Back to the Margins in Search of the Core

Foreign Land's Geography of Exclusion

The Tagus is fairer than the river flowing through my village,
But the Tagus isn't fairer than the river flowing through my village
Because the Tagus isn't the river flowing through my village.

—Alberto Caeiro (Fernando Pessoa's heteronym),
"The Keeper of Flocks"[1]

Lampião was great, but he often became small.

—Dadá, in *Black God, White Devil*[2]

The crisis of the national project in the early 1990s, caused by a short-lived but disastrous government, led Brazilian art cinema, for the first time, to look at itself as periphery and reapproach the old colonial center, Portugal. *Terra estrangeira/Foreign Land* (Walter Salles and Daniela Thomas, Brazil/Portugal, 1995), a film about Brazilian exiles in Portugal, is the best illustration of this perspective shift aimed at providing a new sense of Brazil's scale and position within a global context. Shot mainly on location in São Paulo, Lisbon, and Cape Verde, it promotes the encounter of Lusophone peoples who find a common ground in their marginal situation. Even Portugal is defined by its location at the edge of Europe and by beliefs such as Sebastianism, whose origins go back to the time when the country was dominated by Spain. As a result, notions of *core* or *center* are devolved to the realm of myth.

The film's carefully crafted dialogue combines Brazilian, Portuguese, and Creole linguistic peculiarities into a common dialect of exclusion, while language puns trigger visual rhymes that refer back to the Cinema Novo (the Brazilian New Wave) repertoire and restage the imaginary of the discovery turned into unfulfilled utopia. The main characters also acquire historical resonances, as they are depicted as descendants of Iberian conquistadors turned into smugglers of precious stones in the present. Their activities define a circuit of international exchange that resonates with that of globalized cinema, a realm in which *Foreign Land,* made up of citations and homage to other cinemas, tries to retrieve a sense of belonging.

The poet Fernando Pessoa, a looming figure behind the film's form and content, shows, in the famous verses quoted above, how notions of center and periphery can vary according to the point of view. But while Pessoa's oxymoronic order secures a central position for the author's native village, in *Foreign Land* the view from abroad enables the realization of Brazil's smallness, despite its great territorial dimensions. In this chapter, I will attempt to demonstrate how the dialectic tension between great and small, center and periphery permeates the film at all levels and accounts for its main qualities.

The Perspective Shift

Foreign Land was one of the first signs of cinematic revival after the collapse of Brazilian film production, following the drastic measures introduced by newly elected President Collor de Mello, in 1990. As well as freezing the bank accounts of the entire population, the Collor government downgraded the Ministry of Culture to a mere Secretariat and closed down several cultural institutions, including Embrafilme, the state production and distribution company that had supported two decades of a burgeoning popular film industry. *Foreign Land* is thus a modest, independent production, in sharp contrast to Salles's previous film, *A grande arte/High Art* (Walter Salles, Brazil/USA, 1991), a commercially ambitious, English-language production, aimed at the international market. As the director explains, "I was emerging from a much more hierarchical and painful process, from a personal point of view, which was *High Art. Foreign Land* was a true rediscovery of the pleasure to shoot a fiction film with the same lightness and enthusiasm of my documentary filmmaking, which is where I come from."[3] The film was conceived and developed in a collaborative manner. The script was co-written by Walter Salles, Daniela Thomas, and Marcos Bernstein, with additional dialogue by Millôr Fernandes. Salles also contributed to the editing, alongside Felipe Lacerda. Thomas's cousin, Fernando Alves Pinto, then a beginner, was cast in the lead, and other professional actors, such as Fernanda Torres, Alexandre Borges, Laura Cardoso, and Tchéky Karyo, were hired on the basis of friendship or reduced fees. Black-and-white 16 mm stock, later blown up to

35 mm, was chosen as a more economic and agile format for location shoot. Shooting was completed in just over four weeks, despite taking place in three different continents (South America, Europe, and Africa). This suited the sense of urgency prompted by the national crisis and the need to provide "an immediate response to what we had gone through in the early 1990s," in Salles's words.[4]

The same black-and-white 16 mm stock, combined with ascetic formalism, had been used by Walter's brother and close collaborator, João Moreira Salles, to shoot his confessional film *Santiago* (Brazil, 2007) in 1992, just before preparation work started for *Foreign Land*. Moreira Salles's documentary, which reflects social and personal crises to the extent that it remained unfinished until 2007, is a radical defense of modesty by means of homage to giants such as Ozu, while calling for a detailed scrutiny of individual responsibilities toward Brazil's unequal class structure. By exposing its aesthetic options through self-reflexive voice-over commentary, *Santiago* offers an interesting insight into *Foreign Land*'s respectful cinephilia, which draws on Wim Wenders's early, unpretentious road movies as well as on Wenders's own aesthetic models, such as Ozu, as we will see below.

On the level of the fable, *Foreign Land* is all about defeat and loss of self-esteem. Its storyline combines three basic strands: the nefarious consequences of an unscrupulous government; the fate of an émigré widow, Manuela, living in São Paulo, who dies before realizing her dream to return to her native Basque country; and the misfortunes of Brazilian exiles in Portugal. The time frame is contemporary, the early 1990s, a moment when economic constraints had turned Brazil "into a country of emigration, for the first time in 500 years," in the words of scriptwriters Thomas, Bernstein, and Salles.[5] The main character, Paco, represents one of the 800,000 emigrants who left the country during the less than two-year period of the Collor government. His mother, Manuela, dies of a stroke when she realizes, from a government TV broadcast, that her meager savings, meant to finance her trip back to San Sebastián, in the Basque country, have been confiscated. With the death of his widowed mother, Paco is left completely bereft and falls prey to Igor, a Mephistophelean character who offers him a trip to Portugal. He thus becomes unwittingly embroiled in an international scheme of diamond trafficking. In Lisbon, Paco meets and falls for Alex, another expatriate Brazilian older than he, who has just lost her junkie saxophonist boyfriend, killed in a diamond-related dispute. Paco and Alex make their way toward what becomes for them an ersatz homeland, San Sebastián, but end up in the hands of the enemy.

Its formal modesty and defeatist storyline notwithstanding, the film displays a considerable intellectual thrust. The range of cinematic references resorted to includes Welles's *Touch of Evil* (USA, 1958) for the camera work; Antonioni for the meditative scenes; Truffaut's and Godard's early Nouvelle Vague films for the black-and-white and location shots; Huston's *The Treasure of the Sierra Madre* (USA, 1948) for the lost diamonds at the end, and many others.[6] Literary citations abound, including Goethe, Euripides, Shakespeare, Vinicius de Moraes, and, not least, Fernando Pessoa. Despite his humble origins, Paco, who lives on the earnings of his seamstress mother, intends to become an actor and take the role of no less than Faust in Goethe's classic play. As is well known, Faust is not only Goethe's most ambitious character but also the protagonist of his most central work, a multigenre, multiform piece, which evolved through the author's life for about sixty years. The figure of Faust is characterized by an insatiable thirst for knowledge, which to a great extent reflects that of Goethe himself and draws upon the hero the attention of God and the devil.[7] In the opening scene of *Foreign Land,* Paco is rehearsing the verses from which the film title is extracted, and which expresses Faust's delusions of power:

> Even now my powers are loftier, clearer;
> I glow, as drunk with new-made wine:
> New strength and heart to meet the world incite me,
> The woe of earth, the bliss of earth, invite me,
> And though the shock of storms may smite me
> No crash of shipwreck shall have power to fright me!
> . . .
> I feel thy presence, Spirit, I invoke!
> Reveal thyself!
> Ha! In my heart what rending stroke!
> . . .
> Let them drop down the golden atmosphere,
> And bear me forth to new and varied being!
> Yea, if a magic mantle once were mine,
> To waft me o'er the world at pleasure,
> I would not for the costliest stores of treasure—
> Not for a monarch's robe—the gift resign.[8]

Inspired by these verses, later on in the film, Paco will gather courage to face a bunch of powerful enemies and flee with Alex, thus unleashing the chase sequences that drive the plot to a climax. The "shipwreck" that Goethe's hero remains unafraid of will also reemerge in Paco's story, acquiring special significance, as we will see in a moment. For the time being, let us note that the Brazilian translation of the verses above, utilized in the film to signify Faust's dream of exploring the world in a magic mantle, employs the term *terras estrangeiras* ("foreign lands") for "world at pleasure."

But it is not only Goethe who lies at the origin of the title. Another, more important reference is Brazil's foremost filmmaker, Glauber Rocha, who made a famous "land trilogy" (*trilogia da terra*), which consists of *Deus e o diabo na terra do sol/Black God, White Devil* (Brazil, 1964), *Terra em transe/Land in Trance* (Brazil, 1967),[9] and *A idade da terra/The Age of the Earth* (Brazil, 1981). Rocha's obsession with the national project, as well as his megalomania, are encapsulated in the recurrent use, in his film titles, of the term *terra,* which in Portuguese means at the same time the "land," the "country," and the entire "Earth." And indeed his cosmogonic vision of history progressed from the Brazilian land, in *Black God, White Devil,* to Latin America in *Land in Trance,* to finally encompass the whole planet in *The Age of the Earth.*

As well as quoting Rocha's films by resorting to the word "land" (*terra*), *Foreign Land* re-elaborates crucial aspects of the first two parts of the trilogy, which are Cinema Novo landmarks, *Black God, White Devil,* and *Land in Trance.* These films present a dialectical structure that owes much to Rocha's pioneering move of drawing on the country's foundational mythology as a means of explaining its ongoing political processes. On the basis of sixteenth-century utopian myths derived from the imaginary of discovery, such as the belief in Eldorado in the New World and the island of Utopia itself, Rocha developed a monumental imagery to express his heroes' great expectations in contrast with the country's tragic reality.[10]

Oppositional binaries, inspired by Sartre (*The Devil and the Good Lord*) and Nietzsche (*Beyond Good and Evil*), which echo *Faust's* rivalry between God and the devil, constitute the core of *Black God, White Devil.* Its protagonist, the rebel cowherd Manuel, is torn between two antagonistic leaders, the religious preacher Sebastião and the outlaw Corisco (the right hand of the famous Lampião), who are alternately defined as good and evil, dwarfs and giants, as in the epigraph above. At the end of this film, shot just before the 1964 military coup put an end to the hopes of the Left, aerial shots of the infinite *sertão* (the arid backlands of the Brazilian northeast) are replaced by images of a vast sea in a famous sequence suggestive of the social revolution. However, *Land in Trance,* shot in the disillusioned period that followed the military coup, provides a negative sequel to this ending. The film opens with monumental aerial shots of the sea's gleaming silver surface leading to a country of lush forests referred to as "Eldorado." But paradise regained is only presented to be immediately deconstructed as a privilege of the ruling classes, while utopianism is blamed for the inequality that has reigned in Brazil from its birth.

Nearly thirty years later, *Foreign Land* revisits Rocha's dialectics as a way of reflecting on a new political crisis in Brazil. According to Salles, at the origin of the film are the photographs of a shipwreck on the Cape Verde coast, taken by Jean-Pierre Favreau. Salles took his crew and cast to Cape Verde to shoot the lead couple in their flight to San Sebastián against the backdrop of this shipwreck.[11] Although at this point in the story Paco and Alex are still unscathed and, like Goethe's hero, unafraid of the world, the metaphorical shipwreck indicates their forthcoming defeat. It also provides a visual rhyme to the "old ship" bound for some unknown destination mentioned in the song "Vapor barato" ("Cheap Steamer"), by Jards Macalé and Waly Salomão, sung by Alex in the diegesis and Gal Costa in the extradiegetic soundtrack. These poetic ship metaphors, however, only gain consistency and historical resonance thanks to Rocha and his maritime imagery, resorted to in a key scene of the film.

Paco and Alex find themselves in Cape Espichel, defined in the film as Europe's farthest westerly point,[12] seated at the edge of a precipice beyond

Alex and Paco photographed against the shipwreck in Cape Verde in *Foreign Land* (1995).

which lies the vast open sea. For a moment the sea fills the frame, before the camera drifts back to capture Alex and Paco from behind, looking out to the sea before them. A dialogue follows:

> ALEX: You have no idea of where you are, do you? This is the tip of Europe. (*Flinging her arms open*) This is the end! What courage, don't you think? To cross this sea 500 years ago . . . Just because they thought paradise was there. (*She points left toward the horizon.*) Poor Portuguese . . . they ended up discovering Brazil.
>
> *Paco laughs. Alex remains serious.*
>
> ALEX: What are you laughing about?

Although an unmistakable reference to Rocha, these monumental sea images, connected by the dialogue to the imaginary of the discovery and Brazil's foundational myths, present a decisive difference from their model in that they are territorially attached to Portugal, rather than Brazil. Through this radical perspective shift Brazil's situation is redefined as periphery and its territory reduced to irrelevant, even invisible, proportions within a global context. As a result, Brazil's foundational myth becomes the butt of a joke.

For Marilena Chauí, one of the effects of the foundational myth at the base of Brazilian authoritarian society is to reassert the belief in the country as a gift from God and Nature, whose problems derive from external causes, among them, the colonization by Portugal, rather than another (supposedly "better") European nation (France and Holland are some of the alternative countries that, in the early colonial times, had attempted to capture Brazil from the Portuguese domain without success).[13] By providing a view of Brazil from an external point of view, the maritime scene in *Foreign Land* turns this myth on its head and Brazil becomes the bad luck in Portuguese history, rather than the other way round.

With this majestic maritime scene, *Foreign Land* leads a trend in the Brazilian Film Revival of the mid-1990s of resorting to sea imagery as a way of reconnecting with and revising Rocha's and Cinema Novo's national project, thus becoming a foundational film in its own right. There is no lack of examples: *Baile Perfumado/Perfumed Ball* (Paulo Caldas and Lírio Ferreira, Brazil, 1996), *Corisco e Dadá/Corisco and Dadá* (Rosemberg Cariry, Brazil, 1996), *Crede-mi/Believe Me* (Bia Lessa and Dany Roland, Brazil, 1997), *Bocage—o triunfo do amor/Bocage—The Triumph of Love* (Djalma Limongi Batista, Brazil/Portugal, 1998), *Hans Staden* (Luiz Alberto Pereira, Brazil/

The sea scene in *Foreign Land.* Brazil is reduced to invisible proportions.

Portugal, 1999), up to Walter Salles's own *Abril despedaçado/Behind the Sun* (Brazil/France/Switzerland, 2001).[14]

 Foreign Land thus defines itself as a direct, though modest, heir of past cinematic milestones. Accordingly its protagonist, Paco, is characterized as a downgraded descendant of sixteenth-century heroes. Verbal puns and explicative dialogue make such connections explicit. Paco's full name is Francisco Eizaguirre, a surname that Igor (played by the forceful theater actor, Luis Melo) pronounces detachedly as "Ex-Aguirre," in a reference to Dom Lope de Aguirre, the Spanish conquistador who famously sailed to South America in search of Eldorado. Alongside the historical fact, the relevant reference here is the film *Aguirre, der Zorn Gottes/Aguirre, the Wrath of God* (Werner Herzog, Germany, 1972), which was not only partly shot in Brazil and starred, among others, Cinema Novo filmmaker Ruy Guerra, but was also deeply influenced by Rocha and his megalomania.[15] Igor describes the time of the discoveries as that of "visionaries," just as Herzog, in his early days, used to be described—and enjoyed describing himself.

 Gilles Deleuze has observed the way in which in Herzog's films, including *Aguirre,* the dialectics of the large and the small result in "the sublimation of the large form and the enfeeblement of the small form," something that characterizes Herzog as "the most metaphysical of cinema directors."[16] *Foreign Land*'s powerful imagery, under the direction of the exceptional cinematographer Walter Carvalho, would certainly stand comparison with Rocha's and Herzog's metaphysical visions, were it not for the accompanying self-ironic text through which the hero remains imprisoned within his earthly dimensions. When Igor compares Paco to great names of gold and diamond hunters, this is just a way of enticing the unsuspecting youngster to become a mule in his international smuggling operations. Through Igor's cultivated speech, which includes mentions of Aleijadinho (Brazil's greatest baroque sculptor), one learns about a Brazilian tradition, harking back to the colonial times, of smuggling gold and precious stones inside hollow wooden statues of saints (*santos do pau oco*). Igor's remark cuts to the image of the expatriate Miguel, involved in illegal trafficking, hammering the bottom of a wooden saint to extract a bag of diamonds, thus confirming the degradation of current descendants of past conquistadors.

Wenders and the Elusive Nation

The wiping out of the Brazilian nation through a perspective shift offers the filmmakers an opportunity to reconnect with Wim Wenders, whose early works are structured upon the character of the modern wanderer in search of an elusive homeland. The Salles brothers, and Walter in particular, are self-confessed Wenders admirers.[17] Salles's kinship with the German director can be easily observed in his interest in aimless travelers, reminiscent of the characters in *Im Lauf der Zeit/Kings of the Road* (Wim Wenders, Germany, 1976) and *Alice in den Städten/Alice in the Cities* (Wim Wenders, Germany, 1974). In *Foreign Land,* the option for black and white, though primarily due to economic concerns, is no less tributary to Wenders's avowed preference for this style in his early films. "Life is in color, but black and white is more realistic," declares the cameraman Joe, Wenders's alter ego in the film *Der Stand der Dinge/The State of Things* (Wim Wenders, Germany/Portugal/USA, 1982). And indeed Wenders made a point of shooting this film, set in Portugal, in black and white as a form of protest against Coppola, the producer of *Hammett* (Wim Wenders, USA, 1982), who had him shoot this homage to American film noir in color. Needless to say, *The State of Things* is a decisive influence on *Foreign Land,* with its Portuguese settings and displaced characters lodged in a "shipwreck" hotel half-sunk into the sea. By an intriguing coincidence, Wenders was again exercising his independent filmmaking penchant in Portugal with *Lisbon Story* (Wim Wenders, Germany/Portugal, 1994), at the time when Salles, Thomas, and their team were there working on *Foreign Land*.[18]

Homelessness and loss of identity are typical of Wenders's characters, who in their travels are constantly photographing places, people, and themselves as a "proof that they exist."[19] In *Foreign Land,* the Wendersian photographic proof of identity is translated into didactic images of identity documents, for example when Paco forges his mother's signature in order to withdraw money for her burial, which cuts to a close-up of the late Manuela's identity card. In another passage, Alex, after her boyfriend has spent all her savings on drugs, sees herself obliged to sell her passport to a gang of Spaniards, who pay a pittance for it because "it is Brazilian" ("*es brasileño*"). Another close-up of her Brazilian passport is duly provided. Both Paco and Alex are, in fact, ridding themselves of the "stigma" of being Brazilian, while looking for a sense of belonging, which is nowhere to be found.

Another of the film's common features with Wenders are deserted or estranged landscapes and cityscapes, often adorned with signs or advertisements in the manner of ironic comments. An emblematic example in Wenders's work is the town sign "Paris" in a Texas desert (*Paris, Texas,* France/Germany, 1984), which is reminiscent of Ozu's shots of shop signs in English to hint at the American presence in occupied Japan. Similar compositions can be found in *Foreign Land,* such as the shot of a huge outdoor billboard of the underwear Hope against the backdrop of the Minhocão, or "big worm," a dreadful flyover in the heart of São Paulo constructed in the dictatorship

The word *Hope* on the outdoor functions as an ironic comment on the characters' destinies.

years, next to which Paco and his mother live. Rather than "hope" for the characters involved, what follows is Manuela's death and Paco's trip abroad, which also leads to his end.

The Invention of San Sebastián

On closer inspection, some apparently random options in the film reveal a surprising resonance with both Portuguese and Brazilian history and mythology. One of them is the choice of San Sebastián as Manuela's birthplace, a city that, in the film, is endowed with a sort of mystic aura, given that she dies before going back there and that Paco also fails to reach it on his escape from Portugal and Igor's persecution. San Sebastián may have been an entirely fortuitous choice, due, for example, to its attractive rocky formations stamped on a postcard found among Manuela's cherished assets—or simply because it is popular among filmmakers for its famous yearly international film festival.

However, a few details give it particular significance in this film. Firstly, it is located in the Basque country, known for its long-lasting struggle for independence from Spain and recognition of its own national identity. Its uniqueness is reinforced by the fact that very little is known about the origin of the Basque language, which does not belong to the Indo-European family. Identity, and national identity, are thus coherent, though tacit, links between the place and the film's subject matter.

Secondly, and more importantly, the repetition of the name "San Sebastián" throughout the film as a leitmotiv leads to unavoidable associations with Sebastianism, Portugal's most important patriotic myth. This connection is emphasized by the montage, attentively steered by Salles himself. The first time Manuela pronounces the words "San Sebastián," the image that follows is a ferry crossing the Tagus, in Lisbon. The viewer is thus introduced to Portugal in connection with (and submission to) Spain, even before the story relocates there, after having started overseas in São Paulo. The overlap of Portugal and Spain through the mention of San Sebastián has a second, more profound resonance in that the Sebastian myth was developed during the period when Portugal was dominated by Spain. This association is endorsed in the film by the definition of Portugal as peripheral to Europe, and therefore to Spain, through a number of dialogue lines. For example: shortly before being killed, Miguel tells Pedro that he is going away to "Europe" with Alex, and Pedro retorts: "You'll have to get in Europe first."

As for Sebastianism, it is a myth perpetuated through a number of religious sects over the centuries both in Portugal and Brazil. Its origin harks back to the episode of the disappearance of Dom Sebastião, "o Desejado" (Sebastian I, "the Desired"), King of Portugal, in the battle of Ksar-el-Kebir, in Morocco, in 1578. Because the twenty-four-year-old king was the last heir to the Portuguese throne after a long-lasting hereditary crisis, his death caused a power vacuum. There followed a two-year dynastic dispute that was eventually resolved in 1580 with the victory of Philip II, King of Spain, whose army invaded Portugal. In the following year, 1581, Philip II was recognized as King of Portugal, and the country remained annexed to Spain for the following sixty years.

As a result, a belief took shape in Portugal that Sebastian was not dead and would return to redeem the Portuguese people. The essence of Sebastianism can thus be summarized as nostalgia for the lost homeland. In association with it, the Portuguese word *saudade*—normally translated as "nostalgia," but which includes an element of passive awaiting and longing—has acquired the quality of a national trait. As the humorous remark of Portuguese novelist Eça de Queiroz goes, "*procrastinare lusitanum est,*" or "to procrastinate is typical of the Portuguese."[20]

António Machado Pires describes Sebastianism as an "indolence motivated by the confidence in the King's return,"[21] an attitude that leads to inaction and submission to authoritarian regimes, in the same way described by Chauí about the Brazilian foundational myth. In the apt definition by António Quadros, "Sebastianism is based on . . . the painful awareness (*consciência infeliz*) of the Portuguese reality . . . and places its bet on the hope of regeneration through a personal savior, a leader distinguished by charisma and fate." This "painful awareness," according to Quadros, "is the foremost and clearest feature of *The Lusiads.*"[22] Significantly, *The Lusiads,* by Luiz de Camões, Portugal's greatest epic poem, on the adventures of the navigator and discoverer Vasco da Gama, is dedicated to none other than Sebastian. Thriving through Portuguese literary history, Sebastianism also marks the oeuvre of Almeida Garrett, Father Vieira (who spent most of his life in Brazil) and, not least, Fernando Pessoa, the author of innumerable Sebastianic writings with patriotic undertones, in which Sebastian is defined as the very impersonation of Portugal.[23]

Sebastianism was introduced in Brazil in early colonial times and acquired the form of a conservative attachment to monarchy after the establishment of the republican regime in 1889. The famous rebellions of Canudos and Pedra Bonita, which are restaged by Rocha in *Black God, White Devil,* were Sebastianist movements animated by the hope that Sebastian would return in the person of a messianic savior, redeem the poor, and provide them with a fairer homeland.

In Portugal, Sebastianism has deeper roots, which hark back to a time prior to Sebastian's disappearance. A predecessor of the Sebastian myth is that of the "Encoberto" King, sung by the legendary shoemaker Bandarra in the early sixteenth century. According to the legend, the Encoberto would emerge from the salt sea mounting an unharnessed horse.[24] Euclides da Cunha, the author of one of the most seminal books in Brazilian literature, *Rebellion in the Backlands,* a detailed account of the rebellion of Canudos, records a similar prophecy among the rebels in relation to the return of Sebastian: "In truth I say unto you, when nation falls out with nation, Brazil with Brazil, England with England, Prussia with Prussia, then shall Dom Sebastião with all his army arise from the waves of the sea."[25]

In Rocha's *Black God, White Devil,* inspired to a great extent by Euclides's account, Sebastianism is incarnated by the messianic leader São Sebastião (Saint Sebastian), who utters the apocalyptic prophecy that "the backlands will turn to sea, and the sea into backlands." This slogan leads to the film's famous closure, in which the revolutionary sea replaces the arid backlands. As we have seen, images of the sea have become, ever since, a privileged cinematic representation of the Brazilian Utopia.

Foreign Land's chain of references is thus a construction *en abîme,* as it suggests the cyclical recurrence of the search for the lost homeland throughout history. San Sebastián, a city in search of a land, reflects Sebastianism, originated in a time when Portugal had ceased to be an independent nation in the sixteenth century, a situation that comes to inflect the story of Brazilian expatriates in a moment of national crisis in the present. This occasions the revision of the maritime utopia of the discovery, utilized in Rocha's Cinema Novo films as allegories of Brazil's contemporary problems. In *Foreign Land,* the plight of sixteenth-century discoverers, who risked their lives in search of gold and precious stones, reflects on the lives of current Brazilian emigrants, involved as they are with trafficking in diamonds and drugs.

In its recycling process, the discovery mythology acquires new features and loses a few others. Rocha's concern was mainly political. He had resorted to the mythology of the discovery as a means of analyzing the vicious power structure in present-day Brazil. *Foreign Land,* however, is much more about the end of politics, symbolized by the traumatic TV images of finance minister Zélia Cardoso de Mello announcing the freezing of all bank accounts. The disaster to an individual life that ensues—the abrupt death of Manuela—sends the story from the public back to the private domain. As I have pointed out elsewhere,[26] the focus here is on individual destinies of middle-class characters, affected by a provisional economic recession rather than a structural class struggle. While in a Rocha film such as *Land in Trance* the utopian Eldorado was discarded as part of a baleful foundational mythology, in *Foreign Land* it responds to a positive belief of the middle classes, endorsed (as a loss) by the enunciation. Rocha's symbolic characters, driven by the urge to change the world, are here replaced by common individuals, moved by personal aspirations. Accordingly, the "fatherland" gives way to the "father," politics to religion, and revolution to a love affair.

Whereas on the aesthetic level the filmmakers are searching for affiliation among the great in Brazilian and international cinema, in the story Paco is looking for his missing father in the person of his mother's mythical father back in the unattainable homeland of San Sebastián. Manuela constantly remarks on Paco's resemblance to his grandfather, through which the son coincides with the father in the same way that Jesus equals God by taking his seat on his Father's right-hand side, in the Christian mythology. When Paco, with his arms wide open, tries on the clothes that his mother has been commissioned to make, he is compared by one of her customers to "Christ the Redeemer" (the famous statue on the Corcovado hill, in Rio).

Later on he is photographed under a bare stone cross in a public square, in an unequivocal indication of his sacrificial ending. *Aitá* ("father" in Basque) is the last word Manuela utters before she dies. And Paco finally dies in the arms of Alex, the substitute mother, before he reaches the utopian San Sebastián. But here social cinema has already lost touch with reality to enter the realm of the crime thriller genre and its corresponding rules.

Paco is compared to "Christ the Redeemer."

The Transnational Portuguese

One of the disconcerting discoveries for Brazilians in the film seems to be the realization that they have been a colonized people alongside the Africans. Such a statement may sound surprising for readers unfamiliar with Brazil's colonial history, as they may not be aware that during the Napoleonic wars, in 1808, the entire Portuguese court, including the emperor, John VI, relocated to Rio de Janeiro, which became the capital of the empire until shortly before Brazil declared independence in 1822. Thus the memory of colonialism, for Brazilians, is not as clear and painful as for those who remained under Portuguese domination until the late twentieth century. In the film, Brazilians are repeatedly reminded of the fact that they are former Portuguese subjects. This also brings forth the awareness that Portugal holds the primacy of the Portuguese language. The following comment by Alex shows how her use of vernacular Portuguese has been denaturalized through the contact with native Portuguese: "I'm becoming increasingly aware of my accent, that my voice is an insult to their ears."

Miguel resentfully refers to the bar where he plays saxophone as "the cabaret of the colonies," to which his friend Pedro, the Portuguese bookshop owner reminiscent of Fernando Pessoa, with his round spectacles and proverbial mode of address, retorts: "This is a site where there are folks from everywhere, *pá*, from the *Brasis*, from the *Angolas*, from the *Guinés*, what do you want? This is how it is, *pá*!"[27]

The film then proceeds to focus on real Lusophone Africans residing in Portugal who, in the fictional plot, share with Brazilians their semilegal status. Their spoken Creole Portuguese also offers the Brazilians an opportunity to reflect on the Brazilian vernacular from an external perspective. Daniela Thomas, in the extras of the DVD of *Foreign Land,* talks about the laboratory training she carried out with African immigrants in Portugal in order to become familiar with what she jokingly terms *pretoguês,* a word that amalgamates "black" (*preto*) and "Portuguese" (*português*).[28] Most non-African Portuguese speakers would need a glossary to decipher the rich vocabulary used in the film.[29]

But not only are non-Africans puzzled by Lusophone African speakers, the reverse is also true, as illustrated in this humorous dialogue between Paco and Loli, an Angolan immigrant played by José Laplaine (a Malian filmmaker residing in Paris in real life), upon Paco's return from a night of love with Alex:

PACO: She started it all, you know? Took hold of me and . . . (*embar-*

rassed) ate me.

LOLI: How do you mean?

PACO: She ate me.

LOLI: She ate you?

PACO: She ate me.

Loli laughs a lot.

LOLI: A-ka, Brazilian, so she ate you! Well, I'll go out tonight and dine on some chick. (*laughing a lot*) Ah, you people are really something. Ah! And it's us they call cannibals! Ate you . . .

PACO: She ate me and, the morning after, she acted like we'd never met, man. Since I've been here the weirdest things keep happening.

LOLI: What did you expect from Lisbon, Brazilian?

PACO: I don't know . . . at least to discover something. After all, they set out from here to discover the whole world.

LOLI: (*laughing and pointing to the bridge*) Portugal? It takes them three hours to cross that fucking bridge! You are kidding!

Various interesting elements can be drawn from this conversation. The first of them is that native Brazilians have a past of cannibalism, which had been registered in minute detail by European travelers in the sixteenth century, such as Jean de Léry, André Thevet, and Hans Staden. Their accounts supplied rich pickings for late Cinema Novo films, such as *Como era gostoso o meu francês/How Tasty Was My Little Frenchman* (Nelson Pereira dos Santos, Brazil, 1970–72) and more recently to *Hans Staden.* Cannibalism, or "anthropophagy," inspired by the customs of Tupi Indians, was celebrated by the modernist movement of the 1920s and 1930s as a component of Brazilian national identity and metaphorically translated into a means of devouring European culture and exporting it back to Europe in the form of national artworks. In *Foreign Land,* the curious trace of Brazil's cannibal past found in current Brazilian-Portuguese slang, alongside Paco's naive belief in Portugal's grandeur, draws attention to the fact that Brazilians are still attached to the colonial times, while Africans have a more realistic picture of Portugal's current status. The film as a whole conveys the idea that Brazilians have arrived a few centuries late to board the ship to Utopia. Pedro, in one of his proverbial utterances of Pessoan overtones, says to Paco: "This isn't the right place to find anyone. It is a land of people who left for the sea. It's the ideal place to lose someone or get lost from oneself."

The mutual contact and contamination among the different Portuguese accents entailed by national and international migratory fluxes indicate the dilution of one's nation and identity. Paco has a São Paulo accent that sticks out when confronted with the speech of the two other Brazilians who are already settled in Portugal and enmeshed in the circuit of language exchange. Miguel, with his musical ear, feels at ease playing with the local Portuguese accent. He uses the second person of the singular (unlike Brazilians, who address each other in the third person) and slang typical of Portugal, as well as several Creole terms. In a dialogue with the Portuguese taxi driver and diamond dealer André, both exchange Portuguese and Brazilian accents between themselves, to the point of confusing the viewer as to who comes from where. When Miguel is bargaining with a potential buyer of his diamonds in the back seat of André's taxi, André becomes increasingly suspicious, until he bursts out: "Are we speaking the same language or what?"

Conclusion

As a whole, *Foreign Land* is a subtle corrective applied to the provincial jingoism entailed by the internal point of view. At the same time it declares allegiance to a certain international, self-critical, and self-reflexive cinema, keen on metalanguage and citation. By paying homage to film and literature giants, through the filter of Wenders and Rocha, it universalizes the question of the loss of identity, thus reducing and relativizing the importance of the national imaginary.

However, its anti-utopian imagery and text refer to a degraded middle class for whom the comparison of Brazil to Eldorado had made a certain sense until Collor's recessive coup put a provisional end to it. Rather than the oppressed masses Rocha had focused on, the story here is about characters who led a decent life, with plenty of intellectual and artistic ambitions, before they were forced into exile and lowly jobs, such as waitress in a low-class bar, or even illegal activities, such as dealing in drugs and stones. Paco was a physics student at the prestigious University of São Paulo (as the sticker on his bedroom window indicates), who wanted to be an actor, before becoming embroiled with outlaws. Miguel was a musician and composer whose current illegal activities are primarily due to the poor reception of his music in exile. Even Alex had musical ambitions, as the viewer discovers at the end of the film, when in a rare relaxing moment she sings "Vapor Barato" and says: "This is how I used to be."

And indeed the social problems pointed out in *Foreign Land* proved circumstantial and easy to resolve. Brazil's political and financial situation soon improved, with Collor's impeachment in 1992 and the establishment of the democratic neoliberal government of President Fernando Henrique Cardoso in 1993. The Cardoso government immediately put in place a new film financing system based on tax discounts, which entailed a new boom of films, known as the Brazilian Film Revival, whose first outputs appeared in the mid-1990s. The most representative film of this new batch, awarded the Golden Bear in Berlin and internationally feted as the symbol of Brazil's cinematic revival, was *Central do Brasil/Central Station* (Walter Salles, Brazil/France, 1998). In it, the mythic center that had been lost in Salles's previous film, *Foreign Land,* is regained and clearly identified with Brazil from the film's very title, which in Portuguese means the "center of Brazil" as well as the name of a Rio train station.

Central Station is a celebration of homeland regained in the very territory of poverty, the northeast dry hinterlands, where Glauber Rocha had set two of his most famous films, *Black God, White Devil* and *O Dragão da Maldade contra o Santo Guerreiro/Antônio das Mortes* (Brazil, 1969). As such it turns all the symbolism of *Foreign Land* on its head. A recurrent composition in *Foreign Land* is that of sacrificial sons, who lie in the lap of protective mother figures, such as the scene of Miguel in the lap of Alex, shortly before he is killed, and of Paco, in the lap of the same Alex, who lies dying from a bullet while Alex carries on driving to a hypothetical home in San Sebastián.

The Pietà composition is central in *Foreign Land*'s Christian iconography.

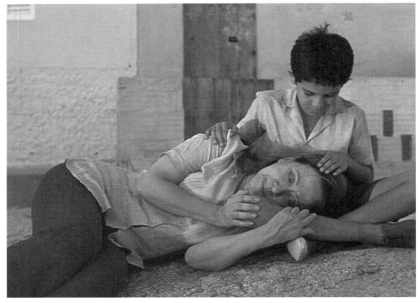

The Pietà tableau is reversed when the center is found, in *Central Station* (1998).

These Pietà tableaux are reversed when, in *Central Station,* the lost boy's substitute mother finally succeeds in taking him back to his homeland in the core of Brazil, the northeastern hinterlands.

At this point, the boy Josué identifies with his missing father, not accidentally called Jesus, and offers his own lap to an exhausted mother figure who has triumphantly accomplished her mission. This is the moment when fiction reencounters religion and the foundational myth, driving the story away from Brazil's real history.

Notes

1. "O Tejo é mais belo que o rio que corre pela minha aldeia, / Mas o Tejo não é mais belo que o rio que corre pela minha aldeia / Porque o Tejo não é o rio que corre pela minha aldeia." Alberto Caeiro, "O guardador de rebanhos," in Pessoa, *Ficções do interlúdio/1—Poemas completos de Alberto Caeiro* (Rio de Janeiro: Aguilar, 1975), 60. I used here Peter Rickard's translation in Pessoa, *Selected Poems,* 125.

2. "Lampião era grande, mas também ficava pequeno." See dialogue list of *Black God, White Devil,* in Rocha, *Roteiros do Terceyro Mundo,* 281.

3. Walter Salles interviewed by Marcelo Carrard Araujo, in Nagib, *O cinema da retomada—depoimentos de 90 cineastas dos anos 90,* 418.

4. Salles interviewed by Araujo, 418.

5. Thomas, Bernstein, and Salles, *Terra estrangeira,* 5.

6. For more on *Foreign Land*'s aesthetic models, see commented track of the film in the DVD *Terra estrangeira,* commemorative edition, 1995–2005, by Videofilmes, at www.vfilmes.com.br.

7. For a study of the embattlement between God and the devil in Goethe's *Faust,* see Campos, *Deus e o diabo no Fausto de Goethe,* 71.

8. Quoted from Goethe, *Faust: A Tragedy,*, 14–15 and 32. These passages are quoted in the filmscript *Terra estrangeira* as follows: "Sinto meus poderes aumentarem, estou ardendo, bêbado de um novo vinho. Sinto a coragem, o ímpeto de ir ao mundo, de carregar a dor da terra, o prazer da terra, de lutar contra as tempestades, de enfrentar a ira do trovão . . . Os espíritos pairam próximos. Me ouvem! Desçam! Desçam dessa atmosfera áurea e levem-me daqui para uma vida nova e variada! Que um manto mágico seja meu e me carregue para terras estrangeiras!" 7.

9. *Terra em transe* has been translated into English in various ways: *Land in Anguish, Earth Entranced,* and the preferred translation here, *Land in Trance.*

10. For a full discussion of Brazil's utopian mythology in relation to Rocha's works and the New Brazilian Cinema, see Nagib, *Brazil on Screen—Cinema Novo, New Cinema, Utopia.*

11. Thomas, Bernstein, and Salles, *Terra estrangeira,* 5.

12. The actual westernmost point in Portugal (and therefore in Europe) is Cape Roca, not far from Espichel.

13. Chauí, *Brasil: Mito fundador e sociedade autoritária,* 8.

14. See chapter 1, "Images of the Sea," in Nagib, *Brazil on Screen.*

15. See Nagib, "Cinema Novo, Glauber, Herzog," in Bax, Béghin, and Araújo Silva, eds., *Glauber Rocha/Nelson Rodrigues,* 88–90, for more on Rocha's influence on Herzog, especially with reference to his megalomaniac characters, such as Aguirre, Fitzcarraldo, and Cobra Verde, all three played by the famously megalomaniac actor, Klaus Kinsky, in films entirely or partly set in Brazil.

16. Deleuze, *Cinema 1—The Movement Image,* 185.

17. Salles interviewed by Araujo, 419.

18. See comments in this respect made by Daniela Thomas in interview to Araujo, in Nagib, *O cinema da retomada,* 485.

19. This line is spoken by Alice, in *Alice in the Cities.* See, in this respect, Buchka, *Augen kann man nicht kaufen—Wim Wenders und seine Filme,* chap. 3.

20. Quoted in Pires, *D. Sebastião e o encoberto—estudo e antologia,* 13.

21. Pires, *D. Sebastião e o encoberto,* 14.

22. Quadros, *Poesia e filosofia do mito sebastianista—o sebastianismo em Portugal e no Brasil,* 39ff.

23. See Quadros, ed., *Obra em prosa de Fernando Pessoa—Portugal, Sebastianismo e Quinto Império* (Mem Martins: Europa América, 1986).

24. Pires, *D. Sebastião e o encoberto,* 38ff.

25. Cunha, *Rebellion in the Backlands,* 194.

26. Nagib, *Brazil on Screen,* 21.

27. In the original: "Isto é um sítio em que vem gente de todo lado, pá, dos brasis, das angolas, das guinés, o que é que tu queres? É assim, pá!"

28. DVD *Terra estrangeira.*

29. Some of the ear-catching Luso-African terms are: *madjé, xota, wafekia, panco, vadiluka, n'gueta, umbivalê, anhaunbitê, kigila, mambo, maka.* They derive from local languages in Cape Verde, Guinea Bissau, Angola, and Mozambique.

Bibliography

Bax, Dominique, Cyrill Béghin, and Mateus Araújo Silva, eds. *Glauber Rocha/Nelson Rodrigues.* Paris: Magic Cinema, 2005.

Buchka, Peter. *Augen kann man nicht kaufen—Wim Wenders und seine Filme.* Munich: Carl Hanser, 1983.

Campos, Haroldo de. *Deus e o diabo no Fausto de Goethe.* São Paulo: Perspectiva, 1981.

Chauí, Marilena. *Brasil: Mito fundador e sociedade autoritária.* São Paulo: Fundação Perseu Abramo, 2000.

Cunha, Euclides da. *Rebellion in the Backland.* Translated by Samuel Putnam. London: Picador, 1995.

Deleuze, Gilles. *Cinema 1: The Movement Image.* Translated by Hugh Tomlinson and Barbara Habberjam. London: Continuum, 1995.

Goethe, Johann Wolfgang von. *Faust: A Tragedy.* Translated by Bayard Taylor. London: Ward, Lock, 1889.

Nagib, Lúcia. *Brazil on Screen: Cinema Novo, New Cinema, Utopia.* London: I. B. Tauris, 2007.

———. "Cinema Novo, Glauber, Herzog." In *Glauber Rocha/Nelson Rodrigues,* edited by Dominique Bax, Cyrill Béghin, and Mateus Araújo Silva, 88–90. Paris: Magic Cinema, 2005.

———. *O cinema da retomada—depoimentos de 90 cineastas dos anos 90.* São Paulo: Editora 34, 2002.

Pessoa, Fernando. *Ficções do interlúdio/1—Poemas completos de Alberto Caeiro.* Rio de Janeiro: Aguilar, 1975.

———. *Selected Poems.* Translated by Peter Rickard. Edinburgh: Edinburgh University Press, 1971.

Pires, António Machado. *D. Sebastião e o encoberto—estudo e antologia.* Lisbon: Fundação Calouste Gulbenkian, 1982.

Quadros, Antônio. *Poesia e filosofia do mito sebastianista—o sebastianismo em Portugal e no Brasil.* Lisbon: Guimarães and Cia., 1982.

Rocha, Glauber. *Roteiros do Terceyro Mundo.* Rio de Janeiro: Alhambra/Embrafilme, 1985.

Thomas, Daniela, Marcos Bernstein, and Walter Salles. *Terra estrangeira.* Rio de Janeiro: Rocco, 1996.

Memories of Underdevelopment

Torremolinos 73, Cinephilia, and Filiation
at the Margins of Europe

Spanish cinema today can hardly be called a *minor* or *peripheral* cinema. Recognized as one of the major Western European industries with global ambitions,[1] contemporary Spanish cinema has made a mark in the art house circuits with a more or less healthy production of quality, character-driven genre films with potential for multiplex crossover (such as *El laberinto del fauno/Pan's Labyrinth* [Guillermo del Toro, 2006]; or *El orfanato/The Orphanage* [Juan Antonio Bayona, 2007]) and a few recognized auteurs, none more overwhelmingly present than Pedro Almodóvar. Almodóvar has contributed, almost single-handedly, to create a brand image of Spanish cinema strongly connoted with undertones of cultural exuberance, overt sexuality, and aesthetic excess. However, there is another side to this success story, which I want to explore in this chapter through a close look at *Torremolinos 73* (Pablo Berger, Spain/Denmark 2003), a comedy that looks back to the early 1970s and thus to a time of far less confidence when it comes to Spain's self-image abroad.

Torremolinos 73 is a significant example of the vitality of a popular cinema that, more often than not, gets overlooked in the international circuits due to the specificity of its indigenous intertexts. The film's excavation of the recent past conflates contesting layers of cultural reality: the lived experiences of an aspiring middle-class in 1970s Spain; the desire for a cultural "beyond" defined by the sophisticated images of Europe circulated by art cinema; and, lastly, coexisting with and traversing both realities, a little-known film culture of sex comedies and soft-core subgenres that connects transnationally with the near-hybridization of art cinema and pornography in the international auteur cinema scene of the 1970s.[2] Far from reaffirming the certainties of the past, the film's complex interweaving of stylistic pastiche and film references draws unexpected connections between canonical and marginalized film histories. My contention is that a sense of cinephilia permeates the reconstruction of the quintessentially Spanish iconography of *Torremolinos 73* in ways that suggest a *strategic* practice instrumental in the debunking of prevalent mythologies in and about Spanish cinema.

Why cinephilia *and* Spanish cinema? The desire for and consumption of cinema has taken force as a peripheral form of film history, subject to practices that are, more often than not, as difficult to document and theorize as they are to regulate.[3] Cinephilia represents the point where industrial, social, and consumer trends meet with personal and idiosyncratic histories, minority tastes, fandom subcultures, and the intersection of the local and the global in processes of citation and appropriation.[4] As a set of cultural practices, cinephilia can therefore help us trace alternative histories that run parallel to and circumvent national borders and official discourses. My purpose in this chapter, though, is more specific; through close focus on *Torremolinos 73,* I want to explore the ways in which cinephilia, as the explicit theme underlying the historicist reconstruction carried out by the film, uncovers what Christian Keathley calls a "counter-factual" history, in which cinephilic moments are "points of entry, clues perhaps to another history flashing through the cracks of those histories we already know."[5] Cinephilia's preference for the odd, the anecdotal, and for the remembered, or even the mis-remembered fragment of a film, is especially helpful to tackle a film culture, such as the Spanish one, shaped by political and cultural upheavals, prolonged state censorship, delays, and interruptions. With this in mind, I want to suggest that *cinephilia* in *Torremolinos 73* entails a quest for a fictional or alternative *filiation,* that is, for ways to reimagine one's (historically and culturally determined) past outside the boundaries of one's national/family history. The above alliteration temptingly obliterates the etymological gap separating the Greek word *philia,* meaning fondness or inclination for, and the Latin noun *filiatio,* which refers to the father-child relationship, to belonging. These are, as the Oxford English Dictionary reminds us, nonrelated words. To link them would be, therefore, a misreading. Yet such misreadings are at the heart of the cinephilic impulse in *Torremolinos 73.* While much of the humor of the film derives from the characters' attempt at making connections that deny actual gaps in cultural understanding, the film's discourse opens up possibilities for a remapping of major national film histories in terms of transnational connections among fragmented histories of popular, minor, and forgotten indigenous traditions.

Cinephilia's Other Histories: Spanish Film Culture in the Era of Desarrollismo

Torremolinos 73 tells, tongue-in-cheek, the "true story"[6] of an average Spanish couple who unwittingly become stars in the underground economy of low-budget amateur porn film. The place is Madrid; the year is 1973. Alfredo López (Javier Cámara) leads a dreary existence as a door-to-door salesman trading an encyclopedic History of the Spanish Civil War that no one wants to buy. His wife Carmen (Candela Peña) works in a beauty parlor and wants, most of all, to have a child. Their dreams of parenthood and prosperity lead them to accept a dubious offer from Alfredo's boss, Don Carlos (Juan Diego), to make "educational" films on the reproductive habits of Spaniards for sale in Scandinavian countries. At first hesitantly, and then enthusiastically, the couple starts making clichéd Super-8 sex movies at home, which in turn start bringing home the kind of money that their modest day jobs could never produce. However, this only awakens Alfredo's desire to become a "real" filmmaker. With the help of a Danish-Swedish crew hired by Don Carlos—who sees in his employee's naive directorial ambitions a profitable business opportunity—Alfredo embarks in the making of an ambitious feature-length film titled "Torremolinos 73," a black-and-white drama inspired by Ingmar Bergman's style, and shot in the eponymous Spanish coastal resort, with Carmen as the star. In the meantime, Carmen has found out that Alfredo is sterile and, desperate to become a mother, she resolves to shoot a scene of explicit sexual intercourse so she can try and get impregnated by the Danish male lead.

Torremolinos 73 is unequivocally informed by the rise of retro styles in the late 1990s in films such as *Boogie Nights* (Paul Thomas Anderson, USA, 1997). Significantly, its release coincided with the international success of *Good Bye Lenin!* (Wolfgang Becker, Germany, 2003), another European comedy that revises the sociopolitical legacy of the recent historical past. As Philip Drake has noted, the retro film "mobilises particular codes that have come to connote a past sensibility as it is selectively re-remembered in the present (that is, 'the seventies' or 'the sixties') as a structure of feeling, and these codes function *metonymically,* standing in for the entire decade."[7] Berger's film capitalizes on indigenous retro trends featured in the unlikely revival of the 1960s and 1970s in Spanish popular culture. This revival has been driven by the huge popular success of the TV series *Cuéntame cómo pasó/Tell Me How It Happened* (TVE, 2001–5)[8] and of film comedies such as *El amor perjudica seriamente la salud/Love Seriously Damages Your Health* (Manuel Gómez Pereira, Spain, 1997) and *Muertos de risa/Death by Laughter* (Álex de la Iglesia, Spain, 1999).[9] These retro fictions are set against the backdrop of the last stages of the dictatorship in Spain, which would come to a close with the death of General Francisco Franco in 1975 and the transition years to democracy, culminating with the Spanish Constitution of 1978. Avoiding direct confrontation with specific historical events, the above films place instead the emphasis on the pastiche of past styles mediated by mass-media images and sounds—including popular music and photographic images along with cinema and television footage of the era. The recycling of archival materials in a present-tense narration thus construes a mode of address informed by the local, specific knowledges provided by the mass media.[10]

Unlike the examples above, *Torremolinos 73* looks abroad rather than at home in order to reconstruct a well-documented moment of cinephilia: the creation of the exportable myth of the film auteur. As Alfredo watches, entranced, the art-cinema classic *Det Sjunde Inseglet/The Seventh Seal* (Ingmar Bergman, Sweden, 1956) on television, the epiphanic moment of revelation[11] is alluded to via a citation of an already canonized signifier of cinephilia: the chess game between Death (Bengt Ekerot) and the Knight (Max von Sydow) that opens Bergman's film. However, the film also foregrounds the peculiarities of the Spanish context for a localized understanding of cinephilia. The late Francoist period (1960–75) was characterized by the end of political isolation and a willful movement toward superficial modernization within the limited freedoms allowed by the regime. As noted by film historians like John Hopewell, by the 1970s "Spain had become a curious mixture of traditional—largely Catholic—values and the behaviour thought proper for a consumer society."[12] Alfredo and Carmen represent the aspirational lower middle-classes in the Spain of *desarrollismo*—a soubriquet earned by the ideology of rapid and uneven economic development that characterized the regime's domestic policy in 1960s Spain.[13]

In the film, the new culture of consumerism is signified by numerous commodities on display. As we watch Alfredo watching *The Seventh Seal* dubbed into Spanish and aired on prime-time national television, the electronic, homely screen is double framed within the film shot. Through this subtly reframing in the mise-en-scène, a milestone of 1960s European cinephilia becomes part of a national landscape populated by a pick-and-mix of visual motifs of the era of *desarrollismo*. These include gray apartment blocks typical of the urbanism of the era; big department stores; the new (minuscule) nationally produced, affordable cars; hunting as the Sunday sport of choice for the well-to-do supporters of the regime; and last but not least, holidays by the sea in resort towns such as Torremolinos. The bleached-out, grayish tones that dominate the film's cinematography, along with the cramped spaces, minimal camerawork, and abundant use of close-ups rather than the medium and long shots of situation comedy give these memories of the 1970s a dismal patina, undermining easy assumptions of nostalgia.

This exercise of reconstruction and reframing connects with cinephilia as a historical and generational phenomenon. The burgeoning film culture in postwar Paris—now reconstructed as the "originary" moment of Western cinephilia—stands as shorthand for what Thomas Elsaesser has called "cinephilia—take one"; a practice located in a specific historical moment and producing its own knowledges and identities.[14] This originary moment can be mapped onto other major urban centers, such as London (where Elsaesser locates, in an autobiographical fashion, his own initiation as a cinephile) as well as New York and, I would add, Barcelona or Madrid. The latter cities produced their own, rivaling "New Waves": the aesthetic-driven experimentalism of the Barcelona School (Escuela de Barcelona), explicitly modeled on surrealism and French New Wave cinema competed with the politically engaged but state-controlled New Spanish Cinema (Nuevo Cine Español) produced by the graduates of the Madrid-based National Film School (Escuela Oficial de Cinematografía).[15] These generational film movements, further supported by film journals such as *Nuestro Cine,* were representative of a burgeoning youth culture engaged in watching, thinking about, and discussing cinema in public forums.

This explosion of cinematic activity took place against a backdrop of controlled freedoms and new forms of cultural expression restricted by state censorship.[16] As the stagnated Francoist regime entered a new phase of "opening" (*apertura*) and friendly foreign policy in search of international recognition and acceptance, the need arose for a new national cinema that could present an acceptable face of Spanish culture at film festivals and on international markets. The tension between the official culture of traditional values predicated by the regime and the controlled exposure to foreign forces of modernization gave birth to a growing culture of dissent, which permeates some of the key films of the late 1960s and early 1970s. A significant example would be Víctor Erice's elliptical masterpiece *El espíritu de la colmena/ Spirit of the Beehive,* made in 1973, in which the memories of cinema filtered through childhood subjectivity provide a densely metaphoric language to refer to an unspeakable past.

The history of this largely frustrated attempt to create a Spanish art cinema for Europe[17] constitutes the offscreen context to the onscreen narrative of *Torremolinos 73.* The film retrieves fragments of a different history of Spanish cinema revolving around the popular success of homespun genre films dealing with the issues of the day. In 1973, with the waning of Francoism, Spanish film reflected both the drive for ideological continuity and the impact of modernization.[18] In sociological terms, this other history presents a more accurate picture of the films Spanish audiences were consuming at the time. However, as is often the case with indigenous popular traditions, this was a cinema that was virtually nonexportable, and that alleviated but also reinforced the perceived sense of cultural isolation. When the couple goes to the movies, Carmen's choice of film is *Adiós, cigüeña, adiós/Bye Bye Stork* (Manuel Summers, Spain, 1970), a comedy-melodrama about teenage pregnancy. This film represents a "Third-Way cinema" (*cine de la tercera vía*), a compromised attempt at a popular cinema with an occasionally risqué and moderately progressive discourse or, as it has been ironically defined: "commercial cinema plus *auteur* cinema divided by two."[19] This attempt at a timidly engaged cinema is dismissed by Alfredo (whose newly discovered passion for Bergman makes him sneer at the sentimentality of the film) but much enjoyed by Carmen, the would-be mother and vocational homemaker.

The conventional gender divide in the cinema consumed by the couple stands in sharp contrast with the cinematic references that pepper the iconography of *Torremolinos 73.* The Third-Way cinema of the Transition was to some extent a reaction to the success of a cycle of down-market sex comedies that were made with the relaxation of censorship between 1969 and 1976. Máximo Valverde, a well-known actor featuring in both the Third-Way dramas and the sex comedies, plays himself in the film,[20] while the characters of Alfredo and his hapless workmate Juan Luis (Fernando Tejero) pay tribute to José Luis López Vázquez and Alfredo Landa, stars in many of the sex comedies. The latter even originated the moniker *landismo.*[21] Oscillating between comedies of manners in the tradition of *costumbrismo* and grotesque farces with sexual undertones, the *landismo* films provide the inspiration for many of the broad comedy situations surrounding Juan Luis's inability to find female sexual partners, and his resistance to the advances of one openly gay member of the Scandinavian film crew.

Whereas the box-office success of the *landismo* sex comedies should be considered in the light of their mixture of "daring" (yet mild) spicy content and reactionary politics,[22] the recuperation of this strand of Spanish popular cinema in *Torremolinos 73* serves to make a wider cultural point on what, for national audiences, would be recognizable stereotypes about Spain still in currency today. As noted by Luis Navarrete, the images provided by the new *españolada,* or indigenous popular film exaggerating traits of the Spanish national character and social mores, connect the old clichés of an invented tradition (gypsies, bandits, passionate women, flamenco, and bulls) with the new clichés integral to Spain's political and social situation during Franco-ism.[23] The latter are abundantly exploited in the *landismo* comedies, often revolving around the sexual frustration affecting the "Spanish little man," and the Spanish "difference" from all things European. Titles such as *Vente a Alemania, Pepe/Pepe, Come to Germany* (Pedro Lazaga, 1971); *Guapo heredero busca esposa/Handsome Heir Seeks Wife* (Luis María Delgado, 1972), *El reprimido/The Repressed Man* (Mariano Ozores, 1974), or *No desarás al vecino del quinto/Thou Shalt not Covet Thy Fifth-Floor Neighbour* (Ramón Fernández, 1971)[24]—cited as the big hit of its day in *Torremolinos 73*—dwell on these new clichés, presenting male characters ridden with inferiority complexes who overcompensate by reveling in male chauvinism, hyperbolic viril-ity, passion for football and women, love of the country and of its religious values characteristic of the new emigrants of late Francoism, and staunch Catholic moral standards (and double standards),[25] all of which intensify the myths of an isolated society craving for but left out of Europeanized modernity.

Torremolinos 73 mobilizes this cultural past through myriad intertex-tual references, and yet it resists the connection between past and present as a continuous, evolving line signposted with familiar cultural stereotypes. Avoiding the pitfalls of nostalgia and irony about "the way we were," *Tor-remolinos 73* operates instead on a different premise, a "what if?" mode that ultimately seeks to undermine the binary opposition between "us," the low national tradition, and a "them" associated with European art cinema and its connotations of cultural capital and sexual freedom. Thus, the film stages the imagined encounter between the "average" Spaniards and the "exotic" Northern Europeans through another intertextual layer: 1970s soft-core pornography. The scene in which Carmen and Alfredo, alongside Juan Luis, are instructed by a couple of Swedish "professionals," Erik (Tom Jacobsen) and Frida (Mari-Anne Jespersen) on how to make films for the so-called Audiovisual Encyclopedia of World Reproduction illustrates this point. This travesty of a scientific enterprise, humorously reminiscent of the sex educa-tion films of the 1960s, is the cover-up for a pornographic distribution outlet in the Scandinavian countries sought by the sleazy Don Carlos. Otherwise unable to raise sufficient income to fulfill their desire to be parents, Alfredo and Carmen decide to take a weekend crash course in which they receive specific training according to their different roles in the production of sex films. Alfredo learns cinematography and direction from Erik, whereas prud-ish Carmen is coached by Frida on how to "undress for man."

The humor of this sequence springs from the clash of brash stereotypes recycled from the *landismo* era. Costume and performance in a series of pointedly shot-reverse-shots highlight the differences between the two couples: the inhibited and sexually naive Spaniards stand in acute contrast to the bohemian and sexually liberated Scandinavians—a perception informed by the pioneering decriminalization of pornography in Denmark and Sweden in the late 1960s and popular misconceptions generated by the flow of tourism from Northern Europe. On the one hand, Frida's lesson in striptease playfully alludes to the "Swedish bombshell" cliché, which became an erotic myth amply exploited, first in the *landismo* sex comedies, and more explicitly in the subsequent raunchy *destape* (sex comedies with nudity) and soft-core porn films, many of which were set in Torremolinos and similar resort towns—at the time a top destination for Swedish tourists.[26] On the other hand, Erik is both coded as a professional of low-budget pornography and presented as a "former assistant to Ingmar Bergman," whom he continuously quotes while instructing Alfredo and Juan Luis on the shooting of sex scenes.

This felicitous gag, which brings side by side the booming market for pornography in Sweden with its most famous highbrow cinematic export, signals a wider post-1960s context in which art cinema would increasingly incorporate what traditionally had been considered X-rated content (and vice versa). Films such as *Last Tango in Paris* (Bernardo Bertolucci, Italy/France, 1972)—a *succès de scandale* cited in *Torremolinos 73; Saló* (Pier Paolo Pasolini, Italy, 1975); *Ai no corrida/The Empire of the Senses* (Nagisa Oshima, Japan, 1976); or, the Swedish *Jag är nyfiken-en film i gult/I Am Curious—Yellow* (Vilgot Sjöman, 1967) acquired notoriety for their explicit sexual content whereas, as Berger has noted, pornographic features such as *The Devil in Miss Jones* (Gerard Damiano, USA, 1973) would experiment under the influence of the aesthetic radicalism of the cinema of Michelangelo Antonioni or Jean-Luc Godard.[27] The name of Bergman also became the site of fusion between art and pornography through a history of international marketing of his films as soft-porn products, forming new layers of reception that indirectly inform the humor—and the drama—of *Torremolinos 73*.[28]

Commercial soft-core pornography had a successful if short-lived run in Spain between 1977 (year in which censorship was abolished and replaced with a classification office) and 1982 with the boom of the *S* film. This classification, granted by Spanish Ministry of Culture to films "likely to wound the sensitivity of the average spectator," served to encompass a mix of subgenres, including horror and soft-core films often made through coproduc-

Torremolinos 73 (2003). Playing out the differences: The Swedish . . .

. . . and the Spaniards.

tion arrangements.[29] Further to the increasing liberalization of social mores, which snowballed after Franco's death, the S film enjoyed a brief bonanza in Spain as a mainstream product. Daniel Kowalski has pointed out that the early S films saw not only a turn to explicit representations of sexuality but also a replacement of the comic relief provided by the male figures of the *landismo* sex comedies by the titillation granted by sexually active female protagonists, most notably the "post-*Franquista* ingénue, who through her sexual wiles overturns and updates the entrenched morals of old Spain."[30] In 1982, under the newly elected Spanish Socialist Party (PSOE), new regulations came into force, ensuring the confinement of these films to X-rated venues and eventually to the home video market.[31] This episode in Spanish film culture is alluded to in the closing titles of *Torremolinos 73,* which note the repackaging and release of Alfredo's Bergmanesque "Torremolinos 73" as the S-classified "Adventures and Mishaps of a Horny Widow" in 1977. The titles add: "it was seen by 1,373 spectators in Spain, and it was a box-office hit across Scandinavia."

The imagined encounter between the S film and art cinema in *Torremolinos 73* helps explain the paradoxes intrinsic to a film culture coming out of forty years of dictatorship. As Elsaesser has noted, cinephilic exchanges entail several kinds of deferral: "a detour in place and space, a shift in register and a delay in time."[32] This rings nowhere truer than in 1970s Spain, where the new era of social permissiveness inaugurated by the Transition years, which brought access to previously censored art and genre cinemas alike, was permeated by a sense of belatedness. As Kowalsky notes, by 1977, the year of the beginning of the S-film boom in Spain, "elsewhere in Europe and the US, the era of mainstream sexploitation had come and gone, and most sexually explicit films were already rated X, their distribution limited to venues licensed to screen these features."[33] The anomalies caused by historical ostracism and marginalization inform the formation of a cinephilic public culture in Spain. Suffice to cite here the preface to a recent compilation of key texts from *Cahiers du cinéma* translated into Spanish, in which critic and academic Josep Lluís Fecé has described the experience of being a cinephile in Spain in the late 1970s as one pervaded by the feeling of arriving late to almost everything: to cinema, to pop music, to the sexual revolution, even to the postcinephilic moment of structuralism and the politicization of film theory.[34] For Spanish cinephiles, Europe—and France in particular—would become the central point of reference for a cinephilia focused on the cult of the auteur reconstructed through television and, later, through video.

Cinephilia Revisited: Transnational Misreadings and the Politics of Self-Inscription

How is this past remembered in contemporary Spanish culture? *Torremolinos 73* emerges in a context in which the renewed accessibility of archival materials through cable television, DVD, and the Internet have facilitated currents of transcultural filmmaking by new cine-literate directors, and thus a second-generation globalized cinephilia (what Elsaesser calls "cinephilia take 2"). For Elsaesser, this return of cinephilia is marked by a generalized crisis of memory that manifests through "the impossibility of experience in the present, and the need to always be conscious of several temporalities."[35] The crisis of memory has brought the ghosts of nostalgia and of the waning of affect, which run through seminal debates on the postmodern and on the loss of history.[36] Indeed, retro cinema and television have contributed to the transformation of highly contentious *lieux de mémoire* such as the Civil War and everyday life under Franco into the subject of recreations that exploit the style and the "authenticity" of archival materials. Commenting on the recycling of media images of late Francoism into successful genre films, Vicente Sánchez-Biosca has argued that these retro trends empty recent history of its political implications. By resorting to flashy pastiche and instantly recognizable archival images (for example, *Love Seriously Damages Your Health* imitates techniques deployed in *Forrest Gump* [Robert Zemeckis, USA, 1994], inserting contemporary actors into historical footage) or to a vague sense of atmosphere supported by stylized black-and-white cinematography and classic film styles (as in *You're the One* [*Una historia de entonces*] [José Luis Garci, Spain, 2000]), the new Spanish retro cinema creates "designer memories," mobilizing visual clichés tinged by nostalgia.[37] But, in the Spanish context, how can nostalgia for the (traumatic) past be other than downright *political*?

I would argue that mediated memories also open the past to, in the words of Andrew Higson, the "contingency or instability of the national," which challenges the notion of the indigenous as either pure or stable.[38] In this respect, the intertextual aesthetic of *Torremolinos 73* dovetails the inward-looking narratives of official film history with the fragments of peripheral traditions that uncover outward connections. The risqué *destape* sex comedies, as well as the pornographic and horror films encompassed under the *S* classification, were seen at the time to undermine a cohesive (and progressive) sense of Spanish national identity and, by extension, to threaten the development of an exportable national cinema of quality.[39] By bringing these "unloved bits and pieces"[40] of the archive into the picture (pieces already under reassessment by film historians), *Torremolinos 73* does not seek so much to make an argument about their intrinsic value, but to complicate linear accounts of Spanish national cinema.

Thus, in the last part of my argument I would like to look more closely at the traces of the "contingency of the national" by bringing to the fore the film's transnational elements. The comic portrayal of a fictional Spanish-Danish joint venture in 1973 invites us to consider the opportunistic[41] coproduction arrangements behind many of the *S* films flooding the Spanish market in the early 1970s in the light of the economic necessity for coproductions in contemporary European cinemas.[42] With this, I am not claiming that the film should be read as a genuine engagement in a pan-European cultural dialogue. *Torremolinos 73* was a moderate success in Spain (where it garnered critical accolades and festival awards, especially on the strength of Cámara's and Peña's performances) but, interestingly enough, it failed for the most part to make an impression among Scandinavian critics as well as audiences, in spite of the participation of Danish star Mads Mikkelsen.[43] Some Swedish reviewers in particular seemed puzzled by the clichés in the depiction of Scandinavian characters and by the film's fixation with Bergman.[44] Rather, *Torremolinos 73* dwells, not without irony, on the problems raised by the desire for a transnational imaginary, namely, cultural dissimilarity, vested interests, and the misunderstanding across national and regional cultures in the context of uneven historical development. In doing so, it tacitly accepts that ideas of nation can only exist in a transnational space in terms of what Elsaesser calls "impersoNation" or "self-othering," that is, the presentation of Self (one's own national culture) through the look of the Other, resulting in the "self-conscious, ironic or self-mocking display of clichés and prejudices."[45] This is one of the dangers confronting national cinema when it comes to acknowledge—and exploit—its own cultural capital as a trading point in the international market, especially through the reworking of the national past as spectacle and "prosthetic media-memory"[46] (a view that connects with the above-mentioned critique on the recent turn to nostalgia in Spanish film and television).

However, the stereotyping processes of "impersoNation" and "self-othering" also allow for unexpected moments of transcultural reworking—that is, "what if?" encounters that disturb the potentially reassuring smugness of "the way we were" snapshots provided by retro comedy. Thus, in the second half of the film, the imaginary of Bergman's art cinema undergoes a surprising relocation to one of the favorite landscapes of the Spanish sex comedies: the beaches and hotels of the resort town of Torremolinos, in Southern Spain. The sequences that recreate the shooting of "Torremolinos 73," the film-within-the-film, exploit the bathetic humor derived from such relocation to the resort town out of season. In a sequence set around the swimming pool of the empty luxury hotel, glimpses of diverse takes belonging to the film-within-the film, shot in crisp black and-white, play against the grayish tones of the actual *Torremolinos 73.*

The sequence pokes fun at Alfredo's effort to make a convincing transcendental drama around Marga/Carmen, a widow spending a holiday in Torremolinos who meets a mysterious man in black who "resembles her late husband." The stranger is played by Magnus (Mads Mikkelsen) as a spoof of the Death figure in *The Seventh Seal.* The appropriation of Bergman as an impossible role model for Alfredo and the painfully wooden acting of Carmen and Magnus results in much of the *Ed Wood*–style (Tim Burton, USA, 1994) humor of the sequence,[47] which highlights the gap between Alfredo's ambitious vision and his endearingly trashy film. The consistent use of medium and long shots to frame Carmen's and Magnus's straight acting against the incongruous backdrop results in an exercise of transculturation in which Bergmanian sublime becomes Bergmanesque cliché. This is reinforced by a montage of different moments in the shoot presented as cinephilic visual jokes for the audience; these include the famous chess game, this time enacted by Magnus and Carmen on a *pedalo;* and the dance of death, which is rehearsed in a tracking shot of cast and crew backlighted against the Mediterranean sea line.

Carmen (Candela Peña) and Magnus (Mads Mikkelsen) in "Torremolinos 73," the film-within-the film.

Relocating Bergman to the Spanish seashore.

Through this exercise in pastiche, the tacky holiday landscapes of the popular comedies of *desarrollismo* are defamiliarized, disclosing a different, downbeat side to the discourses of economic prosperity. The views of Torremolinos in the cold winter light bring to the fore the melancholic undertones of the comedy. As cultural difference becomes postnational pastiche, the appropriation and misreading of art cinema tropes in *Torremolinos 73* provide an alternative imaginary in which Spanish cinema and, by extension, Spanish identity, can project itself, and thus be imagined in dialogue with a desired European identity. Cinephilia both provides a mirror for Spain's exclusion and becomes the means to overcome Spain's historical impossibility to participate fully in the utopia of European modernity.

This fantasy is fully articulated in the ending of the film, which replays the comedy derived from the swimming pool sequence into a poignant denouement. Alfredo's dreams crumble to pieces when he wakes up to the crude reality that he has been manipulated by Don Carlos and by his wife into turning his film into a pornographic picture. Carmen, desperate to have the child that her loving husband cannot conceive, pushes him into accepting her shooting a scene of explicit sexual intercourse with Magnus. As she willfully gets on top of Magnus and strips, she looks straight at the camera—at Alfredo. And, where the money shot could be expected, a (staged) moment of cinephilic frisson happens for the benefit of the diegetic camera—and of the nondiegetic audience. The character mutates from coy Spanish housewife into a sexually adventurous S-film heroine and, ultimately, a transnational "art" film star. Carmen's sustained look at the camera, hair down, lips slightly parted, in a lovingly framed black-and-white close-up lasting several seconds, is reminiscent of the classical close-ups of Bergman's "heroines": Monika of *Sommaren med Monika/Summer with Monika* (Sweden, 1953), or Elisabeth and Alma in *Persona* (Sweden, 1966).

Conclusions: Dreaming of Europe-Cinephilia and Peripheral Filiation

As Alfredo's misguided ambition of becoming a Spanish Bergman gives in to his wife's dream of becoming a mother, the film shifts from comedy into melodrama, and finally into an understated love story. For Alfredo and Carmen, pornography and art cinema provide a space of escape from the colorless reality of Spain in the 1970s—a fantasy space of intellectual sophistication and sexual freedom in which the Spanish couple can try on alternative identities without disrupting the rather traditional dynamics of their marriage. An added level of playfulness can be detected in the fact that, not unlike the conservative sex comedies of the 1960s and 1970s, the abundant display of nudity and sex in *Torremolinos 73* is justified within a narrative that ironically reaffirms marital love and family values.

Superficially a nostalgia piece looking back to Spain in the 1970s, *Torremolinos 73* makes for a cine-literate comedy that confounds deep-seated

A moment of revelation: the "money shot" in "Torremolinos 73."

myths and genre expectations surrounding Spanish culture. The metacine-matic narrative about the love of film in times of cultural scarcity dramatizes the peripheral as a historical condition, while appealing to a transnational imaginary in order for a national cinema to explain itself to its audience. The evocation of despised traditions of sex comedies and pornographic sub-genres side by side with European art cinema brings to the fore alternative imaginaries and ways of conceptualizing the national in Spanish cinema. By creating a fantasy, a "what if?" scenario that imagines the possibility of trans-national cooperation in the past, *Torremolinos 73* signals to a wider historical landscape, that of post-1960s cultural and sexual revolution, from which Spain has been historically excluded.

Torremolinos 73 also points at possible ways of reevaluating marginalized traditions in national film cultures. As Antoine de Baecque reminds us, fol-lowing the inspiration of Serge Daney—perhaps the "original" cinephile as *cine-fils,* or, child of cinema—beyond the fetishistic love for cinema and its *auteurs,* the (hi)stories of cinephilia are also histories of filiation, and there-fore "provided with a true memory."[48] The (false) memories and the leaps of imagination made possible by the peripheral detours of cinephilia thus open the door to the reimagination of film histories. But, what ultimately makes this peculiar fantasy moving are the ways in which the unexpected connec-tions facilitated by cinephilia work as a misreading that allows the losers, if not to rewrite history, at least to replay the archive in order to inscribe them-selves into an imagined history that has sidestepped them.

Notes

I would like to thank Bernard Bentley for sharing with me his extensive knowledge of Spanish popular cinema; this chapter has enormously benefited from his com-ments and suggestions. Thanks as well to Dina Iordanova and David Martin-Jones for feedback at different stages of writing, and to Peter Evans, Andrew Ginger, Chris Perriam, and Isabel Santaolalla for inviting me to present parts of this work while in progress.

1. The special dossiers devoted to Spanish cinema in the February 2007 and Feb-ruary 2008 editions of *Screen International* put forward the image of a national cine-ma vying for a strong global presence by way of increasingly bigger budgets, stars, and global sales boosted through the investment in English-language (co)productions.

2. Darke, "Sexuality, Eroticism and Pornography in European Cinema," 384.

3. In this regard, see Iordanova, "Indian Cinema's Global Reach: Historiography through Testimony," 113–40; and Labanyi et al., dossier on "An Oral History of Cinema-Going in 1940s and 1950s Spain" 105–44.

4. For an overview of this topic, see the collection *Cinephilia: Movies, Love and*

Memory, ed. de Valck and Hagener.

5. Keathley, *Cinephilia and History, or The Wind in the Trees,* 134.

6. The DVD release of the film in both Spain and the United Kingdom includes a promotional "making-of" shot as a mockumentary that affirms the real-story basis of the film. See *Así se hizo "Torremolinos 73"* (Trino Torres, Spain, 2003), *Torremolinos 73,* DVD. Tartan Video, 2005.

7. Drake, "'Mortgaged to Music': New Retro Movies in 1990s Hollywood Cinema," 188.

8. This is the literal translation of the title, although a possibly more appropriate translation would be *Tell Me How It Was For You* (with regard to the show's self-conscious approach to the recent past as memory work). On the relation between retro trends and emotional histories, see Smith, *Spanish Visual Culture: Cinema, Television, Internet,* 14–28.

9. On the recycling of images from the Francoist period in contemporary Spanish cinema and television, see Sánchez-Biosca, *Cine de historia, cine de memoria: La representación y sus límites,* 69–70.

10. Ibid., 77–78.

11. On cinephilia as revelation, see Ng, "A Point of Light: Epiphanic Cinephilia in Mamoru Oshii's *Avalon.*"

12. Hopewell, *Out of the Past: Spanish Cinema after Franco,* 47.

13. Longhurst, "Culture and Development: The Impact of 1960s 'Desarrollismo,'" 17–28.

14. Elsaesser, "Cinephilia or the Uses of Disenchantment," in *Cinephilia. Movies, Love and Memory,* ed. de Valck and Hagener, 27–32.

15. See Guarner, "En pos del conejo blanco: Algunas notas sobre la breve pero portentosa vida de la Escuela de Barcelona," 101–9; Galt, "Missed Encounters: Reading, *catalanitat,* the Barcelona School," 193–210.

16. For a full account of this context, see Triana-Toribio, *Spanish National Cinema,* 71–74 and Hopewell, *Out of the Past,* 63–77.

17. Hopewell, *Out of the Past,* 66.

18. Ibid., 82–84.

19. Quoted in Hernández Ruiz and Pérez Rubio, *Voces en la niebla: El cine durante la transición española,* 140.

20. Thanks to Bernard Bentley for this observation.

21. For a critical assessment of the *landismo* comedies, see Aguilar's entry on *"Cuando el cuerno suena/When the Horn Blows* (Luis María Delgado, 1974)," in *Antología crítica del cine español, 1906–95: Flor en la sombra,* 723–25, and Triana-Toribio, *Spanish National Cinema,* 98–104.

22. Triana-Toribio, *Spanish National Cinema,* 99–100.

23. Navarrete, "La españolada en el cine," 30.

24. As these films have not been released outside Spain, I am providing approximate translations. See also www.imdb.com.

25. See Navarrete, "La españolada en el cine."

26. One of the films that would do the most to spread the myth of sexual freedom in 1960s Sweden, *Jag är nyfiken-en film i gult/I Am Curious—Yellow* (Vilgot Sjöman,

Sweden, 1967) includes a mention of holiday breaks in Spain as one of the political "issues" investigated by the protagonist, who confronts Swedish tourists fresh from Majorca with an indictment of holidays in Franco's Spain as "shameful" and "oppressing Spanish workers."

27. See Callier's interview with Pablo Berger, "Le plus important, est-ce le cinéma ou la vie?"

28. See Steene, "The Transpositions of a Filmmaker—Ingmar Bergman at Home and Abroad," 113, 123.

29. See Bentley on the cinema of the reform in *A Companion to Spanish Cinema,* 226–27.

30. Kowalsky, "Rated S: Soft-Core Pornography and the Spanish Transition to Democracy, 1977–1982," 193.

31. Ibid., 191.

32. Elsaesser, "Cinephilia or the Uses of Disenchantment," 30.

33. Kowalski, "Rated S," 191.

34. Fecé and Pujol, "Prólogo: A propósito del amor," 18.

35. Elsaesser, "Cinephilia or the Uses of Disenchantment" 40.

36. See the influential study by Jameson, *Postmodernism, or, The Cultural Logic of Late Capitalism.*

37. "Diseños de memoria" in the original; my translation (Sánchez-Biosca, *Cine de historia, cine de memoria,* 84). While "memory designs" would be a more literal translation of the original, my choice of "designer memories" attempts to capture the commodification of historical memory by the mass media noted by Sánchez-Biosca.

38. Higson, "The Limiting Imagination of National Cinema," 66–67.

39. On the "non-Spanishness" of the subgenres of the 1970s, see Triana-Toribio, *Spanish National Cinema,* 114–15.

40. Elsaesser: "Cinephilia or the Uses of Disenchantment," 41.

41. See Mette Hjort on opportunistic transnationalism elsewhere in this volume.

42. Berger's first film became possible thanks to the joint forces of Spanish producers Telespan, Estudios Picasso, and Mama Films alongside Danish company Nimbus Films and the support of the Danish Film Institute. This kind of collaboration between private initiatives in different European countries is typical of productions seeking to qualify for supranational funding from the MEDIA and EURIMAGES programs. See Jäckel, *European Film Industries,* 59; Brandstrup and Redvall, "Breaking the Borders: Danish Co-Productions in the 1990s," 149, 156.

43. The volume of theatrical admissions for the film during the 2003–5 period of theatrical exhibition shows a sharp contrast between the 388,614 tickets sold in Spain, and the very low figures of 1,189 in Sweden and 1,883 in Denmark. These figures can be usefully compared with popular hits marketed as representative of one national cinema, such as the Spanish *Todo sobre mi madre/All about My Mother* (Pedro Almodóvar, 1999)—92,590 in Denmark; 204,331 in Sweden, and 2,580.766 in Spain over a 3–4 year period of exhibition—or the Danish *Festen/The Celebration* (Thomas Vinterberg, 1998): 403,642 in Denmark, 136,368 in Sweden and 84,701

in Spain over a similar period. Source: Lumiere—Database of admissions of films released in Europe, at http://lumiere.obs.coe.int/web/search (accessed February 10, 2007).

44. For example, daily *Svenska Dagbladet* gave the film a mostly negative review, criticizing the playful tone of the film as ineffective and the Bergman jokes as repetitious, insisting in the prejudiced view of the Scandinavian characters as overserious and heavy going. For the reviewer at *Dagens Nyheter* the film compares unfavorably with *Boogie Nights,* and it is presented as a failed attempt at the low-budget formula, whereas *TT Spektra* describes *Torremolinos 73* as one of the oddest films in a long time, not the least for its fascination with Bergman and its vision of Scandinavians. See Malmberg, "Lekfullt lättsinne blir till sist likgiltigt," *Svenska Dagbladet;* Gezelius, "Tragedi av komedi. Medvetet lågbudgetgrepp slår fel," *Dagens Nyheter;* Jannerling, Review: *Torremolinos 73.* I am grateful to Lars Kristensen for providing access to and translation of these materials.

45. Elsaesser, "ImpersoNations: National Cinema, Historical Imaginaries," in his *European Cinema: Face to Face with Hollywood,* 61.

46. Ibid.

47. I thank Bernard Bentley for pointing out this connection to me.

48. De Baecque, "Retours de cinéphilia," 174.

Bibliography

Aguilar, Carlos. "*Cuando el cuerno suena/When the Horn Blows* (Luis María Delgado, 1974)." In *Antología crítica del cine español, 1906–95: Flor en la sombra,* edited by Julio Pérez Perucha, 723–25. Madrid: Cátedra/Filmoteca Española, 1997.

Bentley, Bernard P. E. *A Companion to Spanish Cinema (1896–2006).* London: Tamesis, 2008.

Brandstrup, Pil Gundelach, and Eva Novrup Redvall. "Breaking the Borders: Danish Coproductions in the 1990s." In *Transnational Cinema in a Global North: Nordic Cinema in Transition,* edited by Andrew Nestingen and Trevor G. Elkington, 141–61. Detroit: Wayne State University Press, 2005.

Callier, Cédric. "Interview with Pablo Berger: Le plus important, est-ce le cinéma ou la vie?" At www.bazarts.net/article.php3?id_article=442 (accessed November 17, 2006).

Darke, Chris. "Sexuality, Eroticism and Pornography in European Cinema." In *Encyclopedia of European Cinema,* edited by Ginette Vincendeau, 384–85. New York: Facts on File, 1995.

De Baecque, Antoine (1992). "Retours de cinéphilia." Reprinted in *Critique et Cinéphilie,* edited by Antoine de Baecque and Gabrielle Lucantonio, 165–77. Paris: Cahiers du cinéma, 2001.

De Valck, Marijke, and Malte Hagener, eds. *Cinephilia: Movies, Love and Memory.* Amsterdam: Amsterdam University Press, 2005.

Drake, Philip. "'Mortgaged to Music': New Retro Movies in 1990s Hollywood Cinema." In *Memory and Popular Film,* edited by Paul Grainge, 183–201. Manchester: Manchester University Press, 2003.

Elsaesser, Thomas. *European Cinema: Face to Face with Hollywood.* Amsterdam: Amsterdam University Press, 2005.

Fecé, Josep Lluís, and Cristina Pujol. "Prólogo: A propósito del amor." In *Teoría y crítica del cine: Avatares de una cinephilia,* translated by Mariana Miracle, edited by Josep Lluís Fecé, 17–25. Barcelona: Paidós, 2005.

Galt, Rosalind. "Missed Encounters: Reading, *catalanitat,* the Barcelona School." *Screen* 48, no. 2 (2007): 193–210.

Gezelius, Kerstin. "Tragedi av komedi: Medvetet lågbudgetgrepp slår fel." *Dagens Nyheter.* At www.dn.se/DNet/jsp/polopoly.jsp?d=144, July 23, 2004 (accessed December 10, 2006).

Guarner, José Luis. "En pos del conejo blanco: Algunas notas sobre la breve pero portentosa vida de la Escuela de Barcelona." In *Escritos sobre el cine español, 1973–87,* edited by José A. Hurtado and Francisco M. Picó, 101–9. Valencia: Filmoteca de la Generalitat Valenciana, 1989.

Hernández Ruiz, Javier, and Pablo Pérez Rubio. *Voces en la niebla: El cine durante la transición española (1973–1982).* Barcelona: Paidós, 2004.

Higson, Andrew. "The Limiting Imagination of National Cinema." In *Cinema and Nation,* edited by Mette Hjort and Scott MacKenzie, 63–74. London: Routledge, 2000.

Hopewell, John. *Out of the Past: Spanish Cinema after Franco.* London: British Film Institute, 1986.

Iordanova, Dina. "Indian Cinema's Global Reach: Historiography through Testimonies." *South Asian Popular Culture* 2, no. 4 (2006): 113–40.

Jäckel, Anne. *European Film Industries.* London: British Film Institute, 2003.

Jameson, Fredric. *Postmodernism, or The Cultural Logic of Late Capitalism.* Durham, NC: Duke University Press, 1991.

Jannerling, Lisa. "Review: *Torremolinos 73.*" At www.ttspektra.se, July 23, 2004 (accessed December 10, 2006).

Keathley, Christian. *Cinephilia and History; or, The Wind in the Trees.* Bloomington: Indiana University Press, 2006.

Kowalsky, Daniel. "Rated S: Soft-core Pornography and the Spanish Transition to Democracy, 1977–82." In *Spanish Popular Cinema,* edited by Antonio Lázaro-Reboll and Andrew Willis, 188–208. Manchester: Manchester University Press, 2004.

Labanyi, Jo, et al. Dossier on "An Oral History of Cinema-Going in 1940s and 1950s Spain." *Studies in Hispanic Cinemas* 2, no. 2 (2005): 105–44.

Longhurst, Alex. "Culture and Development: The Impact of 1960s 'desarrollismo.'" In *Contemporary Spanish Cultural Studies,* edited by Barry Jordan and Rikki Morgan-Tamosunas, 17–28. London: Arnold, 2000.

Malmberg, Carl-Johan. "Lekfullt lättsinne blir till sist likgiltigt," *Svenska Dagbladet.* At www.svd.se/dynamiskt/rec_film/did_8490753.asp, July 23, 2004 (accessed December 10, 2006).

Navarrete, Luis. "La españolada en el cine." In *Historia(s), motivos y formas del cine español,* edited by Pedro Poyato, 23–31. Córdoba: Plurabelle, 2005.

Ng, Jenna. "A Point of Light: Epiphanic Cinephilia in Mamoru Oshii's *Avalon*." In *Cinephilia in the Age of Digital Reproduction: Film, Pleasure and Digital Culture*, vol. 1, edited by Jason Sperb and Scott Balcerzak, 71–88. London: Wallflower Press, 2009.

Sánchez-Biosca, Vicente. *Cine de historia, cine de memoria: La representación y sus límites*. Madrid: Cátedra, 2006.

Smith, Paul Julian. *Spanish Visual Culture: Cinema, Television, Internet*. Manchester: Manchester University Press, 2006.

Steene, Birgitta. "The Transpositions of a Filmmaker—Ingmar Bergman at Home and Abroad." *TijdSchrift voor Skandinavistiek* 19, no. 1 (1998): 103–28.

Triana-Toribio, Núria. *Spanish National Cinema*. London: Routledge, 2003.

Experience—Information—Image
A Historiography of Unfolding in Arab Cinema

Why do certain images of history reach us, while others remain seemingly forgotten, in the infinite breadth of the past? Why do only certain events seem to matter? I suggest those experiences are not forgotten but enfolded. Looking at the cinemas of the periphery, it is most compelling to understand the way they conceive of history in terms of enfoldment. Being marginal cinemas, usually in a minority position vis-à-vis governments, languages, and other dominant powers, cinemas of the periphery struggle to hold onto local histories and memories. These histories and memories may appear lost forever, wiped out by the colonial or other dominant power, but I want to show that they are simply buried for now, folded away, implicit in the visible face of history. Informed by Gilles Deleuze's revision of Michel Foucault's theory of genealogy, Deleuze's critique of the cliché, and the triadic semiotics of Charles Sanders Peirce as well as the concepts of implicate order from physics and logical depth from mathematics, I have developed an enfolding-unfolding model of the image.

The contemporary politics of historiography can be conceptualized according to the relationship among Experience, Information, and Image; a triadic relationship that I have proposed to understand the nature of the image in the information age. While Experience is infinite, the vast majority of it lies latent. Few Images ever arise from it. In our age, those that do arise tend to be selected, or unfolded, by political and economic interests that deem them to be useful as Information. Nevertheless, anyone can unfold any aspect of Experience to become a public Image. Artists (and others) do so in order to allow other aspects of Experience to circulate, before they enfold, back into the matrix of history. Historiography is this process of unfolding.

As Siegfried Kracauer wrote, a historian should pay attention to the details of the past in order to rescue things from oblivion, "so that nothing should go lost. It is as if the fact-oriented accounts breathed pity with the dead."[1]

This relationship can shed light on many kinds of artworks that deal in some way with the past. This is especially relevant in viewing some remarkable works of Arab cinema, which, like other peripheral cinemas, represent history agonistically. Given the power struggles (neo)colonial and local, in the Arab world in the past century, the telling of history in the Arab world is absolutely fraught: the victors' dominant accounts are patently fraudulent, the accounts produced to please outsiders are simple pandering, and the accounts that people most fervently wish to claim are fragile and difficult to sustain. It should be recognized that these relationships hold in many other parts of the world as well; I hope the model I offer will be useful in analyzing films and other works from many regions, including right at home.

The contemporary cinema of the Arab Mashreq (or eastern Arab world) is, for the most part, a nonindustrial, artisanal, and auteurist cinema. Dependent on a combination of local and foreign funding, it circulates complexly among Arab participants with differing interests and between Arab

Still from *In This House* (Lebanon, 2005) by Akram Zaatari. Courtesy of the artist.

233

and Western audiences, all of whom tend to regard Arab films through the eyes of the others. In the heavily politicized Arab milieu, the Image world is constructed as a selective unfolding of only those aspects of Experience that are deemed to be useful or profitable. For these reasons, filmmakers in the Arab world are highly aware that the perceptible world is constructed by political interests, that it is almost impossible for a filmmaker to picture the world without simultaneously deconstructing or negating it.

Some Arab filmmakers, like filmmakers everywhere, pursue the liberal practice of image critique, fighting images (in the usual sense of the word) with images, in order to reveal that what is apparent is an effect of ideology. The shortcoming of this approach is the failure to realize that images and stories do not arise directly from Experience but from a filter over Experience, which I call Information. Other filmmakers focus on the level of Information, looking neither at history (which is unrepresentable in itself) nor at the available Images of it, but the filters between the two. These filmmakers focus on the blocks to representation, which include censorship and funding restrictions. A radical, ascetic approach, which produces films that barely register in the audiovisual, this Information strategy is quite popular in Arab cinema. Finally, there are those filmmakers who try to get close to the details of history itself, lingering on what I call the level of Experience. Accepting that the resulting films may seem inconsequential, they prefer to carry out their own unfoldings, explicating hitherto latent events, knowledges, and sensations. Thus in these films what official history deems merely personal, absurd, microevents, or not events at all, becomes the stuff of a rich alternative historiography. The latter two processes characterize the work of numerous filmmakers in the Arab world, both in fiction and documentary, a few of whom I will discuss in what follows.

An Enfolded Model of the Image

I began with questions—why do certain images of history reach us, while others remain seemingly forgotten? Why do only certain events seem to matter?— questions that emphasize the unknowability of the past and the seeming arbitrariness by which some aspects of it arise in the present.[2] I suggest the past is not forgotten but *enfolded.* The terms *enfolded* and *unfolded* (or their Latinate synonyms, *implicate* and *explicate*) echo Deleuze's explication of the baroque aesthetics of Leibniz.[3] Leibniz's principle that the smallest element of matter is a fold makes it possible to conceive of what Deleuze and Guattari term the *plane of immanence* as composed of infinite folds. The actual is thus infinitely enfolded in the virtual. The past, then, reaches us or

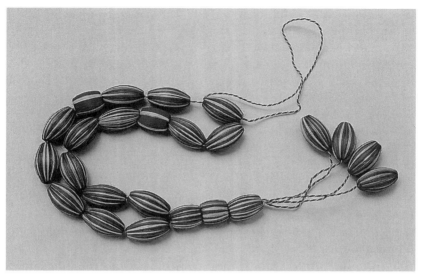

Still from *Khiam* (Lebanon, 2000) by Joana Hadjithomas and Khalil Joreige. Courtesy of the artists.

becomes actual to us through selective unfolding, in a relationship among Experience, Information, and Image. I posit that each of these three levels is a plane of immanence: a membrane in which an infinity of stuff lies virtual, or enfolded.[4] Now and then certain aspects of those virtual events are unfolded, pulled up into the next level. Images, perceptible representations of history, come into the world and retreat back into Experience in a ceaseless flow of unfolding and enfolding.[5]

You may recognize in this model a triad typical of the epistemology of Charles Sanders Peirce. Indeed its three levels, Experience, Information, and Image, have the qualities that Peirce termed Firstness, Secondness, and Thirdness.[6] The first level is Experience. I use this term to signify not personal experience, but Experience in the sense that all experience is experience of something by something, which is the principle at the basis of Peirce's semiology.[7] Experience, then, is the history of all experiences. While Experience is infinite, the vast majority of it lies latent. Few Images arise from it. Most events remain forgotten, and when they do arise, they quickly slip back into the enfolded thickness of Experience.

The second level is Information, which entails a selection from the infinite material of Experience. As a Peircean Second, Information implies a struggle by which certain results are actualized, and not others. As Peirce writes: "In the idea of reality, Secondness is predominant; for the real is something which insists upon forcing its way to recognition as something other than the mind's creation . . . The real is active; we acknowledge it, calling it the actual. (This word is due to Aristotle's use of ενεργεια, action, to mean existence, as opposed to a mere germinal state.)"[8] Applying Peircean categories to film aesthetics, Sean Cubitt considers the *cut* to be the element of Secondness in filmmaking, given that it implies decision and disjunction; he also suggests the cut is where ideology enters.[9] The category of Information I posit here emphasizes that, in information society, the force behind Secondness is institutional. Power consists in the ability to exert some sort of regulatory, instrumental, or ideological force in terms of what aspects of Experience are deemed important. Information is a particular iteration of this phenomenon; it is that aspect of Experience that can be translated into Information that is somehow useful. Information, I would suggest, is the new Spectacle.[10] Power exerts its hegemony by selecting, from the infinity of Experience, only that which can unfold to serve power. It matters little whether this Information produces Images. However, the typical Image that power selects from Experience is the cliché, an Image that confirms ideology and blocks more nuanced and multifarious aspects of Experience. This is why Deleuze so tenaciously critiqued the regime of the cliché, which reinforces commonsense, ideological notions while preventing access to the richness and singularity of Experience.[11] Capital is a particular expression of Information, which in our time determines to a great extent what Experience is selectively unfolded as Information—insofar as it translates directly into a useful investment.[12]

The third level is Image. It is a Peircean Third in that it reflects on the *relation* between Experience and Information, First and Second. There are two kinds of Image: those that directly unfold Experience, and those that are manifestations of Information or Capital. We would think all Images are direct reflections of Experience; but in fact they are selective unfoldings of Experience. In our age, as noted above, those Images that do arise from Experience are often selected, or unfolded, by political and economic interests that deem them to be useful as Information. Nevertheless, anyone can unfold any aspect of Experience to become a public Image, and artists (and others) do so in order to allow other aspects of Experience to circulate. We cannot perceive Experience as such, it has to be mediated through an Image; but films can emphasize the quality of Experience—its presence, detail, strangeness, noninstrumentality, infinity. For example, one of the best-known types of cinema that unfolds directly from Experience is neorealism.

There are many films, often transcendentally beautiful, that linger in the fullness and simplicity of Firstness. Cubitt remarks of Jean Renoir, for example, that he is a filmmaker of Firstness, refusing to submit the evanescent infinity of profilmic reality to the finality of the cut.[13] We can also include in this category filmmakers like Michelangelo Antonioni, Chantal Akerman, Krysztof Kieslowski, and Abderrahmane Sissako.

The second kind of Image is the visible manifestation of Information and Capital; it is the skin of Information, if you like. With such Images, Deleuze's observation that "the film within the film is money" is truer than ever.[14] Cinema that reflects on the Information from which it unfolds, as well as on the Experience that the Information unfolds, includes conspiracy movies, which are Information-driven in a complex and interesting way. Deleuze categorizes such films as films of Thirdness. Many contemporary movies specifically reflect on the Information from which they unfold, from the *Matrix* trilogy (Andy and Larry Wachowski, USA, 1999–2003) to the television series *24* (2001–), and countless other films whose pivotal scenes involve characters hunched around a computer screen. Digital spectacles and films that rely on computer graphics also are Information-driven Images. More generally, a film whose Images directly unfold Information about what is instrumentally useful, such as pornography or propaganda, can be considered an Information-driven film.

The richness of the Image level is that, as a Peircean Third, it shows us how Information has selected, unfolded, and expressed certain aspects of Experience. The Image does not mask Experience (or Information) but puts these two into relation with each other. In my examples from Arab cinema that follow, we will see that what we see and hear in a film tells as much about what remains hidden or inaccessible, and even why it does.

As in all Peircean triads, the relationship among these three terms is fluid. Images and Information are eventually reabsorbed or reenfolded into Experience, the first term of the triad, and return to a state of latency.

What is the enfoldment model of the image good for? For evaluating how artworks (and other things) actively triangulate between Image, Information, and Experience. For the *style* of their selection of what elements to unfold; for example, Akram Zaatari and Omar Amiralay draw attention, in almost diagrammatic fashion, to what they are prevented from showing, while Mohamed Soueid and Yousry Nasrallah are interested in the smallest sights and sounds that usually seem unimportant. Conversely, the enfoldment model permits willing certain elements to remain in a state of latency, as in Joana Hadjithomas and Khalil Joriege's delicate bypassing of well-known facts about prison life. This model does not evaluate art on the basis of its authenticity (which would be to seek a correspondence between Image and Experience, like realism). Likewise, it has no need of the criteria of reflexivity and criticality, for these criteria are also based in a dualist model. Rather it gives a positive or Experience-embracing criterion for criticism: what Experience is privileged, what passed over, in the selection of Information? And what Information is privileged in the selection of Image? Paying attention to the infinity of Experience that remains enfolded is similar to a materialist critique, except that it does not oppose (true) material and (false) ideal, a dualist model, but attends to all the Experience that went into the Information, Capital, and Images that arrive to us. The enfolded model of the Image does not distinguish between material and immaterial.

This model also shows that in our time, much art is concerned with the nature of en/unfolding rather than with producing representations; these artworks (and other things) thus are not so much representational as performative.[15] It is the way they unfold sights and sounds, the struggle to make things apparent, the acknowledgment of censorship and other prohibitions that characterize these and many other contemporary works. The final resulting Image is just the trace of the activity of unfolding.

When I proposed an earlier version of this model in a lecture at the American University of Beirut in April 2003 (at the beginning of the war on Iraq), I privileged remaining enfolded or "invisible" as a political strategy. Artist Walid Sadek objected, "in the Arab world, we are already invisible." He found my suggestion to be more appropriate for artists in Western countries where there are already too many Images, and thus a creative strategy is to refuse to let your art enter the public arena. Lebanese and other Arab artists have a different problem: there are too many ideological, clichéd Images of Arabs, too few alternative representations, too much Experience going uncounted. It is always necessary for the misrepresented to represent themselves. But how to do so without getting pulled along the clichéd, overdetermined unfoldings of capital and state?

The answer may be to deal craftily and stylishly with that striating,[16] instrumentalizing, and homogenizing plane of Information (which empties Experience of everything that is not instrumental), by staying under it *or* by leaping over it *or* by drawing attention to its tracks in the Image.

Funding and Censorship as Information

I consider film funding, and equally film censorship, to exist at the level of Information in the process of filmmaking. Filmmaking in countries without a production infrastructure relies on external or irregular funding, which often comes with crippling strings attached. Similarly, and sometimes in the very same act, filmmaking is subject to external censorship and self-censorship. Funding and censorship striate, homogenize, and selectively unfold Experience. They magnetically draw certain aspects of Experience from its enfolded state. Whether they show it (funding) or hide it (censorship), they perform similar gestures of effacement with regard to the infinity of Experience.

Censorship determines what may not be unfolded from Experience for common viewing, what Images may not be seen. Yet in that very negative attention to Experience, censorship draws attention to what it means to hide something, at the expense of everything else. A most ironic example of this occurs in *Al-Film al-Mafkoud/ The Lost Film* (2003) by Lebanese filmmakers Joana Hadjithomas and Khalil Joreige. It concerns a film of theirs that was never returned after a screening in Yemen, and the filmmakers' fruitless search for it. Ironically, they received several feet of footage in the mail after their return from Yemen, the bits the censors removed—an obscene shout, an obscure gesture. Finally all that was salvaged of their film is that which was selectively unfolded at the level of Information, precisely in order that it *not* be unfolded as Image, namely the censored fragments.

Other than the industrial cinema of Egypt, Mashreq Arab cinema is basically artisanal. These days it is almost entirely dependent on European and other Western funding, including foreign coproductions, European and other television, and NGOs and cultural organizations: the latter include the European Union's EuroMed Audiovisual Programme, UNESCO, the Ford Foundation, the Prince Claus Fund for Culture and Development of the Netherlands, and others. The funding relationship is a delicate one of mutual preemption.[17] Foreign funders want to privilege certain desired aspects of Arab experience, such as attitudes toward the West, Islamic fundamentalism, terrorism, Arab-Israeli cooperation, women's voices, sexuality, and—with voracious fascination—the veil. Arab filmmakers who receive this funding work within its constraints to make films of varying quality. Foreign audiences scrutinize these films for signs of authenticity and for the confirmation or contradiction of received ideas. Local Arab audiences scrutinize them according to what they understand to be Western assumptions, and critique them for how they present the Arab world to the West. So while Western audiences think Arab cinema shows them an Image of Experience, Arab audiences know they are seeing Information.

Funding decides from the outset what aspects of Experience are deemed useful. This is the case in commercial and industrial cinema, of course. But it is especially felt in the funding of small national cinemas, especially in highly politicized regions like the Arab world. Every funder has an interest in producing certain Images, regardless of their correspondence to Experience. Since Experience is infinite, it will always be possible to selectively unfold those aspects of it that correspond to the funder's wish, for example, the many Western funding initiatives to get Arab women to "voice their experience." Such initiatives assume that certain Experience is more authentic and more valuable, and in the process they efface entire other realms of Arab experience. Or, the many initiatives since September 11 that seek to support Arab filmmakers who will explain themselves to the West, such as a Sundance-funded project in 2006 to "award a $50k production grant to an arab docmaker to make a film on solidarity/coexistence between west and middle east," in the words of a Sundance talent scout in Lebanon in a letter to me.

In another example, the EuroMed Audiovisual Programme has goals to enhance cooperation between European and Mediterranean countries in the training, production, distribution, and promotion of audiovisual projects. Another of its goals is regulation, which seems to suggest the EU wants to control the bootlegging rampant in the Arab world. EuroMed's goal in 2006 was to fund twelve projects from a budget of €15 million. One applicant was the little-known Adam Zuabi. Organizer of the Ramallah International Film Festival, Zuabi lost all credibility with Palestinian filmmakers for several reasons: he did not collaborate with respected filmmakers based in Ramallah; he accepted funding from an Israeli organization, the New Foundation for Cinema and Television (NFTC), that refused to take a position against the Occupation (and thus would likely not fund films that were critical of it); the organization was not an NGO but a private company listing Zuabi as sole shareholder; and, in order to seem credible, it listed people on the board of directors who "completely disown[ed] it."[18] All these were signs that Zuabi's festival was not a pro-Palestinian event. Yet Zuabi, in partnership with the NFTC, attracted the interest of EuroMed to open a documentary film center based in Tel Aviv. Forty Palestinian filmmakers protested to EuroMed, and sixty-seven Israeli filmmakers petitioned in support of them. These protests caused Spanish and Turkish partners to withdraw from the pan-Mediterranean documentary project. But EuroMed persevered, so fond of the fantasy of equal Arab-Israeli cooperation that it did not wish to examine the motives and spotty track record of the organizer.[19]

Films of Information

Some thoughtful contemporary Arab cinema is about the paucity of Experience that has not already been neutralized as Information, or the impossibility of extracting an Image from Experience. Films in which there is very little to see or hear, they dwell on the impossibility of producing an Image.

First I offer two examples from Syria, a country where surveillance is a form of censorship that snuffs out Experience the moment it is born. Filmmaking, like any other form of public expression, is strictly surveyed and censored by the Assad government, and even when publicly funded, almost never screens in Syria itself. Yet, as Rasha Salti points out, Syrian filmmakers "have succeeded in carving out an independent, critical and often subversive cinema under the sponsorship of a vigorous state ruled by a single party actively invested in suppressing dissent and coercing an official dogma."[20] Omar Amiralay's documentary *Toufan fi Balad al-Baath/A Flood in Baath Country* (Syria; French funded, 2004), surveys the effect of one of former president Hafez al-Assad's monomaniac public works projects, the Assad Dam on the Euphrates river. Amiralay indicts the self-serving Baath regime with unremitting yet subtle sarcasm. He listens to Bedouins who were displaced by the dam, he films the eerily still water of the artificial lake. In interviews, the officials of the Baath Party hoist themselves on their own petards; Amiralay has only to observe the local official Khalaf el Machi, obsequiously praising current president Bashar al-Assad, through a wide-angle lens to undermine his propaganda. The cute children who comprise the Vanguards of Light, and who in the classroom absorb lessons that the dammed Euphrates

Still from *A Flood in Baath Country* (Syria, 2004) by Omar Amiralay. Courtesy of the artist.

Still from *A Flood in Baath Country* (Syria, 2004) by Omar Amiralay. Courtesy of the artist.

is now "a civilized river," noisily sing a song in praise of Assad. By attending to their antics, the film gleans hints of the wealth of Experience that even the most disciplined children cannot help but express.

Many first films by "third-world" filmmakers are about the impediments to the making of the film. Meyar al Roumi's *Cinéma muet* (Syria/France, 2002), his graduation project from La Fémis in France, takes the rather familiar form of the innocent *ballade* of a young filmmaker who returns to his home country after a Western cinema education, intending to devote his cinematic abilities to his native land, only to be shocked by the actual conditions of filmmaking back home. Al Roumi planned to make a conventional documentary about the Syrian film industry, but he is only allowed to film two shots in the Syrian National Film Organization, and these are banal enough to dash his hopes. Next he visits the great Syrian filmmakers Omar Amiralay, Mohammad Malass, and Ousama Mohammed, with the awe of a spiritual initiate, only to find them frustrated, cynical, and less prolific in cinema than in *arak*-laced sarcasm. The state's censorship system has effectively silenced these filmmakers. Instead we are treated to astonishing clips of some of their great films from the 1970s and 1980s.[21]

A fourth example of a film that focuses on how Information filters Experience is *Fi haza al-bayt/In This House* (Lebanon, 2005), by Lebanese film-

242

Still from *Cinéma muet* (Syria/France, 2002) by Meyar al Roumi. Courtesy of the artist.

maker Akram Zaatari. I discuss this fascinating film in detail elsewhere.[22] Here I will just note that it is exemplary of a filmmaking practice that struggles to produce an Image in the face of censorship on every level, in a country where people have good reason to be paranoid. Recent Lebanese history is so heavily overdetermined by such a host of political factors—even before the assassination of prime minister Rafiq Hariri in 2005 and the devastating conflict that I hesitate to call "the Israeli-Hezbollah war" of 2006—that filmmakers cannot approach history directly. This would be unthinkably naive. Instead they have to delicately hint at Experience by analyzing Information, or against all odds try to get Experience to express itself directly in the Image.

In This House resorts to strategies that *recede* from the audiovisual Image in order to tell the story of the missed encounter, after fifteen years, between a Christian family and the socialist fighter Ali Hashisho, who occupied their house in southern Lebanon for six years during the civil war. The film happens because Zaatari learns that Hashisho buried a letter to the house's owners in the garden, and he sets out to excavate it. Only two characters are willing to appear on camera. One is Hashisho, who was a militia member of the Democratic Popular Party and is now a journalist. He recounts to Zaatari his story of living for six years in the house of Charbel (whose last name we do not learn) when it was on the front with the invading Israeli army. Other characters—the family who live in the house and the three sets of local, police, and army officials who insist on showing up—refuse to appear on camera and barely register their voices. The other character who appears on camera is Faisal, a gardener whom Zaatari hired to dig for the time capsule.

In short, because the people refuse to show their faces to the camera, and because the act itself, of digging for the time capsule, is not very photogenic, the event at the center of *In This House* barely registers visibly. Here is a story suffocated by Information. Zaatari counters with Information of his own: texts, audio tones, and silhouettes that compensate for the absence of the people, render the video barely visible—a line drawing, an abstraction. Experience refuses to arise into Image, and so all that is left is a film about how Information—a filter of official surveillance, self-censorship, and fear—takes the place of Experience. As historiography, *In This House* is extremely revealing, because it shows that present political circumstances heavily affect what kind of access to the past is possible.

Films of Experience

The former are examples of films that operate at the level of Information, observing and rerouting the tortuous passage from Experience to Image. Other Mashreq Arab filmmakers use strategies to tease Experience into unfolding into Image, despite the heavy layer of calculation and cliché barring its passage.

Mohamed Soueid is one filmmaker determined to fish in the teeming sea of enfolded Experience, and to hoist his catch up to the level of Image as a kind of absurd, barely useful Information (which, if it were a fish, might be sardines). His documentary trilogy (Lebanon, 1998–2002) deals personally and obliquely with cinema, love, and the Lebanese civil war and uneasy subsequent state of "peace." This trilogy I also discuss in detail elsewhere,[23] but it is such a key example of a "historiography of unfolding" that I would like to mention it here.

The delicacy of unfolding Experience directly into Image animates the trilogy. The third film in the trilogy, *Harb Ahliya/Civil War* (2002), investigates the mysterious death of Soueid's cinematographer friend Mohamed Douybaess. The film gently skirts the memory of this shy man, who took care

Still from *In This House* (Lebanon, 2005) by Akram Zaatari. Courtesy of the artist.

of his siblings after the death of their father, smoked five packs a day, and did not like to be photographed. Five months after Douybaess disappeared, his body was found in an abandoned building, and it had to be identified by his dental records. A terrible irony is that this Mohamed was obsessed with his dental hygiene and retained at least two dentists. Soueid interviews them and listens as they expound on the teeth of the Lebanese people, circumlocuting the cause of Douybaess's death. According to the dentists, Lebanese have the highest rate of tooth decay in the world. Thoughtfully smoking, the lady dentist Sahar tells how stress causes a sudden "explosion of caries" in mouths that were healthy just six months earlier. Sahar's observation shows that it is not the speaking mouths, but the mute and painful teeth of the Lebanese people that tell the story of their postwar experience: stress, fatigue, living with uncertainty. Although a vast proportion of Lebanese have suffered from posttraumatic stress disorder during and since the civil war, few seek psychotherapy because of the associated social stigma. So the symptoms of stress all come to the surface in the dentist's chair.

This is Soueid's method of unfolding Images directly from Experience.

That teeth can lead to a diagnosis of the causes and effects of war is not the answer to how to understand the history of the civil war. It is one of a potentially infinite number of paths among seemingly unrelated singularities, a kind of counter-Information conducive to a rich and unexpected unfolding of Images.

When you mention the name al-Khiam to Lebanese people, they tend to react predictably. Al-Khiam was an Israeli detention center, named after the town near which it was based, run by proxy on Lebanese soil by the pro-Israeli Southern Lebanese Army from 1985 until the Israeli withdrawal from southern Lebanon in 2000. It is well known as an example of the evil wrought upon Palestinians and Lebanese by the so-called Zionist entity; to some people it has become a cliché. But the documentary *Khiam* (Lebanon, 2000) by Hadjithomas and Joreige spends very little time on the information, already well known to Lebanese though still shocking to foreigners, that the detainees were tortured, humiliated, kept in solitary confinement, held in cells in which it was impossible to stand, sit, or lie, and forbidden any contact with one another. We learn these facts, as well as the facts of their arrest, quickly from the six former detainees, three women and three men. The film is minimal in the extreme, consisting only of medium-shot interviews of each subject against a blank ground and, toward the end, a series of close-ups of objects.

The subject of *Khiam* is not the inhuman and unjust conditions of their detention. It is how they managed to remain human while in detention. It is about creativity—activities so tiny, so embedded in the invisible field of Experience, that one might not notice them at all. One by one, the prisoners begin to tell how they resisted, and kept their sanity, by making things. They tell how, forbidden to speak to one another, and punished if they were found working, the prisoners worked in secret. They produced objects from nothing: needles, a toothbrush. They recount making tiny gifts to be surreptitiously slipped into another's hand: prayer beads carved from hard olive pits, ornaments carved from bits of soap, yarn pulled from their garments and knitted into tiny objects. And, as they describe with rising enthusiasm, they contrived to write.

To prohibit working and writing is one of the central ways that torturers attain the goal of dehumanizing their victims, as Elaine Scarry has described.[24] When the prisoners at Khiam managed to abstract from their material existence, to produce and to write, they maintained their humanity. The detainees' writing is Information that unfolds from the extreme specificity of Experience. For them, writing and making were performative acts that set in motion a strong cycle of unfolding, of Information and Images

Still from *Khiam* (Lebanon, 2000) by Joana Hadjithomas and Khalil Joreige. Courtesy of the artists.

(objects) from Experience, and from these, an enriched understanding of the preciousness of life.

As they tell of their experiments making things, the question that comes to mind is something like, "what makes life worth living?" But it is not until the end of the film, when one by one the objects of their extreme effort are revealed to our eyes, that we understand—in the surprising beauty of these beads, knitted ornaments, and writing implements—that they are not touching or poignant, but works of art. We understand that to live, to love, and to create can occur in the same gesture. The smallness, freshness, and unexpectedness of these objects flowers at the level of Image with a shock, because they mean nothing at the level of Information.

What is special about the tiny things that detainees surreptitiously passed to each other in *Khiam* is that they are not world-making, but signs of love and survival. By contrast, the objects that get smuggled among prisoners usually draw attention only when they are the catalysts of historical action. A contemporary example is the eighteen-point National Accord Document, drawn up after long discussion by Marwan Barghouti, leader of Fatah, and Sheik Abdel Khaliq al-Natsheh, a founder of Hamas, and other imprisoned faction leaders in the high-security Israeli prison Hadarim. The document was made public in late May of 2006. Drafts of this document were rolled into tiny scrolls, stuffed into capsules, and passed in embraces between prisoners and visitors. Virtually a charter for Palestine at a time of desperate danger of civil war, the smuggled document was potentially historic. (It seems at the time of this writing, when civil war has broken out between Fatah and Hamas, that it arrived too late.)

By contrast, the attention *Khiam* places on the act of fabrication itself recalls Robert Bresson's *Un Condamné à mort s'est échappé/A Man Escaped* (France, 1956). There too, though the moral stakes are abundantly clear—the good French resistants are in a prison operated by the bad German occupiers—the film's interest lies in the hand-working of objects, as the protagonist determinedly, even with wretched slowness, manipulates his door, his wire bedsprings, his lantern, and torn rags into tools with which he will be able to escape. As his fellow prisoners urge him on, without volunteering to join him, and as the film mimics his unwavering, obsessive attention to his tasks, the issue that arises from the project is freedom. Why should we care to be free? What risk is it worth? In this existential film free of political ideology, these are veritable questions that arise from Experience. And in *Khiam,* a similar set of questions arises from the physical and temporal experience of the detainees. The detainees' activity during their long imprisonments shows that unfolding is life itself.

Yousry Nasrallah's great four-and-a-half-hour epic *Bab al-Shams/The Door to the Sun* (Egypt and foreign coproduction, 2004) certainly had every pressure on it as the first fiction feature about the Palestinian *nakhba,* or historic dispossession from their land by the Jewish Army in 1948. The pressure is especially intense as the film spans more than fifty years: the massacre, expropriation, and exile of 1948, the PLO-dominated resistance of the 1970s, and present-day refugee existence in Lebanese camps. Certainly, many were awaiting a heroic, clear-cut, emotionally appropriate film, a film that exists as Information (or propaganda) about the *nakhba,* with just enough Experience to give it texture and humanity. However, in this film largely funded by Arte, Nasrallah (the Egyptian director), Elias Khoury (the Lebanese author of the epic book from which Nasrallah's film was adapted), and Mohamed Soueid (who with Nasrallah and Khoury adapted the book into a screenplay) did not have their eyes on the epic prize, but rather on the infinite richness and strangeness of Experience.

The difference is emphasized in the equal weight the film gives to the Palestinian resistance hero Younes, who, forced into exile after 1948, continues to fight, and to his wife Nahila, who remains in Israel, surviving on trade with the Israelis and raising the children the couple manage to conceive de-

Poster for *The Door to the Sun* (Egypt, 2004) by Yousry Nasrallah.

spite Younes's banishment. Their parallel lives are sketched with attention to sensuous fact as well as heroic deeds: Nahila smells of the *zaatar* (thyme) she grows and coffee she grinds for a living; Younes gets instructions on French kissing after watching a Rita Hayworth film in the Shatila refuge camp. The land and its fruits are important reminders of Palestine for the diaspora: one moving scene shows the present-day refugees gorging on oranges gathered from the land they once owned. But the film emphasizes that oranges are not only a symbol but also a sensuous and juicy fact, an embodied emblem of exile.

The difference between epic Information and intimate Experience is also reflected in the shifting of gender roles throughout the film. The dying Younes is cared for with feminine devotion by Khalil, a wounded and failed fighter, pretending to be a doctor. The local two-bit "resistance" leader mocks Khalil for not beating Shams, the woman he loves—since "every husband beats his wife." Their tender and passionate lovemaking opens the film, and it is Shams, the militia leader, who totes the gun. Thus the film *The Door to the Sun,* like the book, critiques and reverses the common tendency to derive Information from masculine activity, while passing over women's Experience as irrelevant. Slogans and militancy speak clearly at the level of Information, while intimacy and sensuality, as well as the unbearable ache of losing them, loiter in the ground of Experience. *The Door to the Sun* dwells passionately on the texture of Experience, on the reasons life is worth fighting for.

So we have a few answers to the question, how can events arise from the infinite breadth of the past and bypass the censorious and idiotic codes that filter them into "meaningful" narratives, to reach us in the present? The best of contemporary Mashreq Arab cinema avoids the sloganeering demanded by censorship and funding alike. It draws attention to the steely grip of Information, our contemporary spectacle, which preempts its engagement with Experience, as in the films of Meyar Al-Roumi, Omar Amiralay, and Akram Zaatari. Or, in the microfocus of Joana Hadjithomas and Khalil Joreige, the fond absurdism of Mohammed Soueid, and the sensuous exuberance of Yousry Nasrallah, Arab cinema yields unanticipated and heart-stopping Images that, in turn, make Experience richer. These filmmakers lift away the Information curtain so that, if only briefly, they and others may tickle Experience itself.

Notes

1. Kracauer, *History: The Last Things before the Last,* 136.
2. This understanding of history as knowable not in itself but only in its repre-

sentations, which are themselves historical, is drawn from Foucault, *The Archaeology of Knowledge,* and from Deleuze's interpretation of Foucault's philosophy of history, *Foucault.*

3. Deleuze, *The Fold: Leibniz and the Baroque.*

4. On the plane of immanence, see Deleuze and Guattari, *What Is Philosophy?* chap. 1.

5. I first introduced this enfolding-unfolding model of the Image in Marks, "Invisible Media," in *New Media: Theories and Practices of Digitextuality,* 3–46. It is explicated in animated diagrams in Marks, "Enfolding and Unfolding: An Aesthetics for the Information Age," pursued in Marks, "Information, Secrets, and Enigmas: An Enfolding-Unfolding Aesthetics for Cinema," and summed up in Marks, *Enfoldment and Infinity: An Islamic Genealogy of New Media Art.*

6. See Peirce, "The Principles of Phenomenology," 74–97.

7. Peirce's definition of the sign—"A sign, or representamen, is something which stands to somebody for something in some respect or capacity"—indicates the ceaseless flow of communication that constitutes the semiotic process. Peirce, "Logic as Semiotic: The Theory of Signs," in Buchler, 99. I take this flow to be the basis of experience itself; note that my use of "Experience" in this essay differs from Peirce's use of the term.

8. Peirce, "The Principles of Phenomenology," 79.

9. Cubitt, *The Cinema Effect,* 64.

10. Guy Debord placed spectacle at the level of the Image, while my model shifts it to the level of Information that is not necessarily perceptible. See Debord, *Society of the Spectacle.*

11. See, for example, Gilles Deleuze, "The Crisis of the Action-Image," in his *Cinema 1: The Movement-Image,* 201–8; and Deleuze, "The Painting before Painting," in his *Francis Bacon: The Logic of Sensation,* 71–80.

12. I discuss this point in more detail in Marks, "Invisible Media."

13. See Cubitt, *The Cinema Effect.*

14. Deleuze, *Cinema 2: The Time-Image,* 78. On conspiracy, see Deleuze, *Cinema 1: The Movement-Image,* 209–14.

15. Indeed the attention to the flow of unfolding and enfolding can help us understand many artworks (and other things) as performative in their origins and their effects in the world. They become fluid and transformative, like the Peircean sign itself.

16. See Deleuze and Guatarri, "The Smooth and the Striated," in their *A Thousand Plateaus: Capitalism and Schizophrenia,* 474–500.

17. See the detailed discussions of NGO and other types of funding in Al-Zobaidi, "Hyper-Nation: Palestine as a Cinematic Real," 19–39; and Marks, "What Is That 'and' between Arab Women and Video? The Case of Beirut," 41–70.

18. Quilty, "'Palestinian film' through an Israeli Lens." These events are documented on the website of the Palestinian Campaign for the Cultural and Economic Boycott of Israel, at www.pacbi.org.

19. Quilty, "Greenhouse: EuroMed Film Center Built on Shaky Ground: Controversy Has Roots in Failed Ramallah Film Festival."

20. Salti, "Critical Nationals: The Paradoxes of Syrian Cinema," in *Insights into Syrian Cinema: Essays and Conversations with Contemporary Filmmakers,* ed. Salti, 21–44.

21. Interviews with some of these filmmakers appear in the excellent book edited by Rasha Salti (ibid.) that accompanies a touring film program she organized. For information about the film program see www.arteeast.org.

22. Marks, "Akram Zaatari's *In This House:* Diagram with Olive Tree," in *Akram Zaatari: Unfolding.*

23. Marks, "Mohamed Soueid's Cinema of Immanence."

24. Scarry, *The Body in Pain: The Making and Unmaking of the World.*

Bibliography

Al-Zobaidi, Sobhi. "Hyper-Nation: Palestine as a Cinematic Real." In *Palestina, Tierra, Exilio, Creación,* 19–39. Cuenca: Fundación Antonio Pérez, 2006.

ArteEast. At www.arteeast.org.

Cubitt, Sean. *The Cinema Effect.* Cambridge, MA: MIT Press, 2004.

Debord, Guy. *Society of the Spectacle.* Translated by Donald Nicholson-Smith. New York: Zone, 1994.

Deleuze, Gilles. *Cinema 1: The Movement-Image.* Translated by Hugh Tomlinson and Barbara Habberjam. Minneapolis: University of Minnesota Press, 1987.

———. *Cinema 2: The Time-Image.* Translated by Hugh Tomlinson and Robert Galeta. Minneapolis: University of Minnesota Press, 1989.

———. *The Fold: Leibniz and the Baroque.* Translated by Tom Conley. Minneapolis: University of Minnesota Press, 1993.

———. *Foucault.* Translated by Séan Hand. Minneapolis: University of Minnesota Press, 1988.

———. *Francis Bacon: The Logic of Sensation.* Translated and introduction by Daniel W. Smith, 71–80. Minneapolis: University of Minnesota Press, 2002.

Deleuze, Gilles, and Félix Guattari. *A Thousand Plateaus: Capitalism and Schizophrenia.* Translated by Brian Massumi. Minneapolis: University of Minnesota Press, 1987.

———. *What Is Philosophy?* Translated by Hugh Tomlinson and Graham Burchell. New York: Columbia University Press, 1994.

Foucault, Michel. *The Archaeology of Knowledge.* Translated by A. Sheridan Smith. New York: Harper and Row, 1972.

Kracauer, Siegfried. *History: The Last Things before the Last.* New York: Oxford University Press, 1969.

Marks, Laura U. "Akram Zaatari's *In This House*: Diagram with Olive Tree." In *Akram Zaatari: Unfolding.* Frankfurt am Main: Portikus Gallery, 2008.

———. "Enfolding and Unfolding: An Aesthetics for the Information Age." An interactive essay produced in collaboration with designer Raegan Kelly. In *Vectors: Journal of Culture and Technology in a Dynamic Vernacular* 1, no. 3 (2007). At www.vectorsjournal.org.

———. *Enfoldment and Infinity: An Islamic Genealogy of New Media Art.* Cambridge, MA: MIT Press, 2009.

———. "Information, Secrets, and Enigmas: An Enfolding-Unfolding Aesthetics for Cinema," *Screen* 50, no. 1, 50th anniversary special issue (2009): 86–98.

———. "Invisible Media." In *New Media: Theories and Practices of Digitextuality,* edited by Anna Everett and John T. Caldwell, 33–46. New York: Routledge, 2003.

———. "Mohamed Soueid's Cinema of Immanence." *Jump Cut* 49 (Spring 2007). At www.ejumpcut.org.

———. "What Is That 'and' between Arab Women and Video? The Case of Beirut." *Camera Obscura* 18, no. 2 (2003): 41–70.

Peirce, Charles Sanders. "Logic as Semiotic: The Theory of Signs." In *Philosophical Writings of Peirce,* edited by Justus Buchler, 98–119. New York: Dover, 1955.

———. "The Principles of Phenomenology." In *Philosophical Writings of Peirce,* edited by Justus Buchler, 74–97. New York: Dover, 1955.

Quilty, Jim. "Greenhouse: EuroMed Film Center Built on Shaky Ground: Controversy Has Roots in Failed Ramallah Film Festival." *Daily Star* (Lebanon), April 22, 2006.

———. "'Palestinian Film' through an Israeli Lens." *Daily Star* (Lebanon), April 25, 2006.

Salti, Rasha, ed. *Insights into Syrian Cinema: Essays and Conversations with Contemporary Filmmakers.* New York: ArteEast, 2006.

Scarry, Elaine. *The Body in Pain: The Making and Unmaking of the World.* New York: Oxford University Press, 1987.

Contributors

KAY DICKINSON lectures in the Media and Communications Department of Goldsmiths College, University of London, and is the author of *Off Key: When Film and Music Won't Work Together* (Oxford University Press, 2008). She has published on Arab cinema in various anthologies and in the journals *Screen* and *Camera Obscura,* as well as working as an education officer and invited guest on the Ramallah International Film Festival (2004) and the Shashat Women's Film Festival in Ramallah, Bethlehem, and Nablus, Palestine (2005). Her current research investigates tropes of travel consciousness in respect to Arab film production and distribution, ideas that are leading toward a book titled *Arab Cinema Travels.*

FAYE GINSBURG is Director of the Center for Media, Culture, and History at New York University where she is also the David B. Kriser Professor of Anthropology. Her work over the years has focused on cultural activism, from her early research on women involved in the abortion debate in the United States to her long-term work on the development of Indigenous media in Australia and elsewhere.

METTE HJORT is Professor and Head of Visual Studies at Lingnan University, Hong Kong, and Affiliate Professor of Scandinavian Studies at the University of Washington, Seattle. She is the author of *The Strategy of Letters* (Harvard University Press, 1993), *Small Nation, Global Cinema: The New Danish Cinema* (University of Minnesota Press, 2005), *Stanley Kwan's* Center Stage (Hong Kong University Press, 2006), and *Lone Scherfig's* Italian for Beginners (University of Washington Press, 2009). She is the editor of *Rules and Conventions* (Johns Hopkins University Press, 1992) and *Dekalog 01: On The Five Obstructions* (Wallflower, 2008), and coeditor of *Emotion and the Arts* (Oxford University Press, 1997), *Cinema and Nation* (Routledge,

2000), *The Danish Directors* (Intellect, 2001), *The Postnational Self: Belonging and Identity* (University of Minnesota Press, 2002), *Purity and Provocation: Dogme 95* (British Film Institute, 2003), *The Cinema of Small Nations* (Edinburgh University Press, 2007) and *The Institution of Cultural Studies* (forthcoming). Mette Hjort is series editor, with Peter Schepelern, of the Nordic Film Classics Series at the University of Washington Press.

DINA IORDANOVA is Professor of Film Studies and Director of the Centre for Film Studies at the University of St. Andrews in Scotland. Her current focus is on the Leverhulme-funded project on *Dynamics of World Cinema* (2008–11). Her monographs include *Cinema of Flames: Balkan Film, Culture, and the Media* (2001), *Emir Kusturica* (2002), and *Cinema of the Other Europe* (2003). She is the editor of BFI's *Companion to Russian and Eastern European Cinema* (2000), and of *Cinema of the Balkans* (2006). She approaches cinema on a metanational level and focuses on transnationalism and works on international film distribution and festivals. She is the editor of the *Film Festivals Yearbook*.

SHELDON H. LU is Professor of Comparative Literature at the University of California at Davis. He is the author of *From Historicity to Fictionality: The Chinese Poetics of Narrative* (1994), *China, Transnational Visuality, Global Postmodernity* (2001), and *Chinese Modernity and Global Biopolitics: Studies in Literature and Visual Culture* (2007). He is the editor of *Transnational Chinese Cinemas: Identity, Nationhood, Gender* (1997), coeditor of *Chinese-Language Film: Historiography, Poetics, Politics* (2005), and coeditor of *Chinese Ecocinema in the Age of Environmental Challenge* (2009).

LAURA U. MARKS is Professor in Contemporary Arts at Simon Fraser University in Vancouver, Canada. She is a media theorist, curator, and author of *The Skin of the Film: Intercultural Cinema, Embodiment, and the Senses* (Duke University Press, 2000), *Touch: Sensuous Theory and Multisensory Media* (University of Minnesota Press, 2002), and *Enfoldment and Infinity: An Islamic Genealogy of New Media Art* (MIT Press, 2009).

BILL MARSHALL is Professor of Comparative Literary and Cultural Studies at the University of Stirling. His authored books include *Quebec National Cinema* (McGill-Queen's University Press, 2001), *André Téchiné* (Manchester University Press, 2006), and *The French Atlantic: Travels in Culture and History* (Liverpool University Press, 2009). His edited works include the volume *Musicals: Hollywood and Beyond* (Intellect Press, 2000), and a three-volume encyclopaedia, *France and the Americas* (ABC-Clio, 2005).

DAVID MARTIN-JONES is Senior Lecturer in Film Studies at the University of St. Andrews, Scotland. He is the author of *Deleuze, Cinema and National Identity* (Edinburgh University Press, 2006), *Deleuze Reframed* (I. B. Tauris, 2008), *Scotland: Global Cinema* (Edinburgh University Press, 2009) and the forthcoming *Deleuze and World Cinemas* (Continuum, 2011). He has published articles in a number of international journals (including *Cinema Journal, Screen* and *CineAction*), and is on the editorial boards of *Film-Philosophy* and *A/V: The Journal of Deleuzian Studies.*

LÚCIA NAGIB is Centenary Professor of World Cinemas and Director of the Centre for World Cinemas, University of Leeds. She is the author of the books *World Cinema and the Ethics of Realism* (Continuum, 2010), *Brazil on Screen: Cinema Novo, New Cinema, Utopia* (I. B. Tauris, 2007), *The Brazilian Film Revival: Interviews with 90 Filmmakers of the 90s* (Editora 34, 2002), *Born of the Ashes: The Auteur and the Individual in Oshima's Films* (Edusp, 1995), *Around the Japanese Nouvelle Vague* (Editora da Unicamp, 1993), and *Werner Herzog: Film as Reality* (Estação Liberdade, 1991). She is the editor of *Realism and the Audiovisual Media* (with Cecília Mello, Palgrave, 2009), *The New Brazilian Cinema* (I. B. Tauris, 2003), *Master Mizoguchi* (Navegar, 1990), and *Ozu* (Marco Zero, 1990).

DUNCAN PETRIE is Professor of Film and Television at the University of York. His previous positions include Head of the Department of Film, Television and Media Studies at the University of Auckland and Director of the Bill Douglas Centre for the History of Cinema and Popular Culture at the University of Exeter. He has published widely on aspects of British, Scottish, and New Zealand cinema, cinematography, and Scottish culture. His books include *A Coming of Age: 30 Years of New Zealand Cinema, Shot in New Zealand: The Art and Craft of the Kiwi Cinematographer, Contemporary Scottish Fictions, Screening Scotland, The British Cinematographer,* and *Creativity and Constraint in the British Film Industry.* He has also served on numerous industry bodies in the United Kingdom including the Scottish Screen Lottery Panel and the board of South West Screen.

PATRICIA PISTERS is Professor of Film Studies in the Department of Media Studies of the University of Amsterdam. Her teaching and research interests focus on questions related to multiculturalism, political cinema, and transnational media, mainly looking at North African cinema and Arab media. Another focus is on film-philosophical questions on the nature of perception, the ontology of the image, and the idea of the "brain as screen" in connection to neuroscience. Publications include *The Matrix of Visual Culture: Working with Deleuze in Film Theory* (Stanford University Press, 2003) and *Shooting the Family: Transnational Media and Intercultural Values* (ed. with Wim Staat; Amsterdam University Press, 2005).

BELÉN VIDAL lectures in Film Studies at King's College London. She has published on the aesthetics of the period film in the journals *Screen* and *Journal of European Studies* and in the edited collection *Books in Motion: Adaptation, Intertextuality, Authorship* (Rodopi, 2005). She is researching a project on cinephilia in Spanish cinema, and has participated in the volume *Contemporary Spanish Cinema and Genre* (Manchester University Press, 2008). Forthcoming work includes the monograph *Heritage Film: Nation, Genre, and Representation* (Wallflower Press).

Index